Family
of Earth
and Sky

Family of Earth and Sky

INDIGENOUS TALES OF NATURE FROM AROUND THE WORLD

EDITED BY

John Elder and Hertha D. Wong

BEACON PRESS
Boston

BEACON PRESS
25 Beacon Street
Boston, Massachusetts   02108-2892

Beacon Press Books
are published under the auspices of
the Unitarian Universalist Association of Congregations.

Library of Congress Cataloging-in-Publication Data

Family of earth and sky : indigenous tales of nature from around the
world / edited by John Elder and Hertha D. Wong.
p.   cm. — (The Concord library)
Includes bibliographical references and index.
ISBN 0-8070-8528-6 (cloth)
ISBN 0-8070-8529-4 (paper)
1. Tales.   2. Nature—Folklore.   3. Mythology.   4. Nature—
Mythology.   I. Elder, John, 1947– .   II. Wong, Hertha Dawn.
III. Series.
GR618.F36   1994
398.21—dc20   93-40539
CIP

99 98 97 96 95   8 7 6 5 4 3 2

TEXT DESIGN BY JANIS OWENS
COMPOSITION BY WILSTED & TAYLOR

Contents

· ·

PART TWO
....

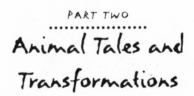

Animal Tales and Transformations

PART THREE
· · · · · · · · · · · · · · · · · ·
Tricksters

CONTENTS ix

PART FOUR
·····················
Tales to Live By

Introduction:
A Trail of Stories

••

What will a reader coming to them for the first time experience in these visions of nature from indigenous cultures around the world? Above all, great *stories*, stories that combine the reverberant simplicity of dreams with the texture of close observation, that freshen the solemnity of religious celebration with gusts of bawdy humor. Stories powerful enough to command one's whole heart and mind are never "just entertainment," as Leslie Marmon Silko has said: "they are all we have to live by." The environmental crises of our day require a multiplying of these crucial resources. Familiarity with the oral traditions of nature from around the world can both reinforce the environmental awareness already fostered by Western nature writing and give it a more global and particular context.

In his celebrated essay on "The Land Ethic," from *A Sand County Almanac* (1949), Aldo Leopold discusses the widening of an ethical circle in the centuries since Homer. He argues that, in spite of the warfare and avarice that continue to shadow our societies, much of the industrialized world has extended basic rights to a broader and broader spectrum of humanity. The movements for equal rights in our own day have contributed to this difficult but inexorable process, while the struggle of nations to find a democratic framework that both enfranchises the individual and protects that individual from the power of the state represents a complementary challenge. Leopold writes, however, that it is now imperative to conceive of an ethical circle within which the rights of *non*human life are encompassed. Believing in such rights, and acting upon such a belief, has become "an evolutionary possibility and an ecological necessity."

The tradition of nature writing in English has contributed in vital ways to the evolution of attitudes toward the intricate web of soil, plants, and animals Leopold refers to as "the land." Thoreau's voice at the beginning of "Walking" sounds a defiant note that echoes through the writing of many of his naturalist successors: "I wish to speak a word for Nature, for absolute freedom and wildness, as contrasted with a freedom and culture merely civil,—to regard man as an inhabitant, or a part and parcel of Nature, rather than a member of society." This recognition that to include nature within the human ethical circle is also to ground humanity within a wilder, more invigorating world is one of the greatest gifts of the nature writers. It prophetically counters the prevalent assumption that there is only one question to ask with regard to "harvesting," "subdividing," or "developing" some wild tract of land: whether, in a strictly monetary sense, the activity will prove profitable. Nature writers, as they register the complex particularity of landforms and the life-forms associated with them, have similarly supplied an antidote to the tendency of many contemporary poets and fiction writers to enclose themselves in rooms, or in automobiles with the windows resolutely rolled up.

Growing numbers of readers have been inspired and encouraged by the vivid inclusiveness of nature writing—not only by the exciting range of works now appearing in this field, but also by the sense that there is a *history*, with its own momentum, behind these "words for nature." Recent anthologies such as *This Incomperable Lande*, edited by Thomas J. Lyon (1989), *The Norton Book of Nature Writing*, edited by Robert Finch and John Elder (1990), and *Sisters of the Earth*, edited by Lorraine Anderson (1991) have framed this literature within several contexts. The Lyon anthology illuminates the distinctively North American origins and continuities of nature writing; the Finch and Elder volume traces the literary form from English naturalists of the late eighteenth century who were inspired by Linnaeus to the genre's current flowering in the United States and elsewhere; and the Anderson collection emphasizes women's contributions, in both poetry and prose, to our literature of nature.

However, as the Western environmental movement goes beyond its emphasis on preserving wilderness areas to a heightened awareness of the *global* nature of all environmental issues, there is also an increasing interest in relating the tradition of nature writing in English to the literature that has emerged from other cultural and linguistic terrains. This desire to explore diverse responses to the earth from the world's different cultures reflects an understanding that the Western literature of nature has been circumscribed in certain ways. "Nature writing" conventionally has been taken to mean personal, reflective essays in a Thoreauvian mode—a species of nonfiction grounded in the appreciation of contemporary science and at the same time remaining open to the physical creation's spiritual and emotional significance. The essays in this genre have been powerful vehicles for integrating observation with revelation, and for bridging the rift between the "two cultures" of science and literature. But they have also projected the voices of solitary—and sometimes alienated—individuals rather more often than they have emphasized how the human *community* might be seen as a part of nature.

Even Leopold's discussion of ethical evolution may finally be seen as bounded by its very breadth. His historical frame of reference is a Western culture that has become increasingly cosmopolitan; within such an international process of cultural evolution, there may be more and more shared *values*, but there are at the same time fewer and fewer shared *landscapes*. Even within the modern, industrialized world of his analysis, however, certain deeply rooted, localized, indigenous cultures have persisted to this day. These "inhabitory" peoples, who have sometimes been viewed as outside the historical mainstream, seem increasingly to bear potent witness to an integrated vision of nature. Because of the fullness of these cultures' identification with their own particular and long-known home grounds, they generally have proven more respectful in their dealings with nature than has the more mobile culture of the industrialized West. Well before Leopold's injunction to act always out of "love, respect, and admiration for land," they maintained a relationship with nature based on far more than "mere economic value."

The main literary form in which such indigenous cultures have expressed their place within nature has been the story rather than the reflective essay—a story that the members of the community gather together to hear rather than an essay written by and read by an individual alone. It is not generally possible to draw a precise distinction between these nature stories and the rest of indigenous literature; the very fact that the West has developed a genre called "nature writing" testifies to a separation between much of human life and the nonhuman world that has developed since the industrial revolution. By contrast, in her essay on "Landscape, History, and the Pueblo Imagination," Leslie Silko writes, "Whatever happened, the ancient people instinctively sorted events and details into a loose narrative structure. Everything became a story." She stresses, further, that "the remembering and retelling were a communal process." Such stories not only included the life of the whole people in a dynamic way, but also integrated features of the landscape or, to describe the relationship from the opposite direction, embedded the collective human experience in those physical objects. In contrast to the distinction implied by the word "landscape," with a writer or painter gazing in admiration at an objectified scene, Silko asserts that the Pueblo way ensured "the human consciousness remains *within* the hills, canyons, cliffs, and the plants, clouds, and sky . . ."

Family of Earth and Sky gathers narratives from around the world that, in their topographical specificity and their emphasis upon community within nature, complement the Western tradition of nature writing. Such voices may help us to extend our ethical circle, as Leopold calls upon us to do, by distinctly conveying the extent to which nature is not only personally meaningful but *personal*. Our selections are obviously neither comprehensive nor systematically representative in any anthropological sense. Rather, we have tried to juxtapose certain related tales from a diversity of cultural backgrounds and geographic regions. While all the tales arise out of indigenous cultures in oral forms, a few of them—Finland's national epic *Kalevala*, Grimm's tales, and the *Jataka Tales* from South Asia—have a prominent history in written forms as well. Our purposes have been to illustrate some of the many possibilities for a response to nature that is grounded in the experience of a specific homeland, and at the same time to highlight continuities among the imaginations of people living in very different bio-regions.

In trying to illuminate some of the larger patterns we found in our reading, we have organized this collection into the following sequence of headings: Origins, Animal Tales and Transformations, Tricksters, and Tales to Live By. The stories in the first of these categories establish in a variety of ways that the earth is our home, not simply "a vast supply depot"—as Gary Snyder has characterized the dominant view of our planet in the secular West. One of the features of living in an indigenous culture seems to be the deep familiarity people experience with the world around them, the recollection throughout life of childhood stories accounting for *those* rocks, *those* trees, and relating them to the grand cycles of sun, moon, and stars.

"Animal Tales and Transformations," the second section, reflects the fact that indigenous stories often present animals who are strikingly human. Underlying the humor, drama, and sexiness of these tales is a strong conviction of the personhood and importance of animals. Personal appreciation of animals provides a vital antidote to the mechanistic view still prominent within the life sciences, and to the education-through-dissection approach that often prevails within the academic study of biology. Interestingly, however, it also accords with an important *counter*-trend in the life sciences today—the tendency toward study of individual organisms in their own habitat, and the increased readiness to register the validity of personal connections, and even of personal identification, within scientific study. In the "Prologue" to his 1984 book *Biophilia* the eminent biologist E. O. Wilson expresses his belief that "to explore and affiliate with life is a deep and complicated process in mental development. To an extent still undervalued in philosophy and religion, our existence depends on this propensity, our spirit is woven from it, hope rises on its currents." "Affiliation," a sense of being connected with other organisms in a deep, personal, and committed way, is Wilson's equivalent to the ethically transformative love for which Leopold's essay also calls. The language of both writers is strikingly similar to many indigenous notions of kinship and reciprocity between human and nonhuman worlds.

Two motifs are especially notable within this sampling of tales about our animal kin. One might be called the moral tale, in which the conduct of animals represents, and is intended to instruct, that of us two-leggeds. The Jataka tales of South Asia often take this form. The other main form here is the tale of transformation, in which a human being becomes an animal or an animal a human being. These stories reflect the mysterious identification we feel with other forms of life, even though there are such obvious differences between us in our physical forms as well as in our behavior. Through both kinds of tales, with their insistence upon the consciousness, individuality, and interrelatedness of all creatures, we may be able to go beyond the distanced and abstract view of nonhuman life that has been so serious an impediment to the development of a more inclusive ethic.

We have made "Tricksters" a separate section—though these are also animal stories—because of the special richness and complexity of this group of tales. Ijapa and Anansi from Africa, Coyote and Br'er Rabbit from North America, manifest powers far beyond the human, and are sometimes even associated with the creation of the earth. At the same time, these tricksters' daring creativity can leave them susceptible to the same foolishness and pride that gets us human beings in so much trouble. Such a combination of traits makes the tales in this section particularly delightful and engaging. The ethical power of trickster stories lies in their suggestion that just when we may feel freest to have our way with the earth, we need to bear our fallibility in mind. Perhaps we will be better able to impose restraints on our collective appetite if the apocalyptic fatalism so prominent within current environmentalism can at least sometimes give way to the sly self-mockery implicit in Coyote and his friends. When we see ourselves as fools we may stop dead in our tracks.

The final section, "Tales to Live By," focuses on contemporary expressions of, and reflections about, the natural visions of indigenous cultures. We wanted in this way to emphasize that indigenous cultures are not relics of the past, but that they persist as lively communities within a world that many others experience as homogenized and rootless. In addition, these concluding pieces bring out most explicitly the pertinence of such visions to the grave environmental problems of our day. A *Sand County Almanac* opens with a specific partridge and the pines surrounding Leopold's Wisconsin "shack," then closes with "The Upshot," a section that illuminates important ethical and philosophic implications of the vignettes that have preceded it. So too are these expressions at the end of this volume meant to press the broad implications of the various stories for our modern way of life. When a story is strong enough, its listeners or readers are literally *moved* by it. When we are led through narrative to reidentify with the particular animals and plants around us, and with the earth on which we all dwell together, then perhaps we can also discern the possibility within our necessity.

▣   ▣   ▣

Both in our book's subtitle and in the preceding section of this introduction we have used "indigenous" to characterize the cultures from which stories in the volume derive. According to the organization Cultural Survival, "indigenous peoples" are "culturally distinct groups that have occupied a region longer than other immigrant groups or colonist groups." Although using the term in this way may signal a real and important distinction, it also raises a set of questions. How long a relationship with a specific place is necessary before a culture group can be considered indigenous? The ancestors of the Diné (popularly known as the Navajo) migrated south, arriving in the fourteenth century in territory where the direct ancestors of the Hopi had resided for several hundred (some say thousand) years. But the Diné and the Hopi are both considered indigenous peoples, original inhabitants of the region. Each culture is intimately associated with what we now call the Four Corners area of the Southwest, situated in the midst of their four sacred mountains—specific geographic sites that shape as well as visually articulate both people's distinct beliefs.

Two related questions are whether the term "indigenous" suits nomadic peoples, who may also have an intimate connection to particular landscapes, and whether it is appropriate to people who have been dispossessed of their land or removed from it. Native people, even when forced to relocate to prescribed land reserves, do not cease to be indigenous after being removed from their homelands. Being indigenous thus appears to be in some sense portable; people are connected to the land in psychological and spiritual as well as in physical ways. These questions are not meant to discredit the term "indigenous," but rather to suggest its historical construction and the dynamic *transitions* of what we now refer to as indigenous cultures. By indigenous, then, we essentially mean early peoples of an area whose traditional cultures are rooted in particular landscapes with which they are essentially and specifically identified, whether they are presently living in those landscapes or not.

It has become almost a cliché to note the distinction between Western and non-Western notions of nature. Westerners, as the generalization is most often articulated, see nature as a force to be conquered and tamed, as a resource to be utilized, and they see themselves as separate from, most often superior to, nature; non-Westerners, particularly indigenous people, view nature as a powerful force to be respected and honored, as a life-giving Mother to be cherished, and themselves as part of the intricate web of the natural world. Such a generalization overstates the case, since there are certainly respecters of nature in Western cultures and exploiters of nature in non-Western cultures. At the same time, the broad dichotomy does describe accurately many of the fundamental assumptions, as well as the dominant behavior, of these two sets of cultures. In part, this difference reflects the kinds of technology developed in these contrasted cultural spheres. But conversely, the drive toward advanced technology, and the applications to which it has been put, may have something to do with what kinds of stories a people has been listening to.

Environmentalists in particular have often looked to the indigenous cultures of the Americas for models of living in harmony with nature—sometimes even putting words in the mouths of native speakers to suit their own purposes. The much-circulated "environmental" speech of Chief Seeathl (better known as Seattle) is a good example of the well-meaning but misguided attempts of non-Natives to borrow selectively from indigenous cultures for the purpose of promoting an environmental agenda. Although the cause may be noble, the result is often appropriation, rather than illumination, of native cultures.

Even though pre-Columbian indigenous people in the Americas may have lived closely and respectfully with the plant and animal life of their environments (possessing what we call today an ecological awareness), pre-twentieth-century indigenous people did not consider themselves "environmentalists." Such a term is historically specific and can be used accurately only to reflect the self-conscious awareness of the fragility, complexity, and interrelatedness of nature, coupled with the fear of its imminent destruction, that has become so prevalent in our own century. What we interpret today as indigenous conservation practices did not arise from fear of the apocalyptic destruction of nature, but rather from a more integral understanding of the reciprocity between humans and all living beings.

Many nineteenth-century and early twentieth-century ethnographic records—the dominant source for most of the oral tales and myths included in this anthology—reflect a now suspect belief in "objective" documentation, often erasing or ignoring historical, cultural, and performance contexts. The written record of indigenous oral narratives recorded by others is inherently problematic because of the multiple translations involved: from the spoken to the written word; often from a native language to English (or another language); from performance to text; from one cultural community to another. Such an ethnographic document is always a translation: a version of a single performance in a particular historical moment and a specific place, shaped by its immediate audience and reshaped by a usually nonindigenous amanuensis-editor. To generalize grandly about such "texts" is suspect, but to dismiss them as unreliable may be to revert to an early romantic or anthropological impulse to locate, record, and thereby preserve the "true," "genuine," "authentic" traditional indigenous person. Often particular recorded versions of myths, tales, and stories have assumed a kind of authority unwarranted in any oral tradition. They can be used, mistakenly, as the "correct" or "authentic" version of the story when, most often, they are simply specific versions of ongoing, ever-changing practices of oral narration. Each storyteller has his or her own special talents for inspiring humor, for instance, or for impersonating characters or turning a phrase; a single storyteller can also tell the same story differently for different occasions, audiences, and purposes.

Some scholars claim that, in such mediated (translated and edited) texts, no indigenous voice is possible; only the voice of the editor, often a member of a colonizing power, remains. Others insist that these cross-cultural collaborative texts are themselves both literary and cultural boundaries and blendings that challenge us to hear the voice of the speaker *as well as* (not instead of) the editorial language of the editor. All too often ethnographers, linguists, folklorists, and other scholars of indigenous cultures have transformed, however unintentionally, the oral traditions of indigenous people into cultural artifacts. Even if we do not consider recorded oral traditions as accurate ethnographic documents, we can still appreciate them as imaginatively translated and constructed collaborative narratives.

The oral myths and tales you read in this anthology were first experienced as storytelling. Part of what gets lost in the translation from the storyteller's performance (and the audience's response) to the editor's written narrative (and the reader's reaction) is the sense of community; of tone of voice, pacing, and timing; and of storyteller-audience interaction or perhaps co-creation. Several scholars have offered strategies for translating storytelling performances into detailed scores and scripts. Dell Hymes, Dennis Tedlock, and Barre Toelken have attempted to record spoken and performed words in forms that reflect the particular performance itself. They note performance cues such as pauses by dashes or ellipses; shifts in thought as line breaks; changes in sound by varied fonts, to note a few. ("**YES**," for instance, would be read in a loud voice, while "maybe" would be read as a whisper.) Since we were concerned first with a good *reading* experience, we have not included such scripts—technically accurate though they may be. Even so, you might wish to read some of these selections aloud to gain a sense of their spoken power.

◉ ◉ ◉

Collectively, then, these selections raise many questions about the complexity of cross-cultural collaboration, the role of performance in storytelling, and the subtleties of "reading" oral and performed narratives translated into written forms. We also believe, however, that the stories gathered here can speak powerfully across the gaps of transcription and translation, and that in their significant parallels and intersections they can also provide meaningful contexts for each other. Therefore, we offer this volume in the hope that it may contribute to more substantial dialogue between the industrialized West and the world's indigenous cultures. As is true for all anthologies, ours represents just one editorial approach—inevitably skewed—to a rich literary terrain. Its success will thus be determined by the degree to which it helps stimulate the discussion and the collections of stories that supersede it.

A number of Western nature writers have already become intensely interested in the power of traditional stories. Barry Lopez is one author who both embeds such stories in his extended essays and, in the recent *Crow and Weasel*, has produced a self-contained narrative informed by Native American models. At the same time, indigenous people writing in English are with increasing frequency adding their voices, on their own terms, to the conversations of Western environmentalists. Sometimes agreeing with the main current of environmentalist thinking, sometimes correcting it—as in their critique of "wilderness" as a concept based on artificial separation between humans and the rest of nature—these writers from indigenous traditions are helping to plot the trail we must take to ensure the survival of *all* our human cultures. That trail, with all its myriad byways, is mapped in the stories. Many indigenous people around the world are engaged in acts of retrieval, recuperation, and, when necessary, reimagining. Reimagining notions of nature and our relation to it and telling stories that awaken and sustain our relationship to the earth are necessary acts of survival as we all struggle to transform ourselves from twentieth- to twenty-first-century global citizens.

PART ONE

Origins

*E*very culture has a web of narratives that answer, in diverse ways, fundamental human questions about how we got here and who created the earth and everything upon, below, and above it. Often referred to as myths, such accounts are traditional stories that the people tell to articulate how and where they originated, what collective transformations they have undergone to come to who and where they are now, and how they should behave toward one another. This section begins with myths about the origins of the earth and of humans, and concludes with narratives describing the origin of death. In between are stories of the creation of plants, animals, celestial bodies, and seasons.

The gods or creators in these myths and tales are rarely distant or infallible; often, in fact, like the Trickster Coyote, they create through trial and error rather than divine wisdom. Very often humans assist their creators in fashioning or completing the world, even becoming co-creators. This responsibility underscores a crucial sense of reciprocity and harmony between and among all aspects of creation, a fundamental orientation to the earth and to all things below and above it.

In native North America, three fundamental types of creation myth are acknowledged widely: the Emergence myth, the Earth-Diver myth, and the Made-from-Earth myth. Each of these myth-types has a rich diversity of traditions, and elements of each are found in the Navajo and Mohawk stories included here. The Navajo Emergence myth tells how early forms of the people emerged from the First World through the Second, Third, and Fourth Worlds and finally into the Fifth World, where First Man and First Woman were created from two ears of corn. Whereas emergence is a movement up and out, the movement of Earth-Diver myths is down and in (and then up and out). In the Mohawk creation story included in this section, an Earth-Diver myth retold in both contemporary pictograms and writing, Sky Woman descends to a water-covered world where, with the help of animals, she forms the earth. In this version, Beaver, Loon, and Muskrat all sacrifice themselves, diving deep into the water to obtain some earth upon which Sky Woman might land. When Muskrat floats up from below with a little earth in his claws, it is placed on the back of Turtle who generously agrees to support it—the origin of the reference to earth as Turtle Island. This Mohawk story also incorporates the third myth-type, where human beings are created from the earth. Here, the Spirit Being fashions humankind from some red clay. The fundamental actions of these myths—emerging from the earth, diving into the water to locate and raise the earth, or being shaped from earth—all work to define humans as related to the earth.

Rather than emerge or dive or shape, some creators enact their thoughts in language. Words, then, are profoundly potent; they create, not merely narrate. In many of the myths, language (the manifestation of thought) has the power to create and shape the world. An Australian aboriginal creation myth, for instance, tells of a time when life existed only as a dormant possibility. As the sun is born, the Ancients come to life and sing the earth into being. After the Ancients have traveled all around and "wrapped the world in a web of song," they return to their transcendent state. Associated with life-giving breath, speech or song gives birth to physical creation.

In addition to creation stories, there are many tales, commonly referred to as etiological tales, about how certain celestial bodies or specific life-forms were created. The Juruna tale from Brazil about how a murderous sun was replaced by a beneficent son/sun is one example here. Sometimes a union between celestial persons gives rise to creation. The Wakaranga from Central Africa, for instance, tell how Moon slept with Morningstar and created all the trees, grasses, and plants; he slept with Eveningstar and from their union sprang goats, cows, sheep, antelopes, birds, then boys and girls. At other times, celestial beings resolve their differences, resulting in good to the universe. In a Nivaklé story, Sun and Moon are competing brothers who finally agree to take on complementary functions by which they still abide. Frequently, a deity creates life from part(s) of herself. In Finland's Kalevala the

Air Spirit Mother/Mother of the Water gives birth to the earth, the heavens, the sun, the moon, to features of the shore, and finally, to Väinämöinen, the "eternal singer" who sings lays in her honor.

There are also stories tied explicitly to particular places. Long ago seventy-some warriors on the way to conquer England were turned to stone by a witch's curse and can be seen today, so the story goes, as the Rollright Stones—a specific rock formation. Similarly, in a Kiowa tale, the tree trunk that lifts the Seven Sisters to safety in the sky (where they become the seven stars of the Big Dipper) is transformed into the Wyoming monolith known today as Devil's Tower. Or, in the secular tale from northern China, Hailibu the Hunter turns to stone to help his people survive. The etiological function—explaining how something came to be—is not necessarily the most important aspect of such tales. Sometimes there is a moral—in Hailibu's case, about the necessity of personal sacrifice for the good of the people. More importantly, such myths and tales unite the people not only with each other, but with the entire natural world. As N. Scott Momaday says in The Way to Rainy Mountain *(1969), when his people look at the Big Dipper, "So long as the legend lives, the Kiowa have kinsmen in the night sky." Such a web of narrative, woven throughout land and sky, reminds the people of the interrelatedness of all creation.*

The Emergence

One
•••••••••••••••••

Of a time long, long ago these things are said.

It is said that at *Tó bił dahisk'id* white arose in the east and was considered day. We now call that spot Place Where the Waters Crossed.

Blue arose in the south. It too was considered day. So the *Nílch'idine'é*, who already lived there, moved around. We would call them Air-Spirit People in the language spoken today by those who are given the name *Bilagáana*, which means White Man.

In the west yellow arose and showed that evening had come. Then in the north black arose. So the Air-Spirit People lay down and slept.

At *Tó bił dahisk'id* where the streams came together water flowed in all directions. One stream flowed to the east. One stream flowed to the south. One stream flowed to the west. One stream flowed to the north.

Along three of those streams there were dwelling places. There were dwelling places along the stream that flowed east. There were dwelling places along the stream that flowed south. There were dwelling places along the stream that flowed west. But along the stream that flowed north there were no dwellings.

To the east there was a place called *Dáá*. In the language of *Bilagáana* the White Man that name means food. To the south there was a place called *Nahodoolá*. It is unknown what that name means. And to the west there was a

place called *Lók'aatsoh sikaad*. In the White Man's language that name means
Standing Reed. Nothing is said about a place to the north.

Also to the east there was a place called *Ásaa'łáá'ii*, which means One
Dish. And also to the south there was a place called *Tó hadziłtił*, which means
A Big Amount of Water Coming Out in the language of *Bilagáana*. And also
to the west there was a place called *Dził łichíí' bee hooghan*. That name means
House of Red Mountain. To the north there are no places that have been
given names.

Then there was a place called *Leeyaa hooghan* to the east. In his language
the White Man would give it the name Underground House. And there was
another place called *Chiiłchintah* to the south. In the language he speaks *Bilagáana* would give it the name Among Aromatic Sumac. And there was another place called *Tsé łichíí' bee hooghan* to the west. In the language of his
people the White Man would give it the name House of Red Rock. We hear
of no places with names to the north.

In those early times dark ants dwelled there. Red ants dwelled there. Drag-
onflies dwelled there. Yellow beetles dwelled there.

Hard beetles lived there. Stone-carrier beetles lived there. Black beetles
lived there. Coyote-dung beetles lived there.

Bats made their homes there. Whitefaced beetles made their homes
there. Locusts made their homes there. White locusts made their homes
there.

Those are the twelve groups who started life there. We call them *Nílch'i-
dine'é*. In the language of *Bilagáana* the White Man that name means Air-
Spirit People. For they are people unlike the five-fingered earth-surface
people who come into the world today, live on the ground for a while, die at a
ripe old age, and then leave the world. They are people who travel in the air
and fly swiftly like the wind and dwell nowhere else but here.

Far to the east there was an ocean. Far to the south there was an ocean. Far
to the west there was an ocean. And far to the north there was an ocean.

In the ocean to the east dwelled *Tééhoołtsódii*, who was chief of the people
there. In the White Man's language he can be called The One That Grabs
Things In the Water. In the ocean to the south lived *Táłtł'ááh álééh*. His
name means Blue Heron. In the ocean to the west *Ch'al* made his home and
was chief of those people. In the language of the White Man he would be

called Frog. And in the ocean to the north dwelled *Ii'ni' jiłgaii*. In the White Man's language that name means Winter Thunder. He was chief among whoever those people were who lived there, it is said.

Two

. . . .

It is also said that the Air-Spirit People fought among themselves. And this is how it happened. They committed adultery, one with another. Many of the men were to blame, but so were many of the women.

They tried to stop, but they could not help themselves.

Tééhoołtsódii The One That Grabs Things In the Water, who was chief in the east, complained, saying this:

"They must not like it here," he said.

And *Táłt'ááh álééh* the Blue Heron, who was chief in the south, also complained:

"What they do is wrong," he complained.

Ch'al the Frog, who was chief in the west, also complained. But he took his complaint directly to the Air-Spirit People, having this to say to them:

"You shall no longer be welcome here where I am chief," is what he said.

"That is what I think of you."

And from his home in the north where he was chief, *Ii'ni' jiłgaii* the Winter Thunder spoke to them also.

"Nor are you welcome here!" he, too, said to them.

"Go away from this land.

"Leave at once!"

But the people still could not help it: one with another they continued to commit adultery. And when they did it yet another time and then argued with each other again, *Tééhooltsódii* The One That Grabs Things In the Water would no longer speak to them. *Táłt'ááh álééh* the Blue Heron would no longer speak to them. Likewise *Ch'al* the Frog would say nothing to them. And *Ii'ni' jiłgaii* the Winter Thunder refused to say anything.

Four days and four nights passed.

Then the same thing happened. Those who lived in the south repeated their sins: the men with the women and the women with the men. They committed adultery. And again they quarreled afterward.

One woman and one man sought *Tééhooltsódii* The One That Grabs Things In the Water in the east to try to straighten things out. But they were driven away. Then they went to *Táłtł'ááh áłééh* the Blue Heron in the south. But they were again driven away. And they looked for *Ch'ał* the Frog in the west. But they were driven away again. Finally they went to the north to speak with *Ii'ni' jiłgaii* the Winter Thunder. He, too, drove them away, breaking his silence to say this to them:

"None of you shall enter here," he said to them.

"I do not wish to listen to you.

"Go away, and keep on going!"

That night the people held a council at *Nahodoolá* in the south. But they could not agree on anything. On and on they quarreled, until white arose in the east and it was again day. *Tééhooltsódii* The One That Grabs Things In the Water then spoke to them:

"Everywhere in this world you bring disorder," he said to them.

"So we do not want you here.

"Find some other place to live."

But the people did not leave right away. For four nights the women talked and squabbled, each blaming the other for what had happened. And for four nights the men squabbled and talked. They, too, blamed one another.

At the end of the fourth night as they were at last about to end their meeting, they all noticed something white in the east. They also saw it in the south. It appeared in the west, too. And in the north it also appeared.

It looked like an endless chain of white mountains. They saw it on all sides. It surrounded them, and they noticed that it was closing in on them rapidly. It was a high, insurmountable wall of water! And it was flowing in on them from all directions, so that they could escape neither to the east nor to the west; neither to the south nor to the north could they escape.

So, having nowhere else to go, they took flight. Into the air they went. Higher and higher they soared, it is said.

Three
....

It is also said that they circled upward until they reached the smooth, hard shell of the sky overhead. When they could go no higher they looked down and saw that water now covered everything. They had nowhere to land either above or below.

Suddenly someone with a blue head appeared and called to them:

"Here," he called to them.

"Come this way.

"Here to the east there is a hole!"

They found that hole and entered. One by one they filed through to the other side of the sky. And that is how they reached the surface of the second world.

The blue-headed creature was a member of the Swallow People. It was they who lived up there.

While the first world had been red, this world was blue. The swallows lived in blue houses, which lay scattered across a broad, blue plain. Each blue house was cone-shaped; each tapered toward the top where there was a blue entry hole.

At first the Swallow People gathered around the newcomers and watched them silently. Nobody from either group said anything to any member of the other. Finally, when darkness came and the exiled Air-Spirit People made camp for the night, the blue swallows left.

In the morning the insect people from the world below decided that someone should explore this new world. So they sent a plain locust and a white locust to the east, instructing them to look for people like themselves.

Two days came and went before the locusts returned. They said that they had traveled for a full day. And as darkness fell they reached what must have been the end of the world. For they came upon the rim of a great cliff that rose out of an abyss whose bottom could not be seen. Both coming and going, they said, they found no people, no plants, no rivers, no mountains. They found nothing but bare, blue, level ground.

Next the two messengers were sent south to explore. Again, two days came and went while they were gone. And they again reported that after traveling for a full day they reached the end of the world. And they reported again that neither in going nor in coming back could they find people or plants, mountains or rivers.

They were then sent to the west. And after that they were sent to the north. Both times they were gone for two days, and they reported each time that they reached the end of the world after traveling for a full day. They also reported that again they could find neither people nor plants and neither mountains nor rivers.

To the others they had only this to say:

"It seems that we are in the center of a vast, blue plain," was all that they could say.

"Wherever we went in this world we could find neither company nor food; neither rivers nor mountains could we find."

After the scouts had returned from their fourth trip, the Swallow People visited the camp of the newcomers. And they asked why they had sent someone to the east to explore.

This is what the insect people from the lower world replied:

"We sent them out to see what was in the land," they replied.

"We sent them out to see if there were people here like ourselves."

Then the swallows asked this:

"What did your scouts tell you?" they asked.

To which the newcomers replied this way:

"They told us that they reached the end of the world after traveling for a full day," they replied.

"They told us that wherever they went in this world they could find neither people nor plants. Neither rivers nor mountains could they find."

The swallows then asked why the insect people had sent their scouts to the south. And they were told that the locusts were sent south to see what was in the land. And when the swallows asked why scouts were sent to the west, they were told again that the locusts were to see what they could find in this blue world. Which is what they were told when they asked why scouts were sent to the north.

To all of which the Swallow People then had this to say:

"Your couriers spoke the truth," they then said.

"But their trips were not necessary.

"Had you asked us what the land contained, we would have told you.

"Had you asked us where this world ended, we would have told you.

"We could have saved you all that time and all that trouble.

"Until you arrived here, no one besides us has ever lived in this world. We are the only ones living here."

The newcomers then had this suggestion to make to the swallows:

"You are like us in many ways," they suggested.

"You understand our language.

"Like us you have legs; like us you have bodies; like us you have wings; like us you have heads.

"Why can't we become friends?"

To which the swallows replied:

"Let it be as you say," they replied.

"You are welcome here among us."

So it was that both sets of people began to treat each other as members of one tribe. They mingled one among the other and called each other by the familiar names. They called each other grandparent and grandchild, brother and sister; they called each other father and son, mother and daughter.

For twenty-three days they all lived together in harmony. But on the night of the twenty-fourth day, one of the strangers became too free with the wife of the swallow chief.

Next morning, when he found out what had happened the night before, the chief had this to say to the strangers:

"We welcomed you here among us," was what he had to say to them.

"We treated you as friends and as kin.

"And this is how you return our kindness!

"No doubt you were driven from the world below for just such disorderly acts.

"Well, you must leave this world, too; we will have you here no longer.

"Anyhow, this is a bad land. There is not enough food for all of us.

"People are dying here every day from hunger. Even if we allowed you to stay, you could not live here very long."

When they heard the swallow chief's words, the locusts took flight. And all the others followed. Having nowhere else to go, they flew skyward.

Into the air they went. Higher and higher they soared. They circled upward until they reached the smooth, hard shell of the sky overhead, it is said.

Four

....

It is also said that like the sky of the world below, this sky had a smooth, hard shell. And like the sky of the world below this one seemed to have no opening. When the insect people reached it they flew around and around, having nowhere to land either above or below.

But as they circled, they noticed a white face peering at them. This was the face of *Nílch'i*. In the language of *Bilagáana* the White Man he would be called Wind. And they heard him cry to them:

"Here!" he cried.

"Here to the south you will find an opening.

"Come this way."

So off they flew to the south, and soon they found a slit in the sky slanting upward in a southerly direction. One by one they flew through it to the other side. And that is how they reached the surface of the third world.

While the second world had been blue, this world was yellow. Here the exiles found no one but Yellow Grasshopper People, who lived in yellow holes in the ground along the banks of a river which flowed east through their yellow land.

At first the Yellow Grasshopper People said nothing. They gathered silently around the newcomers and stared at them. Nobody from either group spoke to anyone from the other. And when darkness finally came and the people from the world below made their camp, the grasshoppers left.

In the morning the wanderers sent out the same two locusts who had explored the second world.

First they flew to the east where they were gone for two days altogether. Then they flew to the south where they were gone for two more days. Then they flew to the west, where they were gone for another two days. And they flew to the north where for two additional days they were gone. Each time they returned with the same report.

For a full day they had journeyed, until by nightfall they arrived at the rim of a cliff that rose from some unseen place far, far below. And neither in going forth nor in coming back could they find people or plants, mountains or waters. The river along whose banks the Grasshopper People lived soon tapered off toward the east until it was a dry, narrow gully. Otherwise there was nothing to see in this world except flat, yellow countryside and the yellow grasshoppers who lived on it.

When the messengers returned from their fourth journey the two great chiefs of the Grasshopper People came to visit. And they asked the newcomers why they had someone fly to the east and to the west, to the south and to the north.

To which the insect people from the world below replied:

"We sent them to see what was in the land," they replied.

"We sent them to see if they could find people like ourselves."

Then the grasshopper chiefs asked:

"And what did they find?" they asked.

Answered the newcomers:

"They found nothing but the bare land," they answered.

"They found nothing but the cliffs that marked the edge of this world."

"They found no plants and no people. They found no mountains and no rivers.

"Even the river along whose banks your people live here in the center of this world tapers off until it is only a dry, narrow gully."

Replied the grasshopper chiefs then:

"You might have first asked us what the land contains," they replied.

"We could have saved your messengers all that trouble.

"We could have told you that there is nothing in this land but what you see right here.

"We have lived here for a long time, but we have seen nothing that you have not seen. And we have seen no other people until you came."

The insect people from the world below then spoke to the grasshopper chiefs as they had spoken to the Swallow People in the second world, saying these things to them:

"Come to think of it, you are somewhat like us," they said to them.

"Like us you have heads. Like us you have wings. Like us you have bodies. Like us you have legs.

"You even speak the way we speak.

"Perhaps we can join you here."

The grasshoppers consented, and the two groups quickly began to mingle. They embraced each other, and soon they were using the names of family and kin together. They called each other mother and daughter, father and son, brother and sister, grandparent and grandchild. It was as if they were all of the same tribe.

As before, all went well for twenty-three days. But as before, on the night of the twenty-fourth, one of the newcomers treated the chief of the grasshoppers exactly as the swallow chief had been treated in the second world.

When he discovered how he had been wronged, the grasshopper chief spoke this way to the insect people:

"No doubt you were sent away from the world below for such transgressions!" is how he spoke.

"No doubt you bring disorder wherever you go. No doubt you lack intelligence.

"Well, here too you shall drink no more of our water. Here too you shall eat no more of our food. Here too you shall breathe no more of our air.

"Get out of here!"

So the insect people took flight again. And again they circled round and round into the sky until they arrived at the smooth, hard shell of its outer crust, it is said.

Five
●●●●●●●●●●●●●●●●●●

It is also said that they again had to circle around for quite some time, looking in vain for some way to get through the sky overhead. Finally they heard a voice bidding them fly to the west and look there. And they noticed a red head peering at them. The voice they heard and the head they saw belonged to *Nílch'i lichíí*. In the language of *Bilagáana* the White Man he would bear the name Red Wind.

Doing as they were told they found a passage which twisted around through the sky's other surface like the tendril of a vine. It had been made this way by the wind. They flew into it and wound their way to the other side. And that is how they reached the surface of the fourth world.

Four of the grasshoppers had come with them. One was white. One was blue. One was yellow. And one was black. To this very day, in fact, we have grasshoppers of those four colors among us.

The surface of the fourth world was unlike the surface of any of the lower worlds. For it was a mixture of black and white. The sky above was alternately white, blue, yellow, and black, just as it had been in the worlds below. But here the colors were of a different duration.

In the first world each color lasted for about the same length of time each day. In the second world the blue and the black lasted just a little longer than the white and the yellow. But here in the fourth world there was white and yellow for scarcely any time, so long did the blue and black remain in the sky. As yet there was no sun and no moon; as yet there were no stars.

When they arrived on the surface of the fourth world, the exiles from the lower worlds saw no living thing. But they did observe four great snow-covered peaks along the horizon around them. One peak lay to the east. One peak lay to the south. One peak lay likewise to the west. And to the north there was one peak.

The insect people sent two scouts to the east, who returned at the end of two days. Those two said that they had not been able to reach the eastern mountain after an entire day's flight. And although they had traveled far indeed they could see no living creature. Neither track nor trail could they see; not one sight of life were they able to detect.

Two scouts were then sent to the south. And when these two returned at the end of two full days they reported that after an entire day's flight they managed to reach a low range of mountains on this side of the great peak which lay in that direction.

They too had traveled very far. They too could see no living creature. But they did observe two different kinds of tracks the likes of which they had never seen before. They described them carefully, and from that description the tracks seemed to resemble those made these days in our own world by deer and turkey.

Two scouts were sent next to the west. And after two full days they returned, reporting that they could by no means reach the great peak which lay in that direction, no matter how fast they could fly in a single day and no matter how far. Neither in going forth nor in returning could they see any living creature. Not one sign of life were they able to see.

Finally, two scouts were sent to explore the land that lay to the north. And when they returned they had a different story to tell. For they reported that they had found a strange race unlike any other. These were people who cut their hair square in front. They were people who lived in houses in the ground. They were people who cultivated the soil so that things grew therein. They were now harvesting what they had planted, and they gave the couriers food to eat.

It was now evident to the newcomers that the fourth world was larger than any of the worlds below.

On the very next day, two members of the newly found race came to the camp of the exiles. They were called *Kiis'áanii*, they said, which in the language of

Bilagáana the White Man means People Who Live in Upright Houses. And they wished to invite the exiles to visit their village.

On the way they came to a stream which was red. The *Kiis'áanii* warned their guests not to wade through it. Otherwise the water would injure the feet of the newcomers. Instead they showed the insect people a square raft made of four logs. One log was of white pine. One log was of blue spruce. One log was of yellow pine. And one log was of black spruce. On this raft they all crossed to the opposite bank, where the people who had arrived from the third world visited the homes of the people who dwelled here in the fourth world.

The exiles were given corn and pumpkins to eat. And they were asked by their new friends to stay. For quite some time, in fact, they stayed in the village of the upright houses. There they lived well on the food that the *Kiis'áanii* gave them. Eventually they all lived together like the people of one tribe. Soon the two groups were using the names of family and kin between themselves. They called each other father and son, mother and daughter, grandparent and grandchild, brother and sister.

The land of the *Kiis'áanii* was a dry land. It had neither rain nor snow and there was little water to be found. But the people who had been dwelling there knew how to irrigate the soil to make things grow, and they taught the newcomers to do so.

Twenty-three days came and went, and twenty-three nights passed and all was well. And on the twenty-fourth night the exiles held a council meeting. They talked quietly among themselves, and they resolved to mend their ways and to do nothing unintelligent that would create disorder. This was a good world, and the wandering insect people meant to stay here, it is said.

Six
· · · · · · · · · · · · · · · · · ·

It is also said that late in the autumn of that year the newcomers heard a distant voice calling to them from far in the east.

They listened and waited, listened and waited. Until soon they heard the voice again, nearer and louder than before. They continued to listen and wait, listen and wait, until they heard the voice a third time, all the nearer and all the louder.

Continuing to listen, they heard the voice again, even louder than the last time, and so close now that it seemed directly upon them.

A moment later they found themselves standing among four mysterious beings. They had never seen such creatures anywhere before. For they were looking at those who would eventually become known as *Haashch'ééh dine'é.*

In the language of *Bilagáana* the White Man, that name means Holy People. For they are people unlike the earth-surface people who come into the world today, live on the ground for a while, die at a ripe old age, and then move on. These are intelligent people who can perform magic. They do not know the pain of being mortal. They are people who can travel far by follow- ing the path of the rainbow. And they can travel swiftly by following the path of the sunray. They can make the winds and the thunderbolts work for them so that the earth is theirs to control when they so wish.

The people who were then living on the surface of the fourth world were looking upon *Bits'íís ligaii*, which name means White Body. He is the one that the Navajo people who live in our own world would eventually call *Haashch'- éélti'í*, which in today's language means Talking God.

And they were looking upon *Bits'íís dootł'izh.* That name means Blue Body. He is the one that the Navajo people in our own world would eventually come to know as *Tó neinilí*, which means Water Sprinkler.

And they were looking upon *Bits'íís litsoii*, or Yellow Body. He is the one that the Navajo people today call *Haashch'éoghan.* Nobody can be sure what that name means in today's language. Some say it means Calling God; some say that it means House God; and some say that it means Growling God.

And they were looking upon *Bits'íís lizhin.* In the White Man's language that name means Black Body. He is the one that the Navajo people living in this world would eventually come to know as *Haashch'ééshzhiní*, which means Black God. Sometimes he is also called the God of Fire.

Without speaking the Holy People made signs to those who were gathered there, as if to give them instructions. But the exiles could not understand their gestures. So they stood by helplessly and watched.

And after the gods had left, the people talked about that mysterious visit for the rest of that day and all night long, trying to determine what it meant.

As for the gods, they repeated their visit four days in a row. But on the fourth day, *Bits'íís lizhin* the Black Body remained after the other three departed. And when he was alone with the onlookers, he spoke to them in their own language. This is what he said:

"You do not seem to understand the Holy People," he said.

"So I will explain what they want you to know.

"They want more people to be created in this world. But they want intelligent people, created in their likeness, not in yours.

"You have bodies like theirs, true enough.

"But you have the teeth of beasts! You have the mouths of beasts! You have the feet of beasts! You have the claws of beasts!

"The new creatures are to have hands like ours. They are to have feet like ours. They are to have mouths like ours and teeth like ours. They must learn to think ahead, as we do.

"What is more, you are unclean!

"You smell bad.

"So you are instructed to cleanse yourselves before we return twelve days from now."

That is what *Bits'íís łizhin* the Black Body said to the insect people who had emerged from the first world to the second, from the second world to the third, and from the third world to the fourth world where they now lived.

Accordingly, on the morning of the twelfth day the people bathed carefully. The women dried themselves with yellow corn meal. The men dried themselves with white corn meal.

Soon after they had bathed, they again heard the distant voice coming from far in the east.

They listened and waited as before, listened and waited. Until soon they heard the voice as before, nearer and louder this time. They continued to listen and wait, listen and wait, until they heard the voice a third time as before, all the nearer and all the louder.

Continuing to listen as before, they heard the voice again, even louder than the last time, and so close now that it seemed directly upon them, exactly as it had seemed before. And as before they found themselves standing among the same four *Haashch'ééh dine'é*, or Holy People as *Bilagáana* the White Man might wish to call them.

Bits'íís dootł'izh the Blue Body and *Bits'íís łizhin* the Black Body each carried a sacred buckskin. *Bits'íís ligaii* the White Body carried two ears of corn.

One ear of corn was yellow. The other ear was white. Each ear was completely covered at the end with grains, just as sacred ears of corn are covered in our own world now.

Proceeding silently, the gods laid one buckskin on the ground, careful that its head faced the west. Upon this skin they placed the two ears of corn, being just as careful that the tips of each pointed east. Over the corn they spread the other buckskin, making sure that its head faced east.

Under the white ear they put the feather of a white eagle.

And under the yellow ear they put the feather of a yellow eagle.

Then they told the onlooking people to stand at a distance.

So that the wind could enter.

Then from the east *Nílch'i ligai* the White Wind blew between the buckskins. And while the wind thus blew, each of the Holy People came and walked four times around the objects they had placed so carefully on the ground.

As they walked, the eagle feathers, whose tips protruded slightly from between the two buckskins, moved slightly.

Just slightly.

So that only those who watched carefully were able to notice.

And when the Holy People had finished walking, they lifted the topmost buckskin.

And lo! the ears of corn had disappeared.

In their place there lay a man and there lay a woman.

The white ear of corn had been transformed into our most ancient male ancestor. And the yellow ear of corn had been transformed into our most ancient female ancestor.

It was the wind that had given them life: the very wind that gives us our breath as we go about our daily affairs here in the world we ourselves live in!

When this wind ceases to blow inside of us, we become speechless. Then we die.

In the skin at the tips of our fingers we can see the trail of that life-giving wind.

Look carefully at your own fingertips.

There you will see where the wind blew when it created your most ancient ancestors out of two ears of corn, it is said.

The Creation

Many Winters in the past (arrow going backward)

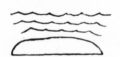

the Earth was entirely covered by a great blanket of water. There was no sun, moon, or stars and so there was no light. All was darkness.

At that time, the only living creatures of the world were water animals such as the beaver, muskrat, duck and loon.

Far above earth was the Land of Happy Spirits where lived Rawennio, the Great Ruler. In the center of this upper world was a giant tree.

This great tree was an apple tree whose roots sank deep into the ground.

One day, Rawennio pulled this giant tree up by its roots.

The Great Spirit called his daughter who lived in the Upper World and commanded her to look into the pit caused by the uprooted tree.

This woman, who was to be the mother of the Good and Evil Spirits, came and looked into the hole by the uprooted tree.

She saw far below her the Lower World covered with water and surrounded by heavy clouds.

"You are to go to this world of darkness," said the Great Spirit. Gently lifting her, he dropped her into the hole.

She floated downward.

Far below on the dark water floated the water animals. Looking upward, they saw a great light, which was the Sky Woman, slowly falling toward them.

Because her body shone as a great light they were at first frightened.

Fear filled their hearts and they dove beneath the deep waters.

But upon coming to the surface again, they lost their fear. They began to plan what they would do for the woman when she reached the water.

"We must find a dry place for her to rest on," said the beaver, and he plunged beneath the water in search of some earth. After a long time, the beaver's dead body floated to the top of the water.

The loon tried next, but his body never came to the surface of the water. Many of the other water creatures dived, but all failed to secure any earth.

Finally, the muskrat went below and after a long time, his dead body floated to the surface of the water. His little claws were closed tight. Upon opening them, a little earth was found.

The water creatures took this earth, and calling a great turtle, they patted the earth firmly on her broad back. Immediately, the turtle started to grow larger. The earth also increased.

This earth became North America, a great island. Sometimes the earth cracks and shakes, and waves beat hard against the seashore. White people say, "Earthquake." The Mohawk say, "Turtle is stretching."

The Sky Woman had now almost reached the earth. "We must fly up and let her rest upon our backs so as to make her landing easy," said the chief of the white swans. Flying upward, a great flock of white swans allowed the Sky Woman to rest upon their backs. Gently, they bore her to earth.

After a time, the Sky Woman gave birth to twins. One who became the Good Spirit was born first. The other, the Evil Spirit, while being born, caused his mother so much pain that she died during his birth.

The Good Spirit immediately took his mother's head and hung it in the sky. It became the sun. The Good Spirit, from his mother's body, fashioned the moon and stars and placed them in the sky.

The rest of his mother's body he buried under the earth. That is why living things find nourishment from the soil. They spring from Mother Earth.

The Evil Spirit put darkness in the west sky to drive the sun before it.

The Good Spirit created many things which he placed upon the earth. The Evil Spirit tried to undo the work of his brother by creating evil. The Good Spirit made tall and beautiful trees such as the pine and hemlock.

The Evil Spirit stunted some trees. In others, he put knots and gnarls. He covered some with thorns, and placed poison fruit on them.

The Good Spirit made animals such as the deer and the bear.

The Evil Spirit made poisonous animals, lizards, and serpents to destroy the animals of the Good Spirit's creation.

The Good Spirit made springs and streams of good, pure water.

The Evil Spirit breathed poison into many of the springs. He put snakes into others.

The Good Spirit made beautiful rivers protected by high hills.

The Evil Spirit pushed rocks and dirt into the rivers causing the current to become swift and dangerous. Everything that the Good Spirit made, his wicked brother tried to destroy.

Finally, when the earth was completed, the Good Spirit fashioned man out of some red clay. He placed man upon the earth, and told him how he should live. The Evil Spirit, not to be outdone, fashioned a creature out of the white foam of the sea. What he made was the monkey.

After mankind and the other creatures of the world were created, the Good Spirit bestowed a protecting spirit upon each of his creations.

He then called the Evil Spirit, and told him that he must cease making trouble upon the earth. This the Evil Spirit refused to do. The Good Spirit became very angry with his wicked brother. He challenged his brother to combat, the victor to become ruler of the earth. They used the thorns of a giant apple tree as weapons.

They fought for many suns (days).

Finally, the Evil Spirit was overcome.

The Good Spirit now became ruler over the earth. He banished his wicked brother to a dark cave under the earth. There he must always remain.

But the Evil Spirit has wicked servants who roam the earth. These wicked spirits can take the shape of any creature that the Evil Spirit desires them to take. They are constantly influencing the minds of men, thus causing men to do evil things.

That is why every person has both a bad heart and a good heart. No matter how good a man seems, he has some evil. No matter how bad a man seems, there is some good about him. No man is perfect.

The Good Spirit continues to create and protect mankind. He controls the spirits of good men after death. The Evil Spirit takes charge of the souls of wicked men after death.

Tangaroa, Maker of All Things

*F*or a long time Tangaroa lived within his shell. It was round like an egg and in the lasting darkness it revolved in the void.

There was no sun, there was no moon, there was no land nor mountain, all was moving in the void. There was no man, no fowl nor dog, no living thing; there was no water, salt or fresh.

At the end of a great time Tangaroa flicked his shell, and it cracked and fell apart. Then Tangaroa stepped forth and stood upon that shell and called:

"Who is above there? Who is below there?"

No voice replied. He called again:

"Who is in front there? Who is behind there?"

Still no voice answered. Only Tangaroa's voice was heard, there was no other.

Then Tangaroa said, "O rock, crawl here!"

But no rock was, to crawl to him.

He therefore said, "O sand, crawl here!"

There was no sand to crawl to him. And Tangaroa became angry because he was not obeyed. He therefore overturned his shell and raised it up to form a dome for the sky, and he named it *Rumia*, that is, Overturned.

After a time great Tangaroa, wearied from confinement, stepped out from another shell that covered him; and he took this shell for rock and sand.

But his anger was not finished, and so he took his backbone for a mountain range and his ribs for the ridges that ascend. He took his innards for the broad floating clouds and his flesh for fatness of the earth, and his arms and legs for strength of the earth. He took his fingernails and toenails for the scales and shells of fishes in the sea.

Of his feathers he made trees and shrubs and plants to clothe the land. Of his guts he made lobsters, shrimps, and eels, for the streams and for the sea.

And the blood of Tangaroa became hot, and it floated away to make the redness of the sky, and also rainbows. All that is red is made from Tangaroa's blood.

But the head of Tangaroa remained sacred to himself, and he still lived, the same head upon a body that remained.

Tangaroa was master of everything that is. There was expansion and there was growth.

Tangaroa called forth gods. It was only later that he called forth man, when Tu was with him.

As Tangaroa had shells, so has everything a shell. The sky is a shell, which is endless space, where the gods placed the sun, the moon, the constellations, and the other stars.

The land is a shell to the stones and to water, and to the plants that spring from it. The shell of a man is woman, since it is from her that he comes forth. And a woman's shell is woman, since it is from her that she comes forth.

No one can name the shells of all the things that are in this world.

In the Beginning . . .

*I*n the Beginning the Earth was an infinite and murky plain, separated from the sky and from the grey salt sea and smothered in a shadowy twilight. There were neither Sun nor Moon nor Stars. Yet, far away, lived the Sky-Dwellers: youthfully indifferent beings, human in form but with the feet of emus, their golden hair glittering like spiders' webs in the sunset, ageless and unageing, having existed forever in their green, well-watered Paradise beyond the Western Clouds.

On the surface of the Earth, the only features were certain hollows which would, one day, be waterholes. There were no animals and no plants, yet clustered round the waterholes there were pulpy masses of matter: lumps of primordial soup—soundless, sightless, unbreathing, unawake, and unsleeping—each containing the essence of life, or the possibility of becoming human.

Beneath the Earth's crust, however, the constellations glimmered, the Sun shone, the Moon waxed and waned, and all the forms of life lay sleeping: the scarlet of a desert-pea, the iridescence on a butterfly's wing, the twitching white whiskers of Old Man Kangaroo—dormant as seeds in the desert that must wait for a wandering shower.

On the morning of the First Day, the Sun felt the urge to be born. (That evening the Stars and Moon would follow.) The Sun burst through the surface, flooding the land with golden light, warming the hollows under which each Ancestor lay sleeping.

Unlike the Sky-Dwellers, these Ancients had never been young. They were lame, exhausted greybeards with knotted limbs, and they had slept in isolation through the ages.

So it was, on this First Morning, that each drowsing Ancestor felt the Sun's warmth pressing on his eyelids, and felt his body giving birth to children. The Snake Man felt snakes slithering out of his navel. The Cockatoo Man felt feathers. The Witchetty Grub Man felt a wriggling, the Honey-ant a tickling, the Honeysuckle felt his leaves and flowers unfurling. The Bandicoot Man felt baby bandicoots seething from under his armpits. Every one of the "living things," each at its own separate birthplace, reached up for the light of day.

In the bottom of their hollows (now filling up with water), the Ancients shifted one leg, then another leg. They shook their shoulders and flexed their arms. They heaved their bodies upward through the mud. Their eyelids cracked upon. They saw their children at play in the sunshine.

The mud fell from their thighs, like placenta from a baby. Then, like the baby's first cry, each Ancestor opened his mouth and called out, "I AM!" "I am—Snake . . . Cockatoo . . . Honey-ant . . . Honeysuckle . . ." And this first "I am!," this primordial act of naming, was held, then and forever after, as the most secret and sacred couplet of the Ancestor's song.

Each of the Ancients (now basking in the sunlight) put his left foot forward and called out a second name. He put his right foot forward and called out a third name. He named the waterhole, the reedbeds, the gum trees—calling to right and left, calling all things into being and weaving their names into verses.

The Ancients sang their way all over the world. They sang the rivers and ranges, salt-pans and sand dunes. They hunted, ate, made love, danced, killed: wherever their tracks led they left a trail of music.

They wrapped the whole world in a web of song; and at last, when the Earth was sung, they felt tired. Again in their limbs they felt the frozen immobility of Ages. Some sank into the ground where they stood. Some crawled into caves. Some crept away to their "Eternal Homes," to the ancestral waterholes that bore them.

All of them went "back in."

Kalevala:
The Mother of Water

It is my desire,   it is my wish
to set out to sing,   to begin to recite,
to let a song of our clan glide on,   to sing a family lay.
The words are melting in my mouth,   utterances dropping out,
coming to my tongue,   being scattered about on my teeth.

Beloved friend, my boon companion,   my fair boyhood comrade,
start now to sing with me,   begin to recite together
now that we have come together,   have come from two directions.
Seldom do we come together,   meet one another
on these wretched marches,   these poor northern parts.
Let us clasp hand in hand,   fingers in fingers,
so that we may sing fine things,   give voice to the best things
for those dear ones to hear,   for those desiring to know them
among the rising younger generation,   among the people which is growing
     up,
those songs got about,   those lays inspired by
old Väinämöinen's belt,   the depths of Ilmarinen's forge,
the point of the sword of [Lemminkäinen,] a man with a far-roving
     mind,   the range of Joukahainen's crossbow,
the remote corners of North Farm's fields,   the heaths of the Kaleva
     District.
These my father formerly sang   while carving an ax handle,
these my mother taught me   while turning her spindle,
me a child rolling on the floor   in front of her knee,

miserable milkbeard,   little clabbermouth.
There was no lack of songs in the Sampo   nor did Louhi lack magic
    charms.
In the songs the Sampo grew old,   in the charms Louhi disappeared,
in the lays Vipunen died,   Lemminkäinen in his frolics.

There are still other songs,   magic words learned of,
plucked from the wayside,   broken off from the heather,
torn from thickets,   dragged from saplings,
rubbed off the top of hay,   ripped from lanes
when I was going about as a herdsman,   as a child in cow pastures,
on honeyed hillocks,   on lovely knolls,
following dusky Blackie,   going along with spotted Frisky.
The cold recited me a lay,   the rain kept bringing me songs.
The winds brought another song,   the waves of the sea drove some to me.
The birds added songs,   the treetops magic sayings.
These I wound up in a ball,   arranged in a clew.
I thrust the ball into my sled,   the clew into my sleigh;
I pulled it home on my sled,   on my sleigh to the threshing barn,
put it up in the storehouse loft   in a round copper box.

For a long time my lays have been in the cold,   housed in darkness.
Shall I pull the lays out of the cold,   draw the songs out of the frost,
bring my box into the house   to the end of the long bench
under the fine ridgepole,   under the lovely roof?
Shall I open my chest of words,   unlock my song box,
clip the end off the ball,   undo the knot in the clew?
Thus I will sing a really fine lay,   intone a beautiful one
out of rye bread,   barley beer.
If no one happens to bring any beer,   serves no table beer,
I will sing from a leaner mouth,   intone on water
to gladden this evening of ours,   to honor this memorable day
or to delight the morrow,   to begin a new morn.

Thus I heard a song being sung,   knew a lay to be composed:
in loneliness do the nights come upon us,   in loneliness do the days shine
    bright upon us;

in loneliness Väinämöinen was born,   the eternal singer emerged
from the maiden who bore him,   from his Air Spirit mother.

There was a virgin, maiden of the air,   lovely woman, a spirit of nature.
Long she kept her purity,   ever her virginity
in the spacious farmyards,   on the smooth fields of the air.
In time she got bored,   her life seemed strange
in always being alone,   living as a virgin
in the spacious farmyards,   in the vast wastes of the air.
Now indeed she comes lower down,   settled down on the billows,
on the broad expanse of the sea,   on the wide open sea.
There came a great blast of wind,   severe weather from the east;
it raised the sea up into foam,   splashed it into billows.
The wind kept rocking the girl,   a wave kept driving the virgin
around about on the blue sea,   on the whitecapped billows.
The wind blew her pregnant,   the sea made her thick through.
She carried a hard womb,   a stiff bellyfull
for seven hundred years,   for nine ages of man.
Nothing is born,   the self-begotten fetus does not come free.

As mother of the water the virgin went hither and yon.   She swims east,
     swims west,
swims northwest, south,   swims along the whole horizon
in the agonies of her burning gestation,   with severe labor pains.
Nothing is born,   the self-begotten fetus does not come free.

She keeps weeping softly and unceasingly,   uttered a word, spoke thus:
"Woe are my days, poor me,   woe is my wandering, wretched child!
Now I have got into trouble: ever to be under the sky,
to be rocked by the wind,   to be driven by the waves
on these extensive waters, boundless billows! It would have been
     better   to live as a virgin of the air
than it is nowadays   to keep floating about as the mother of the water.
It is cold for me to be here,   painful for me to be adrift,
to dwell in the waves,   to be going hither and yon in the water.
O Ukko, god on high,   supporter of the whole sky!
Come here, since there is need,   come here, since you are summoned.

Deliver the maiden from her predicament,   the woman from her labor
    pains!
Come soon, get here without delay;   you are needed without any delay at
    all."

A little time passed,   a little bit passed quickly.
A goldeneye came, a straight-flying bird;   it fluttered about
seeking a place for its nest,   considering a place to live.
It flew east, it flew west,   flew northwest, south.
It does not find such a place,   not even the poorest kind of place,
in which it might build its nest,   take up its dwelling place.
It flits about, soars about,   it ponders, it reflects:
"Shall I build my house in the wind,   my dwelling place on the waves?
The wind will tip the house over,   a wave will carry off my dwelling
    place."

So then the mother of the water,   mother of the water, virgin of the air,
raised her knee from the sea,   her shoulder blade from a billow,
for the goldeneye as a place for a nest,   as an agreeable dwelling place.
That goldeneye, graceful bird,   flits about, soars about.
She discovered the knee of the mother of the water   on the bluish open
    sea;
she thought it a grass-grown tussock,   fresh turf.
She soars about, flits about,   settles down on the knee.
On it she builds her nest,   laid her golden eggs,
six golden eggs,   the seventh an iron egg.
She began to brood the eggs,   to warm the top of the knee.
She brooded one day, brooded a second,   then brooded a third, too.

Now because of that the mother of the water,   mother of the water,
    virgin of the air,
feels burning hot,   her skin scorched;
she thought her knee was burning,   all her sinews melting.
Suddenly she twitched her knee,   made her limbs tremble;
the eggs tumbled into the water,   are sent into the waves of the sea;
the eggs cracked to pieces,   broke to bits.
The eggs do not get into the ooze,   the bits not get mixed up with the water.

The bits were turned into fine things,   the pieces into beautiful things:
the lower half of one egg   into the earth beneath,
the top half of another egg   into the heavens above.
The top half of one yolk   gets to glow like the sun,
the top half of one white   gets to gleam palely as the moon;
any mottled things on an egg,   those become stars in heaven,
anything black on an egg,   those indeed become clouds in the sky.

The ages go on,   the years go by still longer
while the new sun is glowing,   the new moon gleaming palely.
The mother of the water, the mother of the water,   virgin of the air,
    keeps on swimming
on those gentle waters,   on the misty billows,
before her the flowing water,   behind her the clear heavens.

Now in the ninth year,   in the tenth summer
she raised her head from the sea,   lifts up the crown of her head.
She began to perform her acts of creation,   to accomplish her works
on the wide expanse of the sea,   on the wide open sea.
Where she swung her hand,   there she arranged headlands;
where she touched bottom with her foot,   she hollowed out deep spots for
    fish;
where, moreover, bubbles came up,   there she deepened deep places.
She turned her side against the land;   there she made the coasts smooth;
she turned her feet against the land;   there she formed places to seine for
    salmon;
she came with her head against the land;   there she fashioned bays.
Then she swam farther out from land,   lingered on the open sea.
She forms little islands in the sea,   produced hidden reefs
for a ship to run aground on,   to destroy seamen.
Now the islands were arranged,   little islands created in the sea,
the pillars of the sky erected,   lands and continents sung into being,
patterns marbled in rocks,   designs drawn on crags.
Väinämöinen is not yet born,   the eternal singer has not appeared.

Steadfast old Väinämöinen   went about in his mother's womb
for thirty summers,   the same number of winters, too,

on those gentle waters,   on the misty billows.
He ponders, he reflects   how to exist, how to live
in his dark hiding place,   in the cramped dwelling
where he never saw the moon   nor spied the sun.
He speaks these words,   made this utterance:
"Moon, free me; sun, release me;   Great Bear, ever guide
the man out of the strange doors,   the alien gates,
from this little nest,   the cramped dwellings.
Escort the traveler to land,   the child of man to the outer air,
to look at the moon in the sky,   to admire the sun,
to inspect the Great Bear,   to scan the stars."

When the moon did not free him   nor the sun release him,
he thought his time strange,   became impatient with his life;
he moved the gate of the fort   with his ring finger,
suddenly turned the bony lock   with his left toe;
with his nails he got outside the threshold,   with his knees out from the
    door of the entrance.
Then he plunged straight into the sea,   rolled right into the billows;
the man remains on the sea,   the person among the waves.
There he lay outstretched for five years,   both five years and six,
seven years, eight.   At last he came to a stop on the surface,
by a nameless headland,   a treeless land.
With his knees he struggled up from the ground,   with his arms he
    turned himself over.
He got up to look at the moon,   to admire the sun,
to observe the Great Bear,   to scan the stars.

That was the birth of Väinämöinen,   the ancestry of the stouthearted
    singer,
out of the maiden who bore him,   from his Air Spirit mother.

The Origin of Different Water Animals

NAGALAND, INDIA

Once upon a time a crab, a frog, a shrimp, and a minnow were friends. All four were females and they worked together very well. Each helped the others by doing what she could do best. Each day at dinnertime they arranged a fine meal and ate together. Like humans, these animals grew rice. They worked as a group (*aluzunga*) in one another's fields, thus making the work more enjoyable, due to the company. The four took turns cooking. The one whose turn it was to cook would leave the field early and go home to prepare dinner. When it was ready she would call her friends from the fields, asking them to join her.

After a while it was agreed that the crab's cooking was the best. So, they asked the crab if she would cook every day. She would be delighted to, she said, and thereafter this was her job. One day, there was no meat available to make a decent meal. So the crab took off one of its own legs and added it to the vegetables. When the meal was ready she called her friends as usual. They thought the meal was especially good that day and helped themselves to extra portions. They praised the crab for sacrificing its leg and making such a good meal, even in time of want.

The crab was so pleased with the praise she received from her friends that she continued to remove one after another of her legs each day. She put each leg into the curry until only the stump of her body remained. Each day the group praised her again for her cooking and urged her to continue in her role as chef. She gladly accepted, because their praise warmed her heart.

One day, while the group of three friends was working in the field they realized it was already past time for their midday meal. Still they waited patiently for the crab to call them to dinner. But there was no call. Eventually they decided to go home anyway. But the crab was not at the house. The friends called for her but there was no answer. They decided that she must have returned to the river to bathe or perhaps to grow new legs. They were hungry and so they decided to eat without waiting for her. It was already quite late. As they opened the curry pot to serve their food, there was the crab's body right in the middle of the curry, flavoring the whole dish with her tasty meat.

Seeing the sacrifice the crab had made of herself, the other three animals all started to laugh. They laughed and laughed until they couldn't stand up straight. They laughed until they rolled around on the floor. They laughed until evening, when they finally stopped from sheer exhaustion. When the frog tried to get up, however, she could no longer stand erect. Her back had become permanently bent at the base of the spine from laughing so hard. The fish's neck had become so swollen that it no longer had the graceful curves it used to have. Now it was stiff and straight. The shrimp could no longer walk forward, but only backward as she had been doing during her fit of laughter. Unable to continue their work in the fields, all these animals took to the water. And that is where we find them today.

Juruna Kills the Sun

Kuadê, the Sun, was also a person. He lived far away and spoke another language. The Juruna often traveled near his house. Where the Sun lived, there was a hole in the stone that was always full of water. It was a trap for catching animals. Any animal that put its head in the hole to drink got stuck. Every day the Sun went to see if he had caught anything. When he found something, he killed it and took it home to eat. Fishing he did at night only, shining a light from his rump into the water. He would get furious and kill anybody who claimed to have seen his light. There once was a young Juruna who did not know about the Sun's trap, the hole in the stone. Passing by one day, and being thirsty, he went to get a drink, and his hand got caught.

The next day, when he saw the Sun making his daily rounds, the youth pretended to be dead. He lay there stretched out, not moving a muscle. Even his heart stopped beating, out of fear. The Sun came up and inspected him. He opened his mouth and eyes, felt his chest, and saw that everything had stopped as in dead people. So the Sun freed the young Juruna's arm from the hole and put him inside a basket for carrying. But before raising the basket to his shoulders, to see if the youth was truly dead, he scattered ants all over him. The Juruna put up with the ants without moving until they began to bite his eyes, and then he stirred a little. The Sun's cudgel, which was standing nearby, saw him move and was going to smash him, but its master would not let it; he insisted that the Juruna was really dead. Then the Sun carried the basket with the body to a spot near his house and hung it from the branch of a tree. The next day he told his son to bring the basket into the house. The Sun's boy went out, but the Juruna was nowhere to be found. He had escaped during the night. On learning this, the Sun hurled his cudgel after him. The cudgel left flying and at length struck a deer. The Sun said that was not what he wanted and went after the fugitive himself. Finally he found him hidden in the hollow root of a tree. The cudgel went up to the tree and proceeded to pound its trunk. Realizing that he wasn't getting anywhere with this, the Sun cut a stick and started poking around inside the hollow. He wounded the Juruna from head to foot, but still he would not come out of his lair. It was getting late, so the Sun covered up the hole with a stone and said to the cudgel, "Tomorrow we'll come back and finish him off."

At night, with the Sun far away, all kinds of animals—tapirs, wild pigs, deer, monkeys, pacas, agoutis—came to help the young Juruna out of the hole where he had hidden. From inside, he begged them, "Uncover this trunk so I can leave."

The animals started to burrow. Whenever their teeth were ready to break, they would bring other animals to keep on digging. Finally the tapir succeeded in making a little hole. The Juruna put his head out and asked them to dig a little more. The agouti and the tapir made the hole wide enough for him to get out. When the Sun arrived, the Juruna was nowhere to be found. By that time, he was practically in his own house. At home, he told his relatives about his adventure, saying that he had come very close to being killed by the Sun. After three days, he told his mother he was going out to gather coconuts. In tears, his mother begged him to stay. "Don't go, my son, because the Sun will kill you."

The young man cut off all his hair and painted his body with genipap. He went to tell his mother that the Sun would never recognize him as he was now. "Don't worry, the Sun will not recognize me. I'm different now."

He said this and marched off into the forest. He climbed the first inajá palm he could find and stayed up there gathering coconuts. The Sun happened to be passing through the neighborhood and thought he saw a monkey up in the palm tree. But when he realized that it was a person and that, in fact, it was the young Juruna, he said, "I almost killed you the other day, and now you really are going to die."

"I am not the person you think I am. I'm somebody else," said the young man from above.

But the Sun knew and replied, "It's you, all right. Come on down, you're going to die right now."

Then the Juruna, from the top of the palm tree, asked the Sun first to catch the coconut bunch he was about to throw. "First catch this bunch I'm throwing down."

"Throw it," said the Sun.

The youth threw the bunch and the Sun caught it. It was a small bunch, that first one. Up in the palm tree, the Juruna called again, "Catch this one too."

And from up there he threw a huge, heavy bunch. The Sun was waiting with his arms stretched out. The coconuts struck him right in the chest and killed him on the spot. At the Sun's death, everything got dark. The cudgel, at the death of its master, ran away and transformed itself into a snake, the *salamanta* (ringed boa) or *uandáre* (Sun's cudgel). The blood pouring out of the Sun turned into spiders, ants, snakes, centipedes, and other creatures. The snakes and spiders that covered the ground would not allow the Juruna to climb out of the palm tree. So he began to swing from tree to tree, like a monkey, and would not come down until he saw that the ground was clear. Once on solid ground, the youth looked for his trail and went home to his village. When he got there, he said to his mother, "I killed the Sun."

"Why did you do that? I was right to tell you to stay home. Now everything is dark," the frightened mother complained.

The children were all dying in the darkness, since no one could fish or hunt or work. In the Sun's village, his wife realized that he had died. She said to her three sons, who were starving, "Your father died because he liked to kill people. Which of you wants to replace him?"

First she tested the oldest of the three. As soon as this one put on his father's feather headdress, he thought it was awfully hot. He went up and up, and when it was almost dawn, he couldn't stand the heat any longer and came back down. Then it was the second son's turn. He put the feathers on his head and started to ascend. He went a little past where his brother had given up, but in the end he couldn't stand it either and came down complaining of the heat. Now it was the youngest one's turn. His mother asked him if he wanted to replace his father. He said he did. He adorned himself with the feathers and rose up, but since the heat was frightful, he walked very fast and immediately hid himself on the opposite side.

When he came home, his mother said to him, "You stood it pretty well, but next time you'll have to walk slower, to give people a chance to fish and hunt and work. You mustn't run."

The Sun's youngest boy made the walk once again, and this time he went slower. His mother suggested that he rest awhile when he reached the summit in the middle of the route, and that he come down slowly, resting awhile there too, before going in on the opposite side. When the mother saw her son making the entire journey exactly as it should be done, she wept and said, "Now you've taken over your father's place and you'll never come back to me."

The son, in his turn, answered from above, "Now I can no longer return home to live with you. I must always remain up here."

Upon hearing this, his mother wept again.

How Moon Fathered the World

WAKARANGA, ZIMBABWE

God made a man whom he called Moon. Moon first lived at the bottom of the sea. Moon wanted to go and live on the earth, but God warned him: "Life on the earth is hard and you will regret it."

But Moon went to the earth. In those days the earth was void and uninhabited. There were no trees, no plants, no animals. Moon was unhappy and wept. God said: "I warned you, but you did not listen. Nevertheless I will help you. You shall have a wife, who will live with you for two years."

God sent Morningstar to live with Moon. Morningstar brought fire from heaven. At night when she lay down in Moon's hut she lit a fire and lay on one side of it. Moon lay on the other side. But during the night Moon stepped through the fire and had intercourse with Morningstar.

The following morning he saw that Morningstar's body had swelled up. And she gave birth to trees, grasses, and all kinds of plants until the entire world was green. The trees began to grow. They grew and grew until they touched the sky. But when they touched the sky rain began to fall. Moon and Morningstar lived a life of plenty. They ate seeds and roots.

But when the two years were up, God called Morningstar away and sent her to live in the sky.

Moon wept for eight days. Then God gave him a second wife and he said: "She will live with you for two years. But at the end of that time you must die."

Eveningstar went and lived with Moon for two years. Moon slept with Eveningstar and on the following day her belly swelled up. And she gave birth to goats, sheep, and cows. On the second day she gave birth to antelopes and birds. But on the third day she gave birth to boys and girls.

On the fourth day Moon wanted to sleep once again with Eveningstar, but God said: "Let be. The time is near when you must die." But Moon disobeyed and he slept once more with Eveningstar. On the following morning her body had swelled up and she gave birth to lions, leopards, snakes, and scorpions.

And God said: "I warned you, but you would not listen."

Moon saw that his daughters were beautiful and he went to have intercourse with them. They bore many children to him, and he became king of a large realm.

But Eveningstar was jealous of her daughters and she sent snake to bite Moon. When Moon was bitten he became very ill. And at the same time rain ceased to fall. The lakes and the rivers began to dry up. The plants began to die and there was famine. Then the children began to discuss amongst themselves, how they could make the rain return. And they said: "It is Moon's fault."

Then they strangled Moon and they threw him into the ocean and they made another man their king.

But Moon rose from the sea and he pursues Morningstar across the sky, his first wife with whom he had been happy.

Sun and Moon

• •

NIVAKLÉ, GRAN CHACO PLAINS, PARAGUAY

Sun was a very gluttonous man, and no meal ever satisfied him. He had a son-in-law, married to his oldest daughter, who was not a good hunter. The man used to kill only two animals at a time. Sometimes he brought back three rheas. This was very little for his father-in-law. Whenever Sun had finished his ration of meat, there was a lot of complaining to be heard. "What a shame!" And he would force the son-in-law to go hunting again. Once he brought back only one animal. It was not enough to satisfy Sun's hunger, and the other had to go out again. He found nothing. Then Sun killed his son-in-law. He was very greedy. There never was enough meat for him, and therefore he killed his son-in-law.

Afterward, a man who wanted to improve a bit on this performance married Sun's other daughter, the middle one. Later the new son-in-law went hunting, and returned with four wild pigs. This was a little more to Sun's liking. "It seems my son-in-law will turn out all right," he said. "I'm pleased now, for he seems to be a good hunter."

For a long time the young man fed his father-in-law. But once, as sometimes happens, his hunting luck ran out. We all know that this is something that may happen to any hunter, no matter how good he is. He returned with only three animals. "Oh, what a pity!" exclaimed Sun. Nevertheless he enjoyed the meat, which lasted him about four days. Meanwhile his son-in-law had gone hunting again. This time he brought back only two animals. They lasted Sun barely one evening, for he swallowed them whole. Hurriedly the young man went hunting again. He returned with a single animal. It was midnight. Sun finished the roast, and was still hungry. In the morning the son-in-law went hunting. But this time it went very badly for him, and he did not catch anything, as happens not infrequently to hunters. "My son-in-law," Sun reproached him, "you may as well not go hunting tomorrow, for you're good for nothing. It's a pity that you married my daughter." And he struck him on the neck, killing him on the spot. The young man did not even have time to raise his hand.

After this, a youth who wanted to be better than the other presented himself. "I wonder how I will fare with this Sun," he thought. "But I know that I'm an infallible hunter." He married Sun's youngest daughter. "All right, now you're married to my daughter," said Sun, and sent him out to hunt. He left early, and killed many animals, many wild pigs. I think he caught as many as twelve that day. Sun was very pleased. "That young man shall be my son-in-law for a long time, for he's a good hunter."

But once he did not do very well on the hunt, and brought his father-in-law only four wild pigs. Sun was a bit put out, but said nothing. Actually, the youth had done it on purpose, to see the other's reaction. Thus he realized that Sun was threatening to kill him, although not overtly. "No," he said, "I have to get away from Sun, or he will kill me."

The young man left Sun and went to the village of Moon. "Come here," said Moon, "I would like for you to be my son-in-law and bring me meat all the time. It doesn't matter how little it is; personally I'm not demanding. I'm not like my older brother, for whom there's never enough meat. I myself am not like that." Sun and Moon were brothers, Sun being the older and Moon the younger. "My brother is crazy," said Moon. "His sons-in-law were bringing him all kinds of animals. He's not normal. He made his sons-in-law suffer unjustly, although they brought him meat to eat every day. From now on you shall be my son-in-law."

The youth married the youngest of Moon's daughters, and Moon became his father-in-law. Then he went hunting, and killed many wild pigs. With Moon, things were different. He was not such a greedy meat-eater, and thought his son-in-law was extraordinary. But the following day someone went to Sun's village and said: "Your younger brother has a lot of roasted meat. A young man, the one who used to be your son-in-law, married his youngest daughter." "Tomorrow I'll go to my brother to beg," said Sun. "Why didn't I kill that young man in the first place? And now he's become my brother's son-in-law!"

The next morning Sun went to see his brother. The latter greeted him: "Ah, here you are, older brother!" "Yes, I've come, younger brother," replied Sun. Without wasting any time, Moon fetched a large amount of roasted meat and placed it in a heap. "You may eat it right away," he said to Sun, and then asked him: "What is the reason for your visit, brother?" "I followed my son-in-law," replied Sun. "No, you're not going to take him, for now he is my son-in-law. I made him marry my youngest daughter." "That's how it is," agreed Sun.

After this he stuffed his bag with dried meat of rhea, wild pig, and every other kind of animal that Moon had, and began the return journey to his village. After he had traveled some distance it suddenly grew very cold. He was barely able to walk a few more steps before he had to halt and make a great fire. This happened repeatedly. Every time he had warmed himself he continued on his way, and then lit another fire in order to get warm again. Moon was behind all this, testing his brother. "Darn it, my brother is testing me. Just wait, and you'll see what I'm going to do to you!" thought Sun. Because of all the delays his journey took several days; I think he spent five nights on the road. Wherever he slept he lit a fire to keep warm. It was a terrible frost. As he approached his village, he felt very happy. But when he was nearly there a new wave of cold weather set in, much more intense than before, and it nearly killed him. "Poor me, my brother came close to killing me there! He makes me suffer a lot with his cold weather. But just wait, soon he'll find out what I'm made of!"

With revenge in mind, he invited his brother to come and harvest in his garden. His maize plantation already showed a stubble. There were also a lot of squash, watermelons, and all the fruits and vegetables that we usually plant. This invitation was a trap for Moon. "Tell my brother to come," he said to someone who was going to Moon's village. "He can harvest maize, and also squash and watermelons. Let him come tomorrow for a while to take something home."

Very early the next morning Moon arrived at Sun's house. "Ah, my younger brother is here." "Yes, I have arrived, older brother." "Tomorrow we'll harvest the maize," said Sun. The next day they went to harvest. "Here are watermelons, younger brother," offered Sun, and then he asked: "When are you returning home?" "Early tomorrow, older brother." Sun wanted to know when he was leaving, for he had prepared a great heat wave to use against him.

Moon set out toward his village, but he had hardly walked from here to there when Sun's heat came. He had to seek out some shade, and there he sat for a good while until he felt better. To be able to travel he went from shady spot to shady spot along the road; that was how intense the heat was. During the night the heat grew worse, and Moon nearly died of thirst. When he was close to home the heat increased in intensity even more. Almost at the point of death, he reached the village and was able to drink some water. Only then did Sun end the heat wave. "Good!" he thought. "Now at least my brother was taught his lesson. He made me suffer a lot with his cold, but now he knows who I am. It was he who tested me first that time; he showed his older brother who he was. But now he knows me, too."

Sun then sent for Moon's son-in-law, which greatly annoyed Moon. Something tremendous was going to happen. Sun said: "Well, if it's trouble my brother wants, I'll be glad to oblige him." And he went personally to see Moon. When he arrived, they first prepared their honey drinks, and sang to make the *aloja* ferment. Both brothers rejected the other's songs, each singing his own songs, which he claimed to be better. There were many girls listening. "Is it true that you have songs that attract women, my younger brother?" asked Sun. "No, that's a lie," replied Moon. "Well, actually I don't know; maybe it's true." Then each began to sing with his own group of singers in order to make the honey *aloja* ferment properly. But the beautiful songs of the younger brother surpassed those of the other, and this finally caused their mutual hostility to erupt into the open. The two brothers began to insult each other. This happened just when the *aloja* was ready to drink. "Now we should leave," they said. "I don't care in which direction you go."

They stopped insulting each other and went apart a distance like from here to there. Then, from the spot where he stood, each began to attack the other with his magic powers. Sun sent an intense heat against Moon, but the latter countered this with a wave of great cold. Heat and cold remained some distance apart, but did not mingle. Sun's heat did not mingle with Moon's cold. Seeing that they both were equally powerful, neither claimed to have bested the other. They were equal in magic power.

"All right, brother," said Sun, "we've had our test; now I think we should stop this fighting. I'm going into space, and from now on I shall remain there. I shall never leave there, for now we have tested each other. You must never again try something bad against me."

"And you, too, must never try anything against me," replied Moon.

"We've had our test. Now we know that we are precisely equal. Watch out if you try to harm me!" "No, it will never happen again; I'll never harm you, brother. This battle won't be repeated."

They left, both entering space. Suddenly Sun ceased being a man and turned into a piece of live coal. At first he was red. Some men and women surrounded the coal but could not touch it, for it was very hot. "You had better not do what you have in mind!" shouted Sun's children. But he paid no attention to them and remained as a red-hot piece of coal. Finally a great whirlwind came and carried him violently up into the air. The coal flew upward, but still he was Sun. High up he flew, and continued even higher, until he reached the sky. That was when he first appeared as the sun we see today.

Moon was still on the earth, and from up above Sun challenged him one more time, sending him a terrible heat. It killed many of Sun's own villagers, who died of thirst because the heat made all the water boil. Moon nearly died. But when night fell he, too, finally ascended. All of a sudden he disappeared, ceasing to be a man. Later they saw him, when he was already very high up, transformed into a firefly. His daughters cried over him; everybody was crying disconsolately. They had stayed alive because they had taken refuge in their father's frost, standing in the middle of it to save themselves from Sun's heat. That was how the moon which we see at night came about. His children left. They built new houses, and remained permanently in the place where they had established their new village. They shaved their heads, Moon's son-in-law too. Sun's children had disappeared long before, killed by their own father with the heat that he sent down.

This is where it ends.

Morning and Evening

FON, BENIN

Morning and Evening were brothers.

But their father Mahu (God) did not treat them equally. To Morning, his firstborn, he gave innumerable subjects and great riches, while the younger brother, Evening, received only a calabash with two types of beads—nana and azamun—the only two things Mahu had not given to Morning.

One day Morning fell ill. The doctor said he could cure him, but he needed a nana and an azamun bead. So Morning's subjects went out to look for the beads, but none had them except Evening.

"How much money will you give me for these pearls?" Evening asked.

"One hundred cowries for each bead," they replied.

So Evening gave them two beads and Morning was cured.

Left alone, Evening began to think. He began to wish that Morning would fall ill many times, so that he could get many cowries. Then he remembered that whenever Morning approached, the leaves of the calabash rolled up and shut themselves. So he arranged for entirely open calabash leaves to fall under Morning's feet—and Morning fell ill immediately. Thus he made his brother fall ill as many times as he liked, and gradually he gained possession of all his brother's cowries.

Morning's subjects began to desert him, and they gathered round Evening and made him their king. And they gave him twelve pages to accompany him and sing:

A king will let his subjects wait in the sun,
Or else his subjects will revolt;
Evening is the time for the king's court,
Evening is our king.

The Origin of Fishes

FON, BENIN

At the beginning the sun appeared in the sky surrounded by his children, as the moon does at night. But the heat was so terrible during the day that men could hardly leave their huts, and they found it impossible to look for food. Thus they were dissatisfied with their lives.

The moon thought about this. Then she went to see the sun.

"Our children are causing us trouble," she said. "Men are complaining about them. Let us each gather our children into sacks and throw them into the water."

Having said this, the moon collected white pebbles and gathered them into a sack, making the sun believe that the sack contained her children. So the sun gathered his children into a sack, and followed the moon to the river, where they threw their sacks into the water.

But when night came the sun saw that the moon was surrounded by all her children. Furiously he said:

"You have deceived me. Tomorrow I shall take my children back!"

But when the sun took one of his children out of the water, it died. The second also died, and so did the third. They shone still, but they could no longer see their father. So the sun, fearing that he might kill them all, left them in the water.

Since then the sun hates the moon. He pursues her every day, and sometimes he catches her.

How Gluskabe
Brought the Summer

ABENAKI, NORTHEASTERN UNITED STATES
AND SOUTHEASTERN CANADA

Here camps my story.

Gluskabe had been away for some time. When he finally came home, Grandmother Woodchuck was waiting for him in front of their wigwam.

"Grandson," she said, "I am glad you have returned. It has been a hard, hard winter. The snow was so deep it reached the tops of the trees. The game animals died. Many of our descendants died of hunger and cold."

Gluskabe looked around. He saw it was so. The tops of the trees had been eaten by the hungry animals when the snow was so deep it covered everything but the highest limbs.

"Where is this Winter?" Gluskabe said.

"Very far, Grandson. He lives in the land to the north called Pebunki. There it is always filled up with snow. No one can live there but Winter. All others freeze to death."

"I want you to make snowshoes for me, Grandmother," Gluskabe said. "Make me two netted with caribou, two netted with deer, and two netted with moose."

Grandmother Woodchuck did as Gluskabe asked. She made the snowshoes of rawhide with strong frames of maple and cedar. Gluskabe put on the moosehide snowshoes and strapped the others to his waist with a rope made of basswood bark.

Then Gluskabe started. He walked through the snow wearing the mooseskin snowshoes. It grew colder, but he walked on until his snowshoes were worn out. Then he put on the deerskin snowshoes and walked further. It grew colder still and Gluskabe began to shiver but he walked on until the deerskin snowshoes were worn out. Then he put on the caribou snowshoes and went further. All around him everything was white and there were no longer any trees or bushes. There in front of him was a shining white wigwam. The door was open and Gluskabe went inside. Inside the wigwam sat a strange old man. He was dressed in white and his eyes were the color of sleet. Icicles hung from his long nose and thin white hair straggled around his cheeks. He sat before a fire which glowed like the lights of the dancers in the northern sky but gave off no heat.

Gluskabe sat down across from the old man and held out his hands over the cold fire. "*Kuai!*" said Gluskabe, "I greet you, Grandfather."

"*Kuai!*" said the old man, his voice a mocking echo of Gluskabe's.

"I am cold," Gluskabe said. "You must open your door and let me out."

"You are cold," said the old man.

"Grandfather," Gluskabe said, "I am almost frozen."

"You are almost frozen," said the old man.

"Grandfather, I have frozen to death," Gluskabe said.

"You have frozen to death, indeed," said the old man. He picked up Gluskabe's stiff body and threw him out into the snow.

There Gluskabe stayed until the spring came. The sun shone and the snow melted away from around him. Gluskabe woke up.

"I have been asleep," he said. He looked around, but the wigwam of ice was gone. He began the long walk home.

◙ ◙ ◙

When Gluskabe arrived home he said to his grandmother, "I must go again to the North Land. This Winter has too much power. But how can I defeat him?"

"You must go to your father's house," said Grandmother Woodchuck. "That is where Nibuna, the Summer lives."

"Where is this place?" said Gluskabe.

"It is in Sawanaki, the South Land," said his grandmother.

"I will go there," Gluskabe said.

"It will not be easy. Your father may not recognize you. Your brothers there will be jealous. And even with your father's help, it will not be easy to steal Summer. It is well guarded by day and night."

"How will I know my father?" said Gluskabe.

"You will know him when you get there. He has only one eye."

"I must go now," said Gluskabe. "Make me some balls of rawhide string and a pair of snowshoes."

His grandmother did as he asked and Gluskabe set out. He began to walk and the air grew warmer and the snow less deep. When he came to the place where the snow ended he took off his snowshoes and hung them on a tree.

"If my father has only one eye," Gluskabe said, "I should make it easy for him to recognize his favorite son." He took out one of his eyes and placed it in a hollow in the tree. A chickadee sat on a nearby branch.

"You," said Gluskabe, "watch over my eye until I return."

◙   ◙   ◙

Gluskabe walked on. He walked until he heard the sound of voices singing and a drum beating. A big village which shone with a golden light was there.

Gluskabe came into the village. The people, seeing that he had only one eye, took him to their chief's wigwam.

"*Kuai*! Father," said Gluskabe.

"*Kuai*! Son," said Gluskabe's father.

Gluskabe's brothers, though, were not glad. One of them took out a small stone pipe and filled it. He lighted it and handed it to Gluskabe.

"Now smoke," he said to Gluskabe, certain that the magic pipe would kill him.

Gluskabe, though, took a deep breath and emptied the pipe. He took another breath and the pipe burst. "Ah," Gluskabe said, "Nijia, this pipe of yours breaks easily. Let us smoke now with my pipe."

Then Gluskabe took out a very small pipe made of ivory and filled it with tobacco. He lit it and handed it to his brother. "Now smoke," he said.

The brother smiled. This little pipe would be easy. He took a deep breath and the strong tobacco smoke filled his lungs. He took another breath and another, but could not drain the pipe. He became sick and passed the pipe to the second brother. Gluskabe watched as the second brother also smoked. He, too, became sick and passed the pipe to the third brother. The third brother tried, but the pipe was too much for him, also. At last Gluskabe took back his pipe.

"*Kaamoji*!" Gluskabe said. "It is plain you Nibenaki people do not know how to smoke." He inhaled once and drained the pipe.

"Majiwskinnosis," said Gluskabe's father, "your younger brother is a great magician. Do not try to seek his life again or he'll beat you."

The brothers, though, were still jealous.

"We shall play ball," said the second brother. He took out a ball made of stone. Then the three played ball against Gluskabe. They threw the ball trying to strike and kill him, but each time he caught it and threw it back to them. Finally he threw the ball so hard they could not catch it and it broke.

"Let us use my ball, Nijia," said Gluskabe. He took out a small ball made of ivory and threw it to his brothers. But they could not catch the ball and when it struck the ground they could not pick it up.

The third brother was a great gambler. "Let us play the bowl game," he said. He brought out his magic stone dish and placed his counters on the stone. He struck the bowl against the ground once and won.

"I like this game," Gluskabe said. "I shall play now." He struck the bowl against the ground and it shattered. "Your bowl breaks easily," Gluskabe said, "Let us use mine." Then he took out a small bowl made of ivory with counters made of seeds. He threw once and won. He won many times.

The third brother smiled, thinking he would break this small bowl with no trouble. But when his turn came he could not pick up the bowl. His fingernails slipped off it as he tried.

"Nijia," said the oldest brother to Gluskabe, "you have won."

□ □ □

Now Gluskabe had proved himself. He said to his father, "Where is the Summer?"

"It is over the hill where they are singing and dancing," his father said, "but it is well guarded. They do not wish to share the summer with anyone."

"That is not right," said Gluskabe. Then he went to the place where they were singing. Many were gathered around a big dish made of birch bark. The Summer was held in that dish like a jelly. Gluskabe joined in the crowd to watch the dancers.

The two best dancers were women.

"*Kuai!* You dance well," said Gluskabe to them.

"Who is that ugly man?" said one of the women.

"He has only one eye and isn't good to look at," said the other.

So they insulted Gluskabe and ignored him. But each time they danced close to him he reached out a hand and lightly touched their backs. By the fourth time they passed him the looks on their faces changed. They could no longer dance. The people saw two toads sitting there and threw them out of the Summer Lodge.

"It should be dark now," Gluskabe said. Immediately it became very dark inside the wigwam. Gluskabe ran up to the bowl and grabbed the Summer. As soon as he left the wigwam it became light again. The people looked into the bowl and saw the finger marks.

"The strange one," they said. "He has stolen Niben!" They turned into crows and began to chase him.

Gluskabe, though, tied one of the balls of rawhide to his head. When the first crow saw him, it swooped down and grabbed at the rawhide ball.

"I have his head," said the crow, but all it held was an unraveling ball of string.

Now another crow dove down and grabbed at Gluskabe. Again it grabbed one of the rawhide balls. "I have caught him," shouted the crow, but all it held was a ball of rawhide.

One after another the crows tried and failed. Finally they gave up when they saw the snow ahead of them.

Gluskabe took his snowshoes from the tree and reached into the hollow to get back his eye. But the eye was gone.

"Where is my eye?" he asked the chickadee.

"The horned owl stole it," said the chickadee.

"Then the horned owl must come back here," said Gluskabe. And even as he said it the owl came flying back. Gluskabe plucked out one of the owl's eyes and placed it in his own head. "From now on," Gluskabe said, "You will always be winking your eye, remembering how you stole mine. You will only be able to stay awake at night."

▣   ▣   ▣

Gluskabe put on his snowshoes and began to walk to the North Land. Soon he took the snowshoes off, for as he carried the Summer with him the snow melted. Wherever he stepped the grass became green. Before long he came to the ice lodge of Winter. The door was closed, but Gluskabe touched it and it fell open.

"*Kuai*! Grandson," said Winter.

"*Kuai*!" Gluskabe said, mocking him. He sat down by the fire and the fire changed colors and became hot.

Winter began to sweat. Water ran down his stringy white hair. "Grandson," he said, "I am hot."

"You are hot," said Gluskabe.

"I am growing hotter," Winter said. "You must go away now."

"You are growing hotter," Gluskabe said.

Now the old man was growing smaller. His nose fell off. "You are killing me," he said in a weak voice.

"I am killing you," said Gluskabe.

Now the old man could speak no longer. The walls of the ice lodge fell away. He grew smaller and smaller and was gone and where his cold fire burned there was a circle of white flowers.

So Gluskabe brought Summer and drove Winter away. But he did not steal enough for it to last forever. So it is that for only part of the year Winter is gone from the land of the Abenaki.

And so ends this story of Gluskabe.

The Rollright Stones

At the head of his dwindling army, the king strode on. What his name was, or whence he came, there is now no chance of knowing; but that he was on foot, and that his avowed intention was to subdue the rest of England, is tradition that must not be questioned.

The way had been long, and the traveling hard. Of those who had set out with the king, many had regretted their allegiance, and had sneaked off in the darkness toward their tiny homesteads again. Younger men had deserted along the route, tempted by the warmth and comfort of a cottage hearthstone, or the lure of a pair of rounded thighs in the hay or the heather. Still more had fallen out, sick or wounded from skirmishes among themselves as well as among the unwelcoming inhabitants of the lands they had passed through. Now they were reduced to three score and ten, or thereabouts, seventy-two or seventy-three, or even only seventy-one; the king could not be sure.

Among them, though, were their five captains, the petty lords at whose command they had first left hearth and home to follow the king to fresh and greener pastures. As close as brothers were these five, forever finding excuses for putting their heads together and whispering counsels not meant for the king to hear. He was well aware of their intrigue, but kept himself aloof, sure of his own power and of his own judgment, and confident of success in his purpose. Over the next line of hills lay a stretch of countryside vital to his overall conquest. So up the slope he plodded, while the five knights held close together, a little distance away.

When he was nearly at the top, a figure appeared on the brow, facing him as he strode on. It was the figure of an aged woman, gnarled and twisted but with a commanding presence. She held up her hand in a gesture that stopped him in his tracks, and all his followers with him.

"What do you want?" she asked, in a voice of chilling power.

"Passage across the hill. No one stands in my way."

"The hill is mine, and the land all round it," she replied. "What is your purpose?"

"To conquer England, and rule it as one kingdom."

She gave a cackle of mocking laughter, holding out a long finger with which she pointed to the brow of the hill.

"Ah, so I thought," she said.

> *"Seven long strides more take thee,*
> *And if Long Compton thou canst see,*
> *King of all England thou shalt be!"*

The king measured with his eye the distance to the top of the slope, and saw indeed that it was about seven paces. He was now within a few yards of succeeding in his enterprise, if the old beldame could be believed, and he had no reason to doubt her prophecy. So he turned to face his army, and cried out in exultation,

> *"Stick, stock and stone,*
> *As King of England I shall be known!"*

Then he turned about again, and began to pace out his seven long strides toward the top of the hill; but to his great chagrin, there rose before him a long mound of earth that completely obscured the view down into the valley. And there he stood, while his five knights drew close together and whispered at his discomfiture, and his men spread out in a loose semicircle behind him.

Then the witch raised her arm again, and in a loud voice cried,

> *"Because Long Compton thou canst not see,*
> *King of England thou shalt not be.*
> *Rise up stick, and stand still stone,*
> *King of England thou shalt be none.*

Thee and thy men hoar stone shall be,
And I myself an eldern tree!"

Then the king (and every man with him) felt his feet turn cold as stone, and so heavy on the earth that strength could not raise them an inch; and gradually the freezing numbness crept upwards, till king, knights, and men had all been turned to solid blocks of stone.

And there they are to this day, at Little Rollright in the Cotswold country—the Kingstone tall and commanding, a little apart as a king should be; the five knights with their heads together, plotting still; and the men scattered around and about them in a loose, wide circle. Ask not how many men there are, for though the number is thought to be seventy-two, no one is ever able to count them and make the number of them the same on two successive counts.

There are those who believe that the king still waits, like Arthur and King Redbeard, for the curse to be lifted, when he will march forward again with his men to confound his enemies and take over the realm of England. In the meantime, as he waits while age upon age rolls past, he is surrounded by elder trees, progeny of that tree into which the old crone magicked herself upon that fateful day. It is best not to visit the Rollright Stones on Midsummer Eve, for then, they say, if you stick a knife into one of the elder trees, it will not be sap that runs, but blood; and at the sight of it, the stone that was once a king will bend and bow his head, acknowledging still its power.

The five knights still whisper their treachery to each other as the evening breeze drifts round them; but though many have set out in the moonlight to eavesdrop on their whispering, no one yet has stayed long enough to hear what they have to say.

No doubt it is better that way.

Hailibu the Hunter

Once upon a time there was a hunter whose name was Hailibu. He was always ready to help others. Instead of keeping his game all to himself, he always used to share it out among his neighbors. This made him very popular.

One day Hailibu went hunting deep in the mountains. On the outskirts of a thick forest, he spotted a little white snake coiled in slumber under a tree. Not wanting to wake her, he tiptoed past. Just at this moment, a grey crane flew overhead, swooped down on the sleeping snake, seized her in its claws, and soared up into the sky again. Waking up with a shock, the little white snake screamed, "Help! Help!" Hailibu quickly took an arrow, bent his bow, and shot at the grey crane as it rose up the wall of the mountain. The crane swerved to one side, dropped the little white snake, and flew away. Hailibu said to the snake, "You poor little thing. Go home to your parents." She nodded her head to show him her gratitude and then disappeared into some thick undergrowth. Hailibu put his arrows in their quiver, slung his bow over his shoulder, and went home.

Next day, when passing by the place again, Hailibu saw a little white snake crawling up toward him, escorted by a whole retinue of snakes. Amazed, he was about to walk round them and continue on his way when the little white snake said to him, "How are you, my saviour? You probably cannot recognize me. I am the Dragon King's daughter. Yesterday you saved my life. My parents asked me especially to come here and invite you home, so that they can express their gratitude to you in person." The snake continued, "When you get there, don't accept anything my parents offer you but ask for the precious stone my father keeps in his mouth. With that precious stone in your mouth, you will be able to understand the language of the whole animal kingdom. But you must never tell what you hear to anyone else, or your body will turn to stone from head to foot, and you will die."

On hearing this, Hailibu nodded and followed the white snake. The way led into a deep valley, and the farther he walked, the colder he felt. They found themselves in front of a large door, and the little white snake said, "My parents are waiting for you outside, at the entrance to their storeroom. Here they are now." While she was speaking, the Dragon King stepped forward to greet him and said with great respect, "You saved my dear daughter. I thank you from the bottom of my heart. This is the storeroom where I keep my treasure. Allow me to show you around. Take whatever you want. Don't stand on ceremony, please!" With these words, he opened the storeroom and led Hailibu in. It was full of pearls and jewels, brilliant and glittering. The old Dragon King led him from one room to the next. After they had gone through all the 108 rooms without Hailibu having chosen a single piece of the treasure, the old Dragon King said with embarrassment, "Dear sir! Don't you fancy any of the precious things in my storeroom?" Hailibu answered, "They are fine enough but they can only be used for decoration. They are of no use to hunters like myself. If Your Majesty really wishes to give me something as a remembrance, please give me the precious stone in your mouth!" On hearing these words, the Dragon King lowered his head, pondered for a while, then reluctantly spat the precious stone out of his mouth and handed it to Hailibu.

So Hailibu became the owner of the precious stone. As he took his leave of the Dragon King and went on his way, the little white snake followed him out. She warned him again and again, "With the precious stone you can know everything. But you must not divulge the slightest part of what you know. If you do, danger will befall you! Never forget this!"

From then on, it became very easy for Hailibu to hunt in the mountains, for he understood the language of the birds and beasts and knew exactly which animals were on the other side of the mountain. Several years passed in this way. One day he went hunting in the mountains as usual. Suddenly he heard a flock of birds discussing among themselves as they flew through the air: "We must move somewhere else as soon as possible! Tomorrow the mountains around here are going to erupt; the fields will be flooded and goodness knows how many animals will be drowned!"

On hearing the news, Hailibu was very concerned and no longer in the mood for hunting. He hurried home and said to his neighbors, "We must move somewhere else as quickly as possible! We cannot live here any longer! You must believe me! Don't wait until it is too late!"

They were all puzzled by what he had said. Some thought there was no such impending calamity at all; some thought that Hailibu had gone mad. No one believed him. Hailibu, with tears on his cheeks, said to them in despair, "Do I have to die in order to convince you?"

A few old men said to him, "We all know you have never lied to us before. But now you are saying all this about the mountains erupting and the fields being flooded. Won't you tell us what makes you so sure it will happen?"

Hailibu thought to himself: "Disaster is imminent. How can I escape alone and leave all the villagers to perish? If necessary, I shall have to sacrifice myself in order to save them." So he told the villagers the whole story of how he had acquired the precious stone and used it for hunting; how he had heard a flock of birds discussing the disaster and seen them making their escape. He also told them that he was not allowed to tell what he had heard to anyone else; otherwise, his body would turn to stone and he would die. While he was speaking, he turned little by little into stone. The villagers, seeing what had happened, felt great sorrow. They moved to another place at once, driving their herds and flocks with them. While they were hurrying away, the sky became overcast and it poured rain that whole night. The next morning, they heard a rumbling peal of thunder and a great crash which seemed to shake the earth to its very foundations. The mountains erupted, belching forth a great flood of water. Deeply moved, the villagers said, "Had Hailibu not sacrificed his life for us, we would have been drowned by the flood!"

Afterwards, the villagers found the stone into which Hailibu had been transformed and placed it on the top of the mountain. Generation after generation, they have offered sacrifices to this stone in memory of Hailibu, the hero who gave his life to save others. People say that there is still a place called "Hailibu Stone."

The Seven Sisters

KIOWA, CENTRAL UNITED STATES

*E*ight children were there at play, seven sisters and their brother. Suddenly the boy was struck dumb; he trembled and began to run upon his hands and feet. His fingers became claws, and his body was covered with fur. Directly there was a bear where the boy had been. The sisters were terrified; they ran, and the bear ran after them. They came to the stump of a great tree, and the tree spoke to them. It bade them climb upon it, and as they did so it began to rise into the air. The bear came to kill them, but they were just beyond its reach. It reared against the tree and scored the bark all around with its claws. The seven sisters were borne into the sky, and they became the stars of the Big Dipper.

The Toad

· ·

IBO, NIGERIA

When Death first entered the world, men sent a messenger to Chuku, asking him whether the dead could not be restored to life and sent back to their old homes. They chose the dog as their messenger.

The dog, however, did not go straight to Chuku, and dallied on the way. The toad had overheard the message, and, as he wished to punish mankind, he overtook the dog and reached Chuku first. He said he had been sent by men to say that after death they had no desire at all to return to the world. Chuku declared that he would respect their wishes, and when the dog arrived later with the true message he refused to alter his decision.

Thus, although a human being may be born again, he cannot return with the same body and the same personality.

The Chameleon and the Lizard

When Death first entered the world, men sent the chameleon to find out the cause. God told the chameleon to let men know that if they threw baked porridge over a corpse, it would come back to life. But the chameleon was slow in returning and Death was rampant in their midst, and so men sent a second messenger, the lizard.

The lizard reached the abode of God soon after the chameleon. God, angered by the second message, told the lizard that men should dig a hole in the ground and bury their dead in it. On the way back, the lizard overtook the chameleon and delivered his message first, and when the chameleon arrived the dead were already buried.

Thus, owing to the impatience of man, he cannot be born again.

The Origin of Death

HOTTENTOT, SOUTHERN AFRICA

The moon, it is said, once sent an insect to men, saying, "Go to men and tell them, 'As I die, and dying live; you shall also die, and dying live.'"

The insect started with the message, but, while on his way, was overtaken by the hare, who asked, "On what errand are you bound?"

The insect answered, "I am sent by the Moon to men, to tell them that as she dies and dying lives, so shall they also die and dying live."

The hare said, "As you are an awkward runner, let me go." With these words he ran off, and when he reached men, he said, "I am sent by the Moon to tell you, 'As I die and dying perish, in the same manner you also shall die and come wholly to an end.'"

The hare then returned to the Moon and told her what he had said to men. The Moon reproached him angrily, saying, "Do you dare tell the people a thing which I have not said?"

With these words the moon took up a piece of wood and struck the hare on the nose. Since that day the hare's nose has been slit, but men believe what Hare had told them.

PART TWO

Animal Tales and Transformations

Animals talk to, compete with, instruct, and even marry human beings in tales from oral traditions around the world. Though their mode of locomotion or the number of their legs may differ from ours, animals' individual consciousness and intelligence are vividly evident in such stories. The narratives in this collection present intimate relationship, not distanced observation, as the mode through which we humans know the other animals—and through which we understand ourselves too as animals. The transformations woven into these stories—of stars turning into women, a man into an eel, a bear and his hunters into a constellation, a crane into a woman, a frog into a man— convey a mysterious but deeply experienced process of identification with the physical creation. These stories help us recognize that because we live among an antic diversity of life-forms, we humans have vast resources and potent allies as we attempt to negotiate the crises and metamorphoses of our own individual existences.

Some of these animal narratives might best be described as fables. The tale of the Hunter and the Antelope, from the Nupe people of Nigeria, and the Jataka stories of Buddhist Asia, detailing the Bodhisattva's many reincarnations in animal form, both involve fairly straightforward moral instruction. They teach values of gratitude, of modesty, and of compassion in delightful and accessible ways. Animals' enhancement of such fables reflects the fact that, as Western authors like Chaucer also understood, we human beings can sometimes grasp the moral issues of our own lives more firmly when we are entertained by their projection into a nonhuman realm. We laugh, let our guard down, and at the same time pay closer attention than we otherwise might. Beyond the specific morals of animal narratives, however, there is a general effect in these scenes of animals talking among themselves and with human beings, and displaying their various moral virtues or failings. These stories expand the listener's consciousness of nonhuman life; the entire world of these tales becomes animate. Ancient stories of animals from indigenous cultures around the world may thus be an important contribution to Western environmentalists trying to take the next step in developing an inclusive ethical vision.

In some of these stories, marriages transport our connection with animals to an even more intimate level. Though the German fairy tale of the Frog-King and Japan's beloved story of the Crane Wife both strongly convey the values of sympathy and generosity, their mystery reverberates far beyond any discrete morals. The oddity of mating between different species arrests the listener; it produces a gap in the self-evident routine of mundane life. Like a dream it allows deeper dynamics to surface, such as the exotic, sometimes frightening, nature of men and women for each other, or the way in which some human individuals may find in wildness their true heart's home. Marriage with animals does not guarantee a happy ending, as the Nivaklé stories of the Jaguar and the Girl show. Just as the beginning of the girl's relationship with the formidable predator at once saves her from starvation and terrifies her, so too his eventual murder both releases her and destroys a character to whom we, the story's audience, have come to feel much closer than to those murderous humans. In addition, this tragic and instable mating produces physical offspring—thus establishing that all subsequent people will be the relatives of the very animals they hunt. Contemporary writers such as Gary Snyder and Terry Tempest Williams continue to find inspiration in the indigenous tales of their own regions about women and men who have married bears. The tragic kinship between hunter and hunted often reverberates through the intimate tone of stories about hunting. But the "Song of the Bear" from Finland reveals that this relationship may also be celebrated in a comic key. Even after the bear is killed, its wildness, formidable physique, and wonderful coat are exulted in. It is cajoled into the hall like a bridegroom being carried, amid the laughter of friends, to his own wedding.

The Romantic and Transcendentalist influences upon Western nature writing have contributed to an emphasis upon solitude as a particularly valuable way in which to experience nature. Indigenous peoples, by contrast, seem *in many cases to have traveled and lived in groups. These animal tales are both deeply entertaining and instructive fare for people enjoying each other's company in the midst of daily tasks. Beyond the social function of a good story, they also reflect a decidedly social perception of nature itself. Unlike the distinction those in the West often assume between wilderness and the realm of culture, such stories show a world of animal neighbors, whose lives we recognize as like our own in essential ways and into whose stories we advance with every step.*

The Jaguar and the Girl

NIVAKLÉ, GRAN CHACO PLAINS, PARAGUAY

*N*ow you will hear a story about our ancestors, about a jaguar and a girl from those days. She always did many things for which she was punished by her parents. Once her mother and father had beaten her, and because of that she left the village to die. As the sun sank in the sky she headed purposefully toward the forest. She chose an old path and avoided the new ones, traveling along the paths of old which were only used during honey-gathering expeditions. The night was moonlit. It is said that the girl was beautiful. Having traveled far she reached a river, and crossed over to the other side. There was a tree there below which the path passed. Now she climbed the tree, for she was beginning to feel afraid.

A jaguar had been following her tracks. "It must be a girl!" he said to himself. "Soon I will see if I can catch up with her." Reaching the tree in which the girl was sitting, he passed by it. The trail ended. He turned back and began to search under the foliage. When the moon is full it is easy to see a shadow in the shadow of a tree. Concentrating his whole attention he scrutinized the tree's shadow inch by inch. The girl sat there quietly. Suddenly she made an involuntary movement, and the jaguar looked up. "Come down!" he said. "No," she answered. "Although I want to die, I am afraid of you." "Don't be. I won't hurt you if you agree to be my wife." The girl began to cry. "Come down," he insisted. "You are crying for nothing. Don't be afraid of me; I won't hurt you." Finally she agreed to climb down, crying bitterly. "Stop making so much noise!" said the jaguar. "Don't you see that I am not doing anything to you? I will go hunting so you will have something to eat." The girl did not want to go with the jaguar, but was forced to.

He led her toward the river where he had his lair. "How terrible!" said the girl. "We won't have any fire where we are going." The jaguar replied, "We'll see later, when we reach the other end of my river." While they traveled he had shot a deer. Finally they arrived. "Here we will rest today," he said. "But we don't have fire," she protested. "Don't be in such a hurry. Gather some dry grass." She obeyed. Then the jaguar aimed his rump at the grass and broke wind, and immediately it caught fire and a flame sprang up. While they kept the fire going the moon went down. Only then did the girl begin to look closely at the jaguar. Her face was white. She barely had the courage to be his wife, for he had not transformed himself, he still looked like a jaguar! It was not like in those other days, long ago, when jaguars were human.

Meanwhile she began to roast the venison. The jaguar, who knew how to adapt himself to human customs, ate the cooked meat. Only the next day when he had gone hunting and was by himself did he eat raw meat. He returned to his wife with some more game, and she roasted all the meat. "I can hardly believe it," she commented to him. "I am actually getting used to you!" "Of course you are!" he replied. "Look, as soon as we get to my river we will settle down comfortably. We will build a house where we will spend the rest of our lives together. I will spend my time hunting all the animals I always hunt: wild pig, peccary, tapir, deer, puma. Nothing will stop me from killing anything; there is nothing I won't do. If you had married one of your own people he would not have treated you as I do. Your people are good for nothing. I am different, I won't deceive you. And all the more reason if we have a child. Our son won't be a mere idler; he will also know how to hunt."

The girl understood what the jaguar was saying even though he was a real jaguar; he had not turned himself into a man. She understood him because he spoke the language of the ancients, our ancestors. After their conversation they lay down. The following day they continued their journey. Finally they reached the jaguar's river, where they settled down and the girl built a house. "I am completely willing to stay here by myself," said the girl. "I was lucky to meet this man. At first I was afraid of him." "There is no need to be, for you are not hungry," interrupted the jaguar. "If you had remained with your parents you would all be hungry. That is why they punished you." Previously she had told him of all the problems she had had with her family, and thus the jaguar was referring to what he had heard.

Meanwhile four months had gone by, and the girl realized that she was pregnant. The remaining months also passed, and she gave birth to a boy. Not surprisingly, the child was a real jaguar. Only then did the girl begin to have second thoughts. "What shall I do now?" she thought. "That baby is of another species. That won't make my parents happy. What will they say when they see me with him?" Then, for some hidden reason, she thought: "It is autumn now, the time when the prickly pears bear fruit." Aloud she asked the jaguar, "Where are you going today?" "I am going to the river and to those who are over there." "In that case, tell my older brother to come and fetch some peccary meat." "All right, I will tell him." And he did. The jaguar saw the boy, killed him, and dragged him home to the girl. She recognized him and thought: "My poor brother! How miserable I am! I had no idea that this was going to happen." Reflecting deeply as she walked back and forth, she said to herself, "I will see what I must do later, when it is daylight."

The jaguar lay down in the house. The girl continued to walk back and forth, and then she lay down next to him. "Where did you get that paint with which you painted your eyes?" he asked. "I got it from those fruits over there." "Ah, what a beautiful light color that is!" said the jaguar. "I want the same. How I would like to have that, too!" The girl had done everything on purpose. "I would like you to bring me some. I want you to paint me, too." "Of course," she replied. "I will go and get some for you, those that are farthest away, for they are the prettiest."

The girl went to the place in question and picked a prickly pear fruit. When she returned she said to the jaguar, "Put your head on my skirt and I will paint your eyes; that way it won't get rubbed off. And tomorrow when you go hunting you will look very handsome." The jaguar placed his head on her lap. She did like this with the prickly pear thorns. When she had scraped off one whole side of the fruit she stopped pulling out the thorns, and said, "And now the other eye." The jaguar opened his other eye, and again the girl only stopped pulling out the thorns from the fruit when there were no more left. "This is terrible!" wailed the jaguar. "It hurts a lot! I cannot open my eyes!" But she only replied, "It will go away in a while. It always feels like that. It happened to me, too, I could barely see. But once it passes, everything is fine. Raise your head from my legs a little, and it will hurt less." She said this in order to get away from him.

The girl ran off, and behind her the jaguar stood up. But he was in terrible pain, and unable to open his eyes. He walked around a bit, falling every so often. From afar the girl watched him. And that was how she was able to tell her parents the whole story when she arrived home, much to their surprise.

When she did all this to the jaguar it was already late. During the night she slept on the path, and at daybreak she continued on her way to her village, which she had previously left, determined to die. In the meantime the jaguar went on falling down left and right. "Where are you?" he kept asking, groping in the air to find the girl. He continued in this state for a long while, desperate for not being able to see. Meanwhile the girl went on her way unconcernedly. At first she walked rapidly, and then she ran. "How well I did that!" she said to herself. "How miserable I felt yesterday when I saw him drag my brother along the ground!" And she kept running until she reached her parents.

The sun was high in the sky when she got to her house. Her parents saw her all of a sudden, and said, "That girl who is coming, how she resembles our daughter! Maybe she really is our daughter! How she made me cry all last winter!" They had believed that a jaguar had eaten her. Still, a jaguar had been her husband. Immediately the girl now told her parents all that had happened. "I married the jaguar," she said. "It was that same jaguar that ate my older brother. Yes, it is true that he ate him." "We cried over you two," replied her parents. "I have a son who is completely a jaguar," the girl went on. "But I don't know what can have happened to him, for I didn't want to wait for him. I could not get used to that jaguar boy." "Our poor daughter," said her parents. "From now on we won't do anything to upset you again. We were wrong to have punished you that time; that is why you left, wanting to die. Now we are very happy to see you again. What a pity we cannot see your brother, too!"

In the meantime the blind jaguar died. His eyes had burst. The men from the village went to look at him, for the girl had told her uncles where the place was. "Next to the stream," she said. They immediately recognized the place she mentioned, and the men went to look at the jaguar. "This is the one our granddaughter was referring to yesterday," they said when they saw the dead jaguar. He did not have human form but was a real jaguar, a true jaguar. The men cut him into pieces and clubbed him. "What a disgrace that that wretched creature had intercourse with our granddaughter," they said. "It makes me happy to hit him now."

They did not stop striking and cutting him until there were only small pieces left of him. Finally they burned all his bones.

The Woman Who Was
Married to a Jaguar

NIVAKLÉ, GRAN CHACO PLAINS, PARAGUAY

A woman was once out in the forest gathering fruit, and a jaguar set his sights on her and grabbed her. He wanted to marry her. He took her far into the bush, far away from where the other people were waiting for her all day and night until they had no hope left. They said to one another, "What has happened? Something must have happened to her. Probably the jaguar got her and ate her." But he had not eaten her; he took her home with him to marry her.

Four months later she was already very heavy; she was pregnant. The jaguar always went out hunting boar in the forest. He brought them home and made a roast and gave the woman meat to eat. He went out hunting for all kinds of animals, and he always gave the woman food, so she was not suffering; she always had plenty to eat. Finally she was about to give birth, and she thought: "What am I going to do?" Because, of course, she had left behind her mother and father. She went out and got a cactus thorn, and she put it in some *maté*. At noon when the jaguar came home he said: "What can have fallen into my eye? We have to see what I have in my eye; it seems that some dirt has fallen into it." The women made him open his eye wide. She poked the thorn into it, and then she moved away from him. The jaguar tried to grab hold of the woman but she moved out of his reach. He had become blind and bumped into all the trees.

Meanwhile the woman ran away. She finally reached her home where all her people were. But her mother was frightened because it had been a year since she had seen her. "That looks like my daughter. Yes, it is she, and she is pregnant." Three days later she gave birth to a jaguar, and she raised him.

Then he began to get very big and he said, "I am going to go hunting." He already knew how to hunt because he was a fully grown jaguar. He would go hunting in the bush, and when he got wild boar he brought them to his mother to eat.

One day the woman's brother accompanied the jaguar on the hunt. When they got to the bush, they saw a boar, and the man killed it. He skinned the boar, cut the meat into pieces, and put it in the bag, but did not give the jaguar any of it. The jaguar was waiting to be given his part, but the man finished putting the meat into the bag, and then placed it on his shoulder. The jaguar jumped and bit him on the head, and then he ate him. Then he returned home. His mother saw that he was full of blood. "When is my brother coming back?" she asked. "What can have happened to him? Maybe the jaguar ate him. Surely that is what happened." It became late, and night fell. In the morning the man's father went tracking the jaguar. He arrived at the spot and saw that only one of his son's legs remained, and so he returned home. He came into the house and told his daughter, "Tie up the jaguar, but very slowly. He has eaten your brother. It seems that he would not give him a piece of the boar, and so the jaguar became angry and ate him." The woman got a string and tied up the jaguar. While he was sleeping she raised a big stick, hit him, and killed him. She gathered wood, piled it up, and set it on fire, and the jaguar was burned up.

The Woman Married
to Jaguar-Man

NIVAKLÉ, GRAN CHACO PLAINS, PARAGUAY

One day a woman left her village to go to the forest, but when she wanted to go back she no longer knew which way the village lay. Disoriented, she began to walk in the opposite direction. On the road she met Jaguar-Man who at that moment had assumed his human form. She told him, "I left my village, but now I don't know where it is." He replied, "Your village is too far off, but I know in which direction it lies. We'll go to your parents together." However, this man stayed with her in the forest a long time, and they were married. When the girl had her first son, she went with her husband to see her parents.

When her brothers saw her arrive, carrying a child in her arms, the oldest brother asked, "Isn't this our sister? And she has a son." When she came nearer, her brothers recognized her. Her father asked her, "Where is my son-in-law?" and she replied, "Oh, he remained over there." The father then asked, "Why did he not come with you? Is he afraid of us?"

Meanwhile her husband was preparing the jaguar skin that he used as a cape. He put it on and went to see the girl's parents. Once he arrived there, he sat down and talked to them until almost midnight. He asked them if they had not seen tapir tracks, to which his father-in-law answered, "We always see tapir tracks near here. You'll see them here, very near the forest."

The following day Jaguar-Man went out at dawn looking for the tapir tracks. When he got to the forest he turned into a jaguar. He found the tracks and smelled them, and then he found the tapir right away. He began to pursue it, following it through the whole forest.

The father-in-law was listening to how his son-in-law pursued the tapir. He heard the noise of the trees that were falling, knocked down by the animal, for when the tapir runs through the forest he takes no heed of the trees.

He knocks them down because his bones are not hollow; they are as if made of iron.

Nevertheless, the jaguar was able to catch him. He jumped on him, and after biting him on the shoulder he killed him. So that no one would find out that he had bitten and dug his claws into him, he took some arrows and put them into the wounds he had made in the animal. However, he did not carry the tapir back to the hut of his father-in-law because it was too heavy. There and then, he again transformed himself into a man and went back to his wife, his father-in-law, and his wife's brothers, telling them that he had killed a tapir. The father-in-law was very happy and the man asked them to help him bring back the dead tapir. They all went out: the girl's brothers, the father-in-law, and the man who turned into a jaguar.

When they arrived at the place where the body lay, they cut the meat into pieces and returned to the village. Later they made an underground oven and when it was ready they threw wood into it. When the coals were lit they began to cook the tapir meat. They covered the oven with the bark of the bottle tree and then threw earth on top of it.

The next day, they took out the meat which was cooked by now and divided it among the men, but the women ate of it as well.

The girl went out into the forest again looking for kindling, and again she went in the opposite direction from her village, not remembering where she had come from. Once again she met that man who turned into a jaguar and lived with him for many years. For the second time her husband took her to see her parents, and they saw that their grandchild was quite big. When the girl's brothers saw her, they asked, "Isn't that our sister who left here a long time ago and we did not know where she was?"

Again her husband put on his jaguar-skin cape, and the tail and head. Those who saw him thought that he had painted his legs, arms, torso, head, and face with coal. However, he was a jaguar.

They could not sleep at night because of the strange roaring noise their daughter's husband made, and they listened to it attentively. He thought that everyone was asleep, but when they found out that he was turning into a jaguar, they killed him. Then they burned his body, and from it there emerged the jaguar, Ijá·ax.

The Man Who Married Gemini and Who Made a Trip to the World of the Thunderbirds

NIVAKLÉ, GRAN CHACO PLAINS, PARAGUAY

There once lived a man, a Nivaklé, who was a bachelor. He had never had a wife. Every night when he slept out in the open, he would always look up into the sky and gaze at the stars. Each time he would say, "There is Gemini—that is to say, the stars. How I wish that one of them would come down and marry me." Every afternoon, every night of every single day, he would say the same.

One day he went out with his uncle and another nephew, wearing the small stones that the Nivaklé used to wear. He decorated his entire body with them, and then he put on a poncho like a *chiripá*. He went to bathe with his uncle a few kilometers away. He walked and walked and then he took one more step and stepped on the handle of a pair of scissors, which are made of iron. It stuck in his foot, and he fell down. He tried to take it out all afternoon. It got stuck in his foot at noon, and he spent all afternoon trying to take it out. The others did not know what had happened to their uncle, and they left. They did not wait for him or call to him. All afternoon he tried to take it out, when suddenly two women appeared before him. One woman was a bit older than the other. They came up to him from behind. Meanwhile the man was trying to get out the iron handle that had got stuck in his foot. The women came up to him from behind, and one of them asked, "What pricked you?" He replied, "Well, when I stepped on this piece of iron, it got stuck in my foot and now I cannot get it out." The older of the two women came up to him and spat on his foot, and then she pulled out the piece of iron. She was able to get it out right away, whereas he had been unable to get it out. When he tried, it had been stuck too far in. Yet, when that woman spat on his foot it came out right away. After she had pulled it out, she spat on his foot again and then she pressed on it. Then his wound healed. Afterward she told him, "We have come to fetch you, because always, every night, you say that you want to marry us. You say that each night." He did not remember. He thought and thought whether there was a village nearby and there was none. He said to himself, "Where can that woman have come from? I never bother women." The women told him, "You are not going to deny that every night you say, 'How I wish that Gemini would come down and marry me.' Now that we have come down from the sky, you are not going to deny saying that." She invited him to walk with them for a few kilometers, but he did not want to go; he did not want to go for a walk. One of them said, "Let's go there. You will have to choose which one of us you like, my little sister or me." He did not know who was going to marry him. He did not know and he did not say which one he was going to marry. He remained silent; he did not say anything. Then he told them, "I cannot go with you because my paint is going to remain behind— the paint for my basket. Everything that I have will remain here." The woman answered, "We have brought all your things." "Not my coat," he said. "I want to take it too." So the other woman brought him a blanket with which to cover himself. The man did not know what to do, so he went with them, saying, "Well, let's go. I'll go with you." After having gone a ways, one of the women told him, "Bring your basket, and let's go. We'll go to our house, to our village."

Suddenly, from up there, where the stars come out, a ladder descended. It was made from the same kind of reeds that the Indians use for the shafts of their arrows. Suddenly a ladder made of reeds appeared; it reached from the sky down to the ground, right here where we are standing. The younger sister said to the elder, "You go first, and we'll put the man in the middle." Then she climbed up, and so did the man and the younger sister. The three of them left. When they were midway up, the man asked, "You are going to kill me. Where are you taking me?" "No," both of them told him. "Don't be afraid. Don't look down or behind you. You must only look in front of you. We are taking you to our village and we'll get married there." Then they left and disappeared from our view, that is to say, our world, the limits of our universe. They came into a dark world, and when they had left it, they passed into one that was yellow. That was the village of the thunderbirds who live up in the sky, and also of Gemini. When they arrived in the world that is rather black and dark, the man was tired and he could go no farther. He told them, "I can't go on. I think that I'm going to stay here." One of the women answered, "No, you're not. Put your arms around me and I'll carry you up into the sky. I'm going to help you get to the place where there is a road that leads to our village." So the man did as she said, and the two women helped him to reach the world that is yellowish.

When they had arrived, they suddenly got out and saw that the world was yellow, that it let off a yellow light. They went farther and found a road, and one of the women said, "This is the road that leads to our village." Before they had been on their way, when they were still on earth, the star-women had told the man, "That is the world of the thunderbirds; that is where the thunderbirds live. They have a chief. He is short and has a big belly and short legs." He had the shape of a human being, but he had feathers on his arms and was rather black. The star-women were advising the man, telling him that when they got to that village, when the chief of the thunderbirds came out and said, "My friend has come," he should not answer. "If you answer his greeting 'My friend has come' the first time, he will kill you." So when they went there, he did as he had been told. The chief came out and said, "Has my friend come?" He said it very slowly. The man did not answer him and after a while the chief repeated the same words, "Has my friend come?" Again the man did not answer. He repeated this, asking the same thing five times. When he had finished, the star-women made a sign to him and told him, "Now you must answer." So when the chief came up to him again and asked, "Has my friend come?" he answered, "Yes, he has. He came yesterday with two women." Then the chief of the thunderbirds told him, "All right, behave correctly. Don't act like the birds who live where you come from."

So the man went to the house where the star-women lived. It was a very pretty house, a bit farther away from the village of the thunderbirds. When they arrived there, one of the women told him, "Now you have to go and get fish and then we'll eat. But you must only get fish. You must not kill any other kind of animal, and if you see a bird, you must not kill it." The man went and brought back a load of fish. Then the woman told him, "If you want to relieve yourself, here is the bathroom, and if you want to take a bath, here is the tub." She showed him everything. She also told him, "When you go out fishing the next time, you must not go at noon, but later in the afternoon." However, he was very intent on going at noon, but he did not get any fish. All he saw were men and women. They were birds, and they talked and talked and raced each other. They were having fun in many ways, but they yelled out like people. He left, but found nothing to take back. He went farther and farther and suddenly a duck appeared before him. He said to himself, "I'm going to take that duck back for food." The duck was a female. The man shot an arrow at her which penetrated her side. When she screamed out, he suddenly realized that it was the voice of a human being.

When the birds heard that the wife of the duck was wounded, they all flew to the village and told the chief that the star-women's husband had killed her. They said, "The husband of the star-women killed a woman; he killed Duck." Then the chief went to the star-women's house, but they would not allow him to come into the house. They defended their husband. The chief then told them, "Excuse me, I would like to know why he has come here to do us harm. He has made everyone fearful. It has never happened before that such a thing occurred there where we bathe. Why did you bring this person? Why don't you take him back to his world?" This is how he spoke to them. The star-women were on the doorstep, and the man was inside the house. The chief wanted to approach in order to kill the man, but the star-women would not allow it. That is what happened. By morning they had formed an army and wanted to kill the man. One of the star-women asked the red-headed vulture, "Why don't you take this man back to his world? I am so ashamed." Vulture was the only one who was sorry for him, so he answered, "All right. I'll go for my club, in order to defend myself should the need arise." He went into the house, and the man got on his neck and Vulture brought him back to earth. As he was flying him back, before they had reached the river, Vulture told the man, "Before we reach the river you must say, 'I am man.' Before you get down, you must say this, but not another word." He told him that he must not say that he was a bird. Before getting down he had to say: "I am a Nivaklé, I am a Nivaklé." Then he told the man: "Now you can get down." But the man could not and the vulture was flying toward that part of the river that was deepest. He flew farther and farther away, and when they had reached the middle of the river, the man got down. He wanted to say: "I am a Nivaklé," but instead he said another word. He said, "I am an eel." He got into the water and was transformed into an eel. He was turned into a fish.

Gratitude:
The Hunter and the Antelope

NUPE, WEST AFRICA

A hunter went out in the bush. He met an antelope. He killed the antelope. Boaji (the civet) passed by. Boaji said, "Give me some of that meat. I am hungry. I beg you for it. I'll do you a favor some other time." The hunter gave Boaji some of the antelope's meat. Boaji ran off.

The next day the hunter went out in the bush again. He came to a place where the bush was overgrown and it was hard to see where one was going. There, in the middle of the bush, he met a crocodile. The hunter said, "How did you get here? Don't you belong in the water?" The crocodile said, "Last night I went out hunting and now I am far from the river. I cannot find my way back. I beg you, show me the way to the river. If you do I'll give you five loads of fish." The hunter said, "I'll do that gladly." The hunter tied a thong around the crocodile's foot and led him to the Niger. At the water's edge the crocodile said, "Now undo the thong and I'll go into the water and fetch you your five loads of fish." The hunter freed the crocodile; the crocodile went into the water and the hunter waited on the bank.

The crocodile came out of the water with a great big fish and laid it high on the bank. The crocodile slipped back into the water. The crocodile returned with a second load of fish and laid it lower on the bank. The hunter climbed down and carried it higher. The crocodile returned with a third load which he left at the water's edge. The hunter carried the third load up the river bank. The crocodile brought a fourth load and laid it in the shallows. The hunter came down, picked the fish out of the shallows and carried it high up the bank. The crocodile returned with a fifth load of fish which it laid on the edge of the deep water. The hunter came down from the bank, waded through the shallows, and came to the edge of the deep water. As he was about to pick up the fish the crocodile snapped at his foot, caught it fast, and dragged the hunter under the water.

The crocodile brought the hunter to his brother crocodiles who lay on a sandbank in midstream. The crocodile called all his friends and said, "We have caught a hunter. We are going to eat him. Come, all of you." The crocodiles came from every side and swarmed around the hunter. The hunter said, "Is that fair? This crocodile lost his way in the bush. I brought him back to the river. And now he wants to eat me." The crocodiles said, "We will ask four other people what they think about it."

Down the river floated an Asubi (colored, oval mat woven by the Benue in the Kutigi region). The Asubi was old and torn. The hunter cried, "Asubi, help me!" The Asubi said, "What is the matter?" The hunter said, "This crocodile here was lost in the bush and I brought him back to the river. I saved his life and now he wants to take mine. Is that fair?" The Asubi said, "You are a man. I know men. When a mat is young and useful, they keep it clean, do not step on it with their feet, roll it up when they have used it, and lay it carefully to one side. But when a mat is old they forget what it used to be like. They throw it away. They throw it into the river. The crocodile will do well if he treats you as men have treated me." The Asubi drifted on. The crocodile said, "Did you hear what the Asubi said?"

A dress, old, torn, and worn, came floating down the stream. Someone had thrown it away. The hunter cried, "Dress, help me!" The old dress said, "What is the matter?" The hunter said, "I brought this crocodile here, who had lost his way, back to the river. And now he wants to eat me. I saved his life and now he wants to rob me of mine. Is that fair?" The dress said, "You are a man. I know men. So long as a dress is young and beautiful they wear it everywhere, accept its beauty for their own, and say, 'Aren't we lovely?' But it is the dress which is lovely. And the people know that they lie for they fold the dress carefully, smooth out the wrinkles, and wrap it up. But as soon as the dress is old they forget what it used to be before. They throw it in the river. The crocodile will do well if he treats you as men have treated me." The old dress drifted on downstream.

The crocodile said, "Did you hear what the old dress said?"

An old mare came down to the river to drink. The mare was old and thin. Her masters had turned her out because she was no longer of any use to them. The hunter cried, "Oh mare, help me!" The old mare said, "What is the matter?" The hunter said, "I brought this crocodile here, who had lost his way, back to the river. Now he wants to eat me. I saved his life and now he wants to rob me of mine. Is that fair?" The old mare said, "You are a man. I know men. When a mare is young they build a stall for her. They send out boys to cut her the best grass. They give her the best grain and when she is in foal they give her double of everything. But when a mare is old and cannot foal, when she is weak and ill they drive her out into the bush and say, 'Take care of yourself as best you can.' Just look at me. The crocodile will do well if he treats you as men have treated me." The mare trotted off. The crocodile said to the hunter, "You heard what the old mare said?"

Boaji came down to the bank of the Niger to drink. It was the Boaji whom the hunter had helped the day before. The hunter cried, "Boaji, help me!" Boaji said, "What is the matter?" The hunter said, "I brought this crocodile here, who had lost his way in the bush, back to the river. And now he wants to eat me. I saved his life and now he wants to rob me of mine. Is that fair?" Boaji said, "That is difficult to decide. First I must know everything. I do not want to hear only your side of the story but the crocodile's side too,—that is, if the crocodile is willing to accept my decision." The crocodile said, "I will tell you." Boaji said, "How did the hunter bring you here?" The crocodile said, "He tied a thong around my foot and dragged me after him." Boaji said, "Did it hurt?" The crocodile said, "Yes, it hurt." The hunter said, "That is not possible." Boaji said, "I cannot decide that until I have seen it. Come ashore here and show me what you did." The crocodile and the hunter went to the shore. Boaji said to the hunter, "Now tie the thong around his foot, just as you did before, so that I can judge whether it hurt him or not." The hunter bound the thong around the crocodile's foot. Boaji said, "Was it like that?" The crocodile said, "Yes, it was like that. And after a while it begins to hurt." Boaji said, "I cannot judge that yet. The hunter had better lead you back into the bush. I will come with you." The hunter picked up the thong and led the crocodile into the bush. Finally they came to the place where he and the croc-odile had met. The hunter said, "It was here." Boaji said, "Was it here?" The crocodile said, "Yes, it was here. From here on the hunter dragged me behind him to the river." Boaji said, "And you were not satisfied." The crocodile said, "No, I was not satisfied." Boaji said, "Good. You punished the hunter for his bad treatment of you by grabbing his foot and dragging him to the sandbank.

So now the matter is in order. In order to avoid further quarrels of this kind the hunter must unbind the thong and leave you here in the bush. That is my decision."

Boaji and the hunter went off. The crocodile stayed in the bush. The crocodile could not find the way back to the river. The crocodile hungered and thirsted. The hunter thanked Boaji.

There comes a time for every man when he is treated as he has treated others.

The Celestial Bear

A long time ago there was a village surrounded by a great forest. Every day the men of the village went into the forest and brought back game for the people. One fall the hunters noticed that the game had become scarce, and they decided, from the tracks that were discovered, that a giant bear was driving away the game. The bear began to range around the edge of the village every night, either killing animals or driving them away. The men of the village feared that if this continued the people would starve, and so the hunters tried to think of a way to rid themselves of the bear. Eventually the hunters went into the woods and there was a great battle with the bear. The bear drove the men back into the village where they were stranded.

There were three brothers living in the village, and one night each dreamed that he had found the bear. This appeared to be a significant omen, and the brothers took on the task of tracking the bear and destroying it. They took along with them their dog Ji yeh. The dog was an able tracker and eventually led the brothers to the great bear.

When the bear saw the hunters he immediately prepared to attack. The faithful dog Ji yeh ran around to the front of the bear, however, and distracted him with barking and biting. In this manner, the men were able to shoot the bear with arrows. The bear tried to attack the dog and fend off the arrows at the same time, but became confused and fled. The men chased him again, and again the bear was confused with the biting dog in front and the men with their arrows behind.

The three brothers and the dog followed and harassed the bear in this way for a long time and they covered a great distance. Each time they shot at the bear, blood was drawn which dropped onto fallen maple leaves. As each leaf was touched by a drop of blood, its color was changed from green to yellow or gold or a deep red.

The brothers continued to chase the bear until they reached the very edge of the world. The bear then climbed a great mountain, with the hunters right behind him and the barking dog directly in front. The terrified bear reached the peak of the mountain and, still attempting to escape, leaped into the sky. The dog jumped up in front of him. The three hunters also jumped off the top of the world and followed the bear and the dog into the sky. The giant bear became four great stars. Ji yeh the dog became Ji yeh the star. Behind the bear followed the three hunters, now stars also.

Now every fall when the leaves begin to change color, Ji yeh, the great bear and the three hunters dip down close to the edge of the world where they must have jumped off.

Trading Teeth
with the Beaver

MOHAWK, NORTHEASTERN UNITED STATES
AND SOUTHEASTERN CANADA

Once long ago our people tried to trade teeth with the beaver. It was well known that of all the animals, the beaver had the strongest and straightest teeth, and the people wished the same for their children. A parent would throw a child's baby tooth as far as possible in hopes that the beaver would trade it for one of his own.

The beaver had at first agreed to the exchange, but after some thought decided that, with a child's tiny teeth, he would be unable to cut down trees to build his home and he would be unable to eat.

The Creator was right, of course, to have given each the teeth he did, because the beaver manages better with his teeth, and people manage better with their own. The people, still hopeful that the beaver might change his mind and trade teeth, continued the practice of throwing a child's baby teeth for a long time.

The Song of the Birds

Years ago the Mohawk people, who are known as the People of Flint, lived in the Mohawk Valley. Beside them lived their neighbors the Oneida. In the valley along the old Mohawk River, the campfires often burned in the evenings and the ôn:kwe?, the people, chanted and sang their songs. They were happy and seemed always to have a song.

There came a day when the Great Spirit was visiting the Great Council Rock and many birds were flying about. The Great Spirit called to a few of them and asked if they would like to be able to sing like the people. The birds became very excited and asked for their own songs. The Great Spirit instructed the birds to tell all the other birds to meet with him on a certain day. At the time he would tell them what they were to do.

The news quickly passed throughout the countryside, and the great invitation was given to all birds to come and gather at the Council Rock. On the day that the Great Spirit was there he was joined by multitudes of birds. Birds of every color, size, and shape were gathered in anticipation of the time when they would be able to sing as ôn:kwe?.

Then the Great Spirit said to the birds, "At dawn as the sun breaks over the horizon, you will fly into the sky. You will continue to soar until you cannot fly any higher. As you turn to come back to the earth, you will pick up your song and when you return you will be able to sing."

Among the gathered birds stood the mighty eagle. The eagle thought that he would be the one to attain the greatest height, and so the best song. Alongside the eagle was a tiny bird called the hermit thrush. He thought that he had little chance of getting a good song because he was in competition with many large birds. Just before the sun rose, however, an idea entered his mind. He jumped onto the eagle's back when he wasn't looking. He crawled under the eagle's feathers and there he hid.

Soon the sun rose and the birds were given their grave commission to fly. Away they flew into the sky until the earth became darkened with the cloud of birds ascending into the heavens. The birds flew higher and higher. Before long, some could not continue because they had tired. As they turned to come back to the earth, the robin and many other birds picked up the songs which they would sing for the Great Spirit.

The day ended and the night came on, yet some birds continued to fly. Soon the eagle took the lead, flying on into the night until the next dawn. The eagle looked around and realized he was alone. He thought that he would be the one to receive the greatest song and he continued to climb. Eventually, however, he began to tire as the air was thin. He knew that he would be unable to go much farther. He thought that with two or three more flaps of his wings he would have tried his very best, and he would return to earth.

Just as he had completed the last great flap of his wings and had reached his ultimate height, the tiny passenger on his back awoke. The hermit thrush poked out his head, looked around, and flew off. He was fresh and strong and ready to fly. As the eagle turned to come back he felt something. He looked up and saw the little thrush flying higher. Anger came into the eagle's heart, and he wanted to stop the bird that had flown higher than he. He was furious but too weak to continue, and he returned to earth. Being so full of anger, the eagle picked up a squawk instead of a beautiful song. The hermit thrush flew higher but became tired quite quickly and made his turn toward earth. As he turned, he picked up one of the most beautiful bird songs ever heard.

The returning birds gathered at the Great Council Rock and there, in the presence of the Great Spirit, began to sing their wonderful songs. The little hermit thrush had just coasted down and was almost back among the family of birds when he saw the eagle standing in their midst. The eagle looked ugly and cross. The thrush thought that if he landed among the birds the eagle would attack him. So instead of rejoining the other birds he veered off into the bushes, and from there he began to sing his song. When the Great Spirit heard the beautiful song he stopped the songs of the other birds and told them to listen. They did, and from the bushes came the melodious song. No one knew from whom the song came. They searched everywhere but could not find the bird.

The eagle was angry because he lost. He had no song, only a complaining squawk. The hermit thrush received a special song because he had flown the highest. He cheated in getting his song, however, and that is why today we can hear the hermit thrush singing, but we always fail to find the reclusive bird.

The Blossom Tree

At the time of the Buddha, Benares had been the holy city of India for many centuries, and Hinduism was its ancient religion. The city was famous for fine temples, many built in beautiful leafy parks with pools of clear, undisturbed water, while the streets of Benares were full of jostling people going about their business, for trading had brought the city much wealth. Merchants had built themselves magnificent houses, and had furnished them with goods they acquired on their commercial travels.

In many ways Benares was like any city in the world today, for then, as now, men sought happiness in making money and in a multitude of other good and evil ways, while some searched for happiness in religious creeds or philosophical paths. Leaders of many new teachings came to Benares, among them the Buddha.

It happened that one day a wealthy merchant was checking the harness of his horse in the courtyard of one of the larger houses, while shouting men and women strapped packs onto the wooden saddles of braying mules, their constantly moving feet kicking up clouds of dust. A little dog barked excitedly, running through the legs of the mules, dodging angry nips from their teeth. In the midst of the preparations for the caravan the merchant's neighbors drank his health and wished him well on his long journey, for it would take many months along the trade routes of Central Asia to China and Arabia.

On his travels he often met people who would ask to accompany him, for his caravan was well protected against attacks by brigands. The merchant had heard many stories from travelers he met on the way, stories of distant lands and strange customs—some spoke of the mighty empire of Rome. Artists showed the merchant ways of writing, painting, and sculpting, unknown to his own people, and philosophers told him of the many ways in which men sought to know the meaning of life. So the merchant's caravan carried much more than wool, cotton, silks, jades, and brocades from country to country— it carried ideas.

One of the merchant's neighbors filled a goblet with wine for him, and asked, since he had no family, who would look after his fine house and warehouse while he was away? The merchant indicated a middle-aged man who was checking the bales of wool. "Jigme will care for my household," he said.

At first the merchant's friends laughed, thinking he was joking; then, realizing that he was serious, they could not believe it. "But Jigme is only a herdsman," one exclaimed. "It is unwise to trust a poor man with wealth," another insisted.

The merchant shook his head. "Jigme is my friend," he said, "he is wise and has a kind heart." But the neighbors still thought the merchant was being very foolish. After all, they muttered among themselves, Jigme was not one of them, he was of inferior rank; some were jealous of Jigme and the trust the merchant placed in him. After arguing unsuccessfully with the merchant one of the men said, "The wise man they call the Buddha is preaching nearby. Will you let us ask for his advice? Remember, your warehouses have our goods in store as well as yours!"

Reluctantly, the merchant agreed. He went with his companions and found the Buddha seated in a palm grove preaching to his followers. Welcoming the merchant and his companions, the Buddha asked them to sit with him while he listened to their story. When the Buddha heard how unwise the merchant's neighbors thought he was, he said he would tell them a story of ancient times, when King Brahmadatta was the king of Benares.

"The king's palace," the Buddha began, "was in a beautiful park, where the king spent many happy hours gardening, and he liked especially to tend his blossom tree. It was the jewel of the park, and he used to look after it very carefully, but neither the king, nor those he took to see the blossom tree, noticed the little clump of kusha grass growing at the roots of the tree trunk. But the spirit of the blossom tree knew all about the kusha grass and its spirit, for the two had been friends for longer than time.

"The blossom tree was mighty and strong, with thick roots that went deep, deep into the earth, reaching into the dark places of demons and monsters. Its trunk was strong, straight, and very high, so that people said its great canopy of branches and foliage reached the heavens.

"No one knew how old the blossom tree was, but it was ancient before Benares had become a great city, indeed, before Benares was even built, and no one knew how long ago that was! And so it was said that the blossom tree was as old as the world itself.

"Everyone saw the blossom tree differently. Some saw it as a mighty and mysterious tree, others as a magic tree, and some, like the king, enjoyed listening to the wind rustling its leaves, which sounded like heavenly music.

"When he was in its shadow, the king was aware of the life of the blossom tree, and it reminded him that everything was like the tree, which grew in the spring and summer, thrusting out leaf-covered branches and new roots, and shriveling in the autumn and winter, leafless, seemingly barren, yet its life went on, and the next year it would burst forth anew. So it told the story of life and death, and life reborn.

"Legend told that the blossom tree, for some who could see, blossomed with the fruit of the secret of life. And sometimes the king had glimpsed for a few seconds among its leaves the most beautiful of blossoming flowers!

"One day, when the king was having tea with the queen in his palace, he was surprised to see something floating in his cup. He looked up at the roof of the room and frowned; small flakes of plaster were falling from the ceiling. He saw that the main wooden pillar which supported the ceiling had cracked and was moving!

"The queen cried out in fear and tried to pull her husband from the room, for she thought that the whole ceiling was going to collapse. But the king asked his wife to leave while he stayed and inspected the damage. He saw that the pillar would have to be replaced as it was beyond repair, and it had to be done very quickly or it would very soon split from top to bottom! He ordered his servants to search the palace grounds for a suitable tree from which the new pillar could be made.

"All that day the servants searched the park, and very carefully measured trees to find a suitable one for the new pillar. After inspecting all the trees in the park, the king's servants realized that there was only one tree that could be used. Sadly, they returned to the palace, and told the king that his beloved blossom tree was the only one fine enough, and strong enough, to replace the old pillar.

"The king was shocked. 'There must be another,' he insisted. 'Maybe one not as strong as the blossom tree, but strong enough to replace the old pillar?' 'Your Majesty,' the servants said sorrowfully, 'in stature and strength, the blossom tree is the only one suitable to make a new pillar.'

"The king was very unhappy, and undecided as to what he should do. If the old pillar split, his whole palace would fall, and his family and many others would be without a home. But there was no other tree in his park as beautiful as the blossom tree. With the queen and their servants, the king went to see the blossom tree.

"Although it was early evening, and the sun still shone, the evening star was so bright that they could see it quite clearly as they walked through the park. The king inspected the blossom tree, and other trees, and even he could see that in comparison it was indeed the best from which to make the pillar. 'Perhaps,' he thought, 'I am being very selfish in trying to keep this beautiful tree which I love, when it could save the home of many. After all,' he thought very sadly, 'it is only a tree, even if it is a special one.'

"So, the king gave the order to his servants, and they prepared sacrifices of penance to the blossom tree's spirit. It was night when the king and queen burned incense and offered sweet tasting delicacies at the foot of the tree. The queen was weeping loudly, as the smoke from the incense fires rose into the velvety blackness. The blossom tree's spirit did not know what to do to save its home, and the gentle breeze quickly carried news of the plight of the blossom tree spirit to all the other tree spirits.

"They gathered around the blossom tree spirit, trying to comfort her and to think of some way of saving her home. Everyone made suggestions, but none was really likely to save the blossom tree. All night long, after the king had left, the tree spirits argued as to what should be done to save the blossom tree, until the poor blossom tree spirit was crying in despair. Then she heard the kusha grass spirit say, in a soft voice, 'Do not worry, my friend, for I have an idea which will save your home.'

"At daybreak, the king's woodsmen walked through the park carrying two great axes. They were not singing as they usually did, and the woodsmen noticed that the birds were not singing either. The whole park seemed to be waiting in silence, expectantly.

"The sun remained hidden behind the clouds, shedding only a grey light, and there was no pleasant breeze as they began to inspect the blossom tree to find the best place to start chopping. They were surprised to see that the bark of the tree looked quite different from the day before. Carefully, the head woodsman went round the tree, studying more closely. When he touched the bark it felt soft. 'This tree has gone rotten here,' he said to his companions. He tested another part of the tree, and that too had gone soft! They peered up at the branches of the blossom tree. All its leaves hung limply, as if they were sick and wilting. 'We cannot use this tree to make the pillar,' they said. 'The wood is too soft . . .' 'I don't understand,' one of the woodsmen said blankly. 'It looked so healthy last night, it was the finest tree in the park.' 'I do not think,' the woodsman said thoughtfully, 'that we were meant to cut the blossom tree down.'

"As they walked through the park to tell the king that they had no choice, they would have to make the pillar from one of the other trees, though not such a fine one, the sun shone through the clouds, and the birds began singing, and the little creatures of the park bustled about their business.

"All were happy that the blossom tree was safe, and happiest of all was the blossom tree spirit. All the tree spirits of the park watched the kusha grass spirit with delighted laughter, for before the woodsmen came it had changed into a large chameleon. It had given the secret of how chameleons could change their color to the blossom tree so it was able to change the color of its bark to look rotten when the woodsmen came.

" 'But how,' the tree spirits wanted to know, 'were you able to make your trunk seem soft when the woodsman touched you?' The blossom tree laughed, as the kusha grass spirit, in chameleon form, moved over the tree trunk, quicker than the eye could see. Thus, the woodsman thought that the soft body of the chameleon was the bark of the tree.

"The blossom tree spirit sang the praises of the kusha grass spirit: 'Spirits of the trees, for all our mighty power, we knew not what to do, while the humble kusha grass spirit had wit to save my home for me. Truly, we should choose our friends without considering whether they are our superiors, equals, or inferiors, making no distinction. Whether they be tree, bird, or grass, each according to his strength, can help a friend in his hour of need.'

"And so she instructed all the tree spirits, and the assembled devas, saying, 'Wherefore such as would escape from an evil plight must not merely consider whether a man is equal or superior, but must make friends of the wise, whatsoever their station in life.' "

As he finished his story, the Buddha smiled at the merchant, who was laughing, for his neighbors, who had thought him so foolish, had received their answer.

The Buddha ended by saying, "In an earlier life, Ananda, my chief disciple, was then the tree spirit, and I, the spirit of the kusha grass."

The Young Man Who
Refused to Kill

Once there was a young man named Tashi who was not very skilled in the ways of the world. Try as he might the young man's father could not make him hunt for food—the son would refuse to take a life and would not even eat the meat that his poor father brought home for the family pot.

Tashi had three sisters, all of whom had married rich men, and often his father and mother would lament their bad luck for having been left with a son who would not be able to take care of them in their old age, a son who would not hunt for game or fowl and who was so meek and mild in his ways.

"He should have been a monk," his mother would cry, "for what good is he to us, this son of ours? When we are old we will have to beg from our daughters and neighbors to save us from starvation." Such was his parents' constant plaint, but still the boy refused to take a life. "All life is sacred," he would say. "I cannot kill another living being."

One day Tashi's father insisted that the boy accompany him on a hunting trip. They walked for many miles and the father was getting very weary for it was a poor day and all he had managed to catch was a small rabbit. The father thought, "It is this son of mine; he brings bad luck."

The young man was sitting on a rock eating his meager ration of fruit and cheese and carving the prayer of Chenrezik into the rock beside him: OM MANI PADME HUM. All along the path there were similar prayers carved into the rocks by travelers, for the path led up to a holy shrine which would be visited by travelers as they passed on their way. Chenrezik, the patron saint of Tibet, Lord of Compassion, commanded a great devotion from the people, and even Tashi's father, when he saw what his son was doing, silently mouthed the powerful prayer over and over again, moving the worn beads of his rosary through his fingers as he did so. Taking life was against his Buddhist beliefs, but he had to provide his wife with food, and he did try to kill the animals as humanely as possible, praying for them as he did so. It was plain to the father that he would never make his son see sense, the boy would never take a life, no matter how hungry they were, and he could see no way out of the situation.

Father and son walked on a little farther, the father keeping a watch out for small animals and birds. Suddenly, through the trees, the father saw a sight that made him catch his breath. There in the field that bordered their path he saw a large hare. It was indeed the best thing that had come his way for many a week, and he was determined not to miss it. Taking up his sling the father crept through the trees to get a better view of the large brown animal. The hare was running toward them, his powerful hind legs pushing him forward at such a rate that it was impossible for the father to get a clear aim.

Suddenly, the hare stopped, as if sensing that there was danger. He twitched his nose, turned his head from side to side, and pricked his ears, listening. He was so near now that the boy could see the hare quite clearly, and so could his father who was just ready to send a large stone flying from his sling when the boy stood up and shouted, "No, father, no; do not kill him!" The hare leaped into the air and was gone in a second, running for cover into a barley field which provided welcome refuge from his angry assailant.

The father stood spellbound for a few minutes, his face had turned ashen white, and anger surged through his body. "Why?" he said to his son. "Why did you do that?" Tashi felt uncomfortable. He knew that his father was angrier than he had ever seen him before and that he could probably expect the beating of his life.

The father could control himself no longer. Taking a large rock from the side of the pathway he walked toward his son. "I will kill you," he said, "I will kill you, my only son." So saying, the father made to throw the rock at Tashi's head, but Tashi backed away, frightened now and pleading with his father to spare his life. Just on one side of the path was a rocky incline, and on the side of the slope was a small cave. The opening was just a small crack, and the young man backed toward it, just managing to squeeze himself into the cave before his father sent the rock hurtling toward his head. The rock struck his leg and he screamed out in pain.

Once inside the cave Tashi knew he was safe, since the opening was far too small for his father to enter. Tashi could not tell how large his rocky prison was, for it was dark and very difficult to see inside the cave. Inching his way along one of the jagged walls he reached the end of the cave just a few yards away from the entrance, and there, his leg pouring blood, he lay down and soon lapsed into unconsciousness.

It was many hours later when Tashi, roused into consciousness by the sound of footsteps, sat up and painfully recalled the events that had led up to his being injured and seeking refuge from his angry father. The footsteps grew louder. He called out for help, but his voice was weak and only a feeble whisper left his lips. Mustering all the energy he could, Tashi called again, this time louder. The footsteps stopped and he could hear voices softly murmuring outside the cave.

Suddenly, a head appeared at the opening, two eyes peered in at him and a voice shouted for him to come out of the cave. "I cannot move," he replied. "I am injured and find it difficult to move the few yards to the opening of the cave."

The head disappeared and was soon replaced by another. Then a small robed body maneuvered itself through the crack and crawled along the cave to Tashi. He could see that it was a monk moving toward him with outstretched hands to support him and lead him to safety. Once outside the cave Tashi saw that there were three monks, traveling together on pilgrimage to the holy shrines.

They carried him to a soft bank of grass, set him down, and tended to his leg. Then, after sharing their food with him, the monks asked Tashi to tell them his story, how he had come to be in such a sorry situation. The boy related his tale, telling them about his unwillingness to hunt for food, and how finally his father, driven to despair, had tried to kill his only son.

The monks listened without speaking; then the head monk invited the boy to accompany them on their travels. This he did, dressed in the robes of a mendicant monk.

After a few days they came to the house of Tashi's eldest sister. The head monk approached the door, knocked, and when the sister appeared, asked for alms. The sister went to fetch food for the wandering monks, but just as they were leaving she asked, "Have you seen my lost brother on your travels? He has been missing for many days and we are worried about him."

The head monk replied that they had not met with her brother on the way, but if they did they would surely tell him of her concern. The eldest sister did not recognize her brother dressed in the robes of a monk.

Soon they came upon the house of the young man's second sister. Once again the head monk approached the house and asked for alms, which he was given, and once again he was asked whether or not they had met with the lost brother. The head monk replied that they had not met with the young man and they went on their way.

When they came to the house of Tashi's youngest sister to ask for alms she immediately recognized her lost brother and hugged him, begging him to stay with those who loved him.

The three sisters gathered at the youngest sister's house and a feast was held to celebrate Tashi's return. The monks were given many gifts and were asked to stay as guests for as long as they pleased, but they declined and left the youngest sister's house to resume their travels.

Tashi thanked his sisters for their help and concern, but asked them to give him their blessings for he wanted to leave and make a life of his own. The sisters were sad to see their only brother go out into the world, and they gave him a gift of a magic horse which could speak. Tashi took the horse and made his way toward the remote regions of the land.

Before he had gone very far Tashi came to a vast plain. The horse spoke to him. "Kill me," he said. "Put my skin on the plain and scatter my hair all around so that the wind will carry it to the far corners of the plain."

The young man was horrified and refused to kill the horse. Instead he set down his pack, ate the food his sisters had given him, and prepared to rest for the night. During the night the horse threw himself over a steep precipice and was instantly killed.

When Tashi woke the next morning he looked for the horse, but he was nowhere to be seen. Searching all over the plain the young man came to the precipice, and peering down saw the shattered body of the horse. Feeling a great sadness and thinking of their conversation the night before, Tashi decided to do what the horse had asked. He took the skin, spread it out in the center of the plain, then scattered the horse's hair all around, throwing it up in the air so that the wind caught it and carried it to the farthest corners of the plain.

Instantly, the horse's skin became a huge mansion, and the hair became herds of sheep and yaks, grazing on the plain as far as the eye could see. The horse appeared before the boy and spoke once more. "You have shown only compassion toward other living beings; this is your reward." As soon as he had spoken the horse galloped off into the distance and disappeared. The young man noticed that where the horse's hooves had touched the ground little patches of gold appeared.

Looking around his new home, Tashi thought about his parents and wondered how they were managing to survive. He decided to go and see them and bring them home to live with him in the mansion. "My father and mother will never want for food again," he thought.

Tashi dressed in monk's robes again, for he did not want his parents to know of his new-found wealth, then he packed two bread pancakes and made his way to his parents' home. He climbed onto the roof of their house, peered down through a small window, and saw his mother and father crouched in front of the fire. Tashi threw down a bread pancake. His mother seized it, declaring, "Gifts from heaven." The father snatched it from her and began to eat greedily. Tashi threw down the second pancake for his mother.

Then Tashi climbed down from the roof and knocked on the door of his parents' house. His mother answered and immediately recognized her son. Taking him in her arms she hugged him and begged him not to leave them again. The young man's father, too, was overcome with emotion and asked his son's forgiveness.

Tashi told his parents about his new home and his wealth and took them with him to the mansion on the plain. There he set his mother on a throne of purest gold, his father on a throne of purest silver, and he, their only son, sat on a throne of the pinkest shell.

Kalevala: Song of the Bear

The news got to North Farm,   the report to the cold settlement
that Väinämöinen's district had recovered,   the Kaleva District freed
of those magically induced plagues,   of those unusual diseases.

Louhi, mistress of North Farm,   gat-toothed dame of North Farm,
she got very angry at that.   She uttered a word, spoke thus:
"I still remember another trick,   indeed know another way.
I will conjure up a bear from the heath,   one with curved claws from the
    backwoods
to attack the livestock in Väinämöinen's district,   the cattle in the Kaleva
    District."
She conjured up a bear from the heath,   a bear from desolate parts
to attack those clearings of Väinämöinen's district,   the cattle lands of the
    Kaleva District.

Steadfast old Väinämöinen   uttered these words:
"Good friend, craftsman Ilmarinen,   forge me a new spear,
forge a spear with a three-cornered point,   with a copper shaft.
There is a bear to be taken,   a bear with a valuable pelt to be laid low
to stop it from harming my geldings,   wanting my mares,
laying low my cattle,   scattering my cows."
The craftsman forges a spear,   neither long nor short;
he forged a middle-sized one: a wolf was standing on the blade,
bruin on the steel tip,   an elk was shuffling along on the ferrule,

a colt was wandering along on the shaft,   a wild reindeer was kicking on
   the grip.
New snow was then falling,   a little fine fresh snow
as much as a ewe born in the autumn,   a hare born in the winter.

Old Väinämöinen said,   uttered a word, spoke thus:
"It is my desire,   my desire to go to Woodland,
to the forest's girls,   to the hazy-blue maidens' farmyards.
I am setting out to the forest away from men,   away from people for
   outdoor work.
Take me on, forest, as one of your men,   as one of your people, Tapio.
Help me to have good luck,   to lay low the fine fellow of the forest.

"Darling, mistress of the forest,   Tellervo, Tapio's wife,
fasten up your dogs,   keep your curs
in a woodbine shanty,   in an oakwood shed.

"Bear, apple of the forest,   chunky honey-paws!
When you hear me coming,   hear the splendid man stepping along,
make fast your claws in your fur,   your teeth in your gums
so that they will never touch me,   never stir when you are on the move.
My bear, my darling,   honey-paws, my beauty,
throw yourself flat on a tussock,   on a lovely crag
while the tall evergreens are swaying above,   firs being heard above.
Then bear, turn around,   honey-paws, turn yourself about,
as does a ruffed grouse on her nest,   a wild goose about to brood."

Then old Väinämöinen   heard the dog barking,
the hound baying loudly   in tiny-eye's farmyard,
in stub-nose's cattle yard.   He uttered a word, spoke thus:
"I thought a cuckoo was calling,   the lovely bird singing;
no cuckoo is calling,   no lovely bird singing at all.
Here my dog is doing finely,   my animal excellently
at the door of the bear's house,   in the farmstead of the distinguished
   man."
Steadfast old Väinämöinen   then encountered the bear;

he upset the satiny beds,   overturned the lovely couches.
He says these words,   made this remark:
"Thanks be, God,   be praised, sole Creator,
for having given me the bear as my share,   the gold of the wilderness as
   my booty."

He looks at his gold.   He uttered a word, spoke thus:
"My bear, my darling,   honey-paws, my beauty,
do not get angry without any reason.   It was not I who killed you;
you slipped from a shaft-bow,   you misstepped from an evergreen branch,
your wooden pants torn through,   your evergreen coat ripped across.
'Autumn weather is slippery,   the cloudy days dark.'
Golden cuckoo of the forest,   lovely shaggy-haired one,
now leave your home deserted,   leave your dwelling place empty,
your birch-branch home,   your cottage of willow withes.
Start, splendid one, to go,   glory of the forest, to step along,
light-shod one to go,   blue-stockings, to trip along
away from this little farmyard,   from these narrow trails
to a crowd of people,   a group of men.
There no one will ill-treat you,   you will not live in poor style;
there one is fed honey,   fresh mead is given to drink
to a stranger who arrives,   to one who wants to be invited.
Set out now from here as if you were really setting out   from this little
   nest
to under a splendid rooftree,   to under a beautiful roof.
Slide along quietly on the snow   like a water lily on a pond,
float along lightly on the evergreen branch drag   like a squirrel on a
   branch."

Then old Väinämöinen, eternal singer,
walked over the clearings playing,   over the heaths singing loudly
with his splendid guest,   with his furry fellow.
The music is already heard as far as the house,   the noise clear to under
   the roof.
The people in the house suddenly said,   the handsome group spoke up:
"Hear this noise,   the words of the musician of the wilderness,

the warbling of a crossbill,   the sound of the pipe of a forest maid."
Steadfast old Väinämöinen   got to the farmyard.
The people came tumbling out of the house,   the handsome group
    remarked:
"Now the gold is coming,   the silver wandering along,
a lovely piece of money stepping along,   a coin stepping along the trail.
Did the forest give up a honey-eater,   the master of the wilderness yield
    up a lynx
since you come singing,   shuffling along caroling on skis?"

Steadfast old Väinämöinen   then said these words:
"The otter has been charmed,   God's game enchanted;
for that reason we come singing,   shuffling along caroling on skis.
But it will not be an otter,   neither an otter nor a lynx;
the splendid fellow himself is coming along,   the glory of the wilderness
    stepping along,
the old man wandering along,   the broadcloth coat moving along.
If our guest happens to be wanted,   fling open the doors;
but if the guest is hated,   slam them to."

In answer the people say,   the handsome crowd speaks:
"Hail, bear, your arrival,   hail, honey-paws, your paying a visit
to this clean farmyard,   this lovely farmstead!
I always hoped for that,   ever since I have been grown up
I have looked forward to Tapio's ringing out,   to the forest's pipe shrilly
    sounding,
to the gold of the woodland coming along,   the silver of the wilderness
    coming
to this little farmyard,   to these narrow trails.
I have been hoping for this as for a good year,   been looking forward as to
    the coming of summer
just as a ski to new-fallen snow,   a left ski to good smooth skiing,
a maiden to a young suitor,   a pink-cheeked girl to a mate.
Evenings I used to sit by the windows,   mornings on the storehouse steps,
for weeks by the gates,   for months at the entrance to the lanes,
winters in the cattle yards.   I stood on the snow so that it got hard-
    packed,

till the hard-packed snow got to be wet ground,   till the wet ground got to
    be gravelly places,
the gravelly places to be loamy places,   the loamy places to be verdant.
I reflected every morning,   every day reflected
as to where the bear was lingering so long,   the lovely fellow of the
    wilderness spending his time,
whether he might have gone to Estonia,   run away from Finnish soil."

Then old Väinämöinen   uttered these words:
"Where shall I take my guest,   lead my golden one?
Shall I perhaps take him to the shed,   put him in the hay barn?"
In answer the people say,   the handsome group spoke up:
"You will take our guest yonder,   lead our golden one
under the splendid ridgepole,   under the lovely roof.
There food has been prepared,   drinks got ready,
all the floorboards cleaned,   the floors swept;
all the women are dressed   in fresh clothes
with pretty head ornaments,   in white clothes."

Then old Väinämöinen   uttered a word, spoke thus:
"My bear, my bird,   honey-paws, my bundle,
you still have ground to cover,   heath to clamber upon.
Set out, now, gold, to get going   dear one, to step along the ground,
black-stockings, to go along boldly,   cloth pants, to go ahead,
to walk along the chickadee's path,   the sparrow's course
to under five rafters,   to under six rooftrees.

"Look out, wretched women,   lest the cattle be frightened,
the small livestock scared,   the mistress's livestock suffer harm
while the bear is coming into the dwellings,   hairy-muzzle pushing his
    way in.
Away, lads, from the porch,   girls, away from the doorjambs
while the fellow is coming into the house,   the splendid man stepping
    along.

"Bear of the forest, apple,   handsome chubby fellow of the forest,
do not fear the maidens   or be afraid of the girls with luxuriant hair;

do not fear the women,   do not feel sorry for those with stockings down at
   the heels.
Whatever women are in the house,   they will all retire to the inglenook
when the man comes into the house,   when the big boy walks in."

Old Väinämöinen said: "Welcome here, God,
under the splendid rooftree,   under the lovely ceiling!
Where shall I now take my darling,   lead my furry fellow?"
In reply the people say: "Welcome, welcome on your arrival!
Put your bird over there,   lead your golden one
to the end of the deal bench,   to the tip of the iron bench
for the pelt to be examined,   the fur to be looked over.
Do not worry about that, bear,   do not take it amiss
when the hour comes to feel your fur   the time comes to view your coat.
No one will damage your fur   nor by looking change your coat
into the rags of miserable people,   into the clothes of poor wretches."

Then old Väinämöinen   took the pelt off the bear,
laid it away up in the storehouse loft;   he put pieces of the meat in a
   cauldron,
into a gilded copper kettle, a copper-bottomed pot.
The pots were already on the fire,   the copper-sided vessels on the flame,
brimful, crammed full   of pieces of meat;
in with them lumps of salt   which had been imported from rather far
   away,
lumps of salt got from Germany,   from the headwaters of Dvina river,
brought by rowing through the Öresund,   unloaded from a ship.
When the stew had been cooked,   the kettles taken off the fire,
then indeed the booty is brought,   the crossbill carried
to the end of the long deal table   to golden bowls
to drink mead in long draughts,   to partake of beer.
The table was made of pine,   the dishes cast of copper,
the spoons of silver,   the knives fashioned of gold.
All the bowls were brimful,   the dishes full to overflowing
with pieces of the lovely gift of the forest,   of the booty of the wilderness
   gold.

Then old Väinämöinen   uttered these words:
"Old man of the knoll with your golden chest,   master of Tapio's farm,
Woodland's honeyed wife,   lovely mistress of the forest,
handsome man, Tapio's son,   handsome man with a red-peaked hat,
Tellervo, Tapio's maid,   together with the rest of Tapio's people!
Come now to your steer's wedding party,   to your shaggy one's feast!
Now there is plenty ready to eat,   plenty to eat, plenty to drink,
plenty for yourself to keep,   plenty to give a neighbor."

Thereupon the people speak thus,   the fair company said:
"Where was the bear born,   where did the valuable pelt grow up?
Do you think it was born on straw,   grew up in the inglenook of a sauna?"
Then old Väinämöinen   uttered these words:
"The bear was not born on straw   nor on the chaff of a kiln.
The bear was born,   honey-paws given birth to
at the Moon's, in the womb of the Sun,   on the shoulders of the Great
    Bear,
at the virgin's of the air,   at Nature's daughters.
A virgin was treading the border of the sky,   a maiden the heavenly pole;
she was walking along the edge of a cloud,   along the border of the
    heavens
in blue stockings,   in particolored shoes with heels
with a basket of wool in her hand,   a basket of down under her arm.
She threw a tuft of wool onto the waters,   dropped the down onto the
    billows.
That the wind rocked,   the turbulent air moved,
the spirit of the water swayed,   a wave drove ashore,
to the shore of a honeyed wilderness,   to the tip of a honeyed headland.
Darling, mistress of the forest,   keen-eyed wife of Tapio's Domain,
seized the tuft of wool from the waters,   the soft bits of wool from the
    billows.
Then she placed it cunningly,   swaddled it nicely
in a maplewood box,   in a fine swinging cradle.
She picked up the diaper strings,   carried the golden straps
to the bushiest bough,   to the broadest leafy branch.
After she got there, she swung,   rocked her darling

under a luxuriant crown of a fir,   under a flourishing pine tree.
Then she brought forth the bear,   brought up the fine-coated one
on the edge of a honeyed copse,   inside a honeyed wilderness.
The bear grew to be handsome,   grew up to be very fine looking
with short legs, with bandy legs,   with a soft stubby muzzle,
a broad head, a snug nose,   a fine shaggy coat.

"Not yet had either teeth   or claws been fashioned.
Darling, mistress of the forest,   uttered these words:
'I would form claws for it,   try to find teeth, too,
if it would not get into wrongdoings,   not take to evil deeds.'
Accordingly the bear swore an oath   on the knees of the mistress of the
     forest,
in the presence of illustrious God,   looking up at the face of the
     Almighty,
to do no evil,   begin no bad deeds.
Darling, mistress of the forest,   keen-eyed wife of Tapio's Domain,
set out to search for a tooth,   to inquire about claws
from firmly rooted rowans,   from rough junipers,
from matted roots,   from hard resinous pine stumps.
Not a claw did she get there,   not a tooth did she find.
An evergreen was growing on a heath,   a fir rising on a knoll;
on the evergreen was a silver branch,   a gold branch on the fir.
These the maiden seized with her hands,   from them made claws,
attached them to the jawbone,   set them in the gums.
Then she let her furry fellow go,   sent her darling forth;
she put him to rove a fen,   to run over a copse,
to walk on the edge of a clearing,   to clamber on the heath.
She bade him walk nicely,   to run along gracefully,
to live joyous times,   to spend splendid days
on the expanses of the fen, in the farthest parts of the world   beyond the
     playing fields,
to go without shoes in summer,   without short socks on in the autumn,
to survive the worser times,   to take it easy in winter cold spells
inside a chokecherry house,   on the side of an evergreen stronghold,
at the foot of a lovely fir,   in the corner of a juniper grove,

under five woolly mantles,   under eight cloaks.
From there I just now got my booty,   brought this quarry of mine."

The young people speak thus,   the old people keep saying:
"Why was the forest favorably disposed,   the forest favorably disposed,
   the wildnerness amenable,
the master of the wilderness delighted,   lovely Tapio obliging
that he gave his precious one,   lost his honey darling?
Was it obtained by a spear   or fetched by an arrow?"
Steadfast old Väinämöinen   uttered these words:
"The forest was very favorably disposed toward us,   the forest favorably
   disposed, the backwoods amenable,
the master of the wilderness delighted,   lovely Tapio obliging.
Darling, mistress of the forest,   Tellervo, Tapio's maid,
maiden of the forest, fair of form,   little maiden of the forest
set out to show the way,   to make blazes,
to point out the sides of the trail,   to direct the journey.
She cut blazes along on the trees,   made marks on the hills
to the doors of the splendid bear,   to the edge of its preserve.
Then after I had got there,   reached my destination,
there was no obtaining by spear,   no going about shooting;
it fell from a shaft-bow,   stumbled from an evergreen branch;
dead branches broke its breastbone,   twigs split open its belly."

Then he uttered these words,   remarked, spoke thus:
"My bear, my pet,   my bird, my darling!
Now leave your head ornament here,   stick out your teeth,
thrust out your sparse teeth,   open your jaws wide!
Do not take offense   if something should happen to us,
a crash of bones, a cracking of skulls,   a loud rattling of teeth.
I will now take the nose from the bear   as a help to my present nose;
I am not taking it as something unlucky   nor will it be all by itself.
I will take an ear from the bear   as a help to my present ear;
I am not taking it as something unlucky   nor will it be all by itself.
I will take an eye from the bear   as a help to my present eye;
I am not taking it as something unlucky   nor will it be all by itself.

I will take the forehead from the bear   as a help to my own forehead;
I am not taking it as something unlucky   nor will it be all by itself.
I will take the muzzle from the bear   as a help to my own muzzle;
I am not taking it as something unlucky   nor will it be all by itself.
I will take the tongue from the bear   as a help to my own tongue;
I am not taking it as something unlucky   nor will it be all by itself.

"Him I would now call a man,   rate as a lucky person
who would enchant the tight-locked teeth loose,   get the set of teeth
from the steely jaw   with an iron grip."
No one else came,   there was no such man.
He himself enchants the tight-locked teeth,   exorcises the set of teeth
     loose,
kneeling on it with his bony knees,   holding it with his iron grip.
He took the teeth from the bear,   he uttered a word, spoke thus:
"Bear of the forest, apple, handsome chubby fellow of the forest!
Now you have a journey to make,   a trip to make boldly
from this little nest,   from a lowly cottage
to a finer home,   a roomier dwelling.
Set out now, gold, to go,   lovely in your fur, to step along
the side of pigs' trails,   across the tracks of young pigs
toward the scrub-grown hill,   to the high hill,
to the bushy pine,   to the hundred-branched evergreen.
It will be nice for you to live there,   lovely to pass your time
within hearing of a cowbell,   near the tinkling of a little bell."

Steadfast old Väinämöinen   now came home from there.
The young people speak thus,   the handsome crowd remarked:
"Where did you take your booty,   where did you bring your prey?
Perhaps you left it on the ice,   sank it in the slush,
knocked it down into the ooze of the fen,   buried it in the heath."
Steadfast old Väinämöinen   uttered a word, spoke thus:
"Indeed I did not leave it on the ice,   sink it in the slush;
there dogs would keep disturbing it,   bad birds would be all over it.
Nor did I knock it down into the fen,   bury it in the heath;
there grubs would destroy it,   black ants devour it.

I took my booty, brought my trifling prey
to the top of a golden knoll, to the shoulder of a copper ridge.
I put the skull in a fine tree, in a hundred-branched evergreen,
on the bushiest bough, on the leafiest spray
as a joy to men, as an honor to passers-by.
I laid it with the gums to the east, I left it with the eyes to the
    southwest.
I did not put it right in the crown; had I put it in the crown,
there the wind would damage it, the cold spring wind treat it badly.
Nor did I put it on the ground; had I put it on the ground,
pigs would have shifted it, the creatures with lowered snouts would have
    turned it over."

Then old Väinämöinen burst out singing
in honor of the splendid evening, as a source of joy for the closing day.
Old Väinämöinen said, remarked, spoke thus:
"Stay now, torch holder, alight so that I may see to sing.
My turn to sing is coming, my mouth desires to ring out."
Then he sang so that it resounded, sang joyfully throughout the evening.
At last he said his say, finally said:
"Grant us another time, God, in the future, steadfast Creator,
to rejoice at such festivities, to do it another time
at the festivities of a chubby lad, at the feast of a long-haired one.
In any event allow, God, another time, true Creator,
blazes to be made, trees to be marked
among the manly folk, the manly bands.
In any event allow, God, another time, true Creator,
Tapio's horn to sound, the woodland pipe to sound out shrilly
in this little farmyard, in this confined farmstead.
By day I would it might be sung, by night that joyous music be made
in these parts, in these districts, in these great farms of Finland,
among the rising generation, among the people growing up."

The Legend of
the Elephant

*I*n those days, and that was very long ago, further back than one can think, mankind lived all together in one big village, and the animals did the same, each in his village, each according to his race; the antelopes with the antelopes, the boars with the boars, the leopards with the leopards, the monkeys with the monkeys.

But in each village, as chief, there lived an elephant, and the elephants were thus scattered, each family of elephants commanding a different village. The chief of them all, the father elephant, lived alone in the forest, but when there was a palaver everyone appeared before him, and he judged with wisdom. When the father elephant thought that his time had come, he passed on his spirit to his successor and disappeared. Never, never was he seen again, but his spirit remained alive.

The men lived apart, far, far in the forest, and no animal lived with them, not one, not even a dog. I know nothing at all about the chickens, but I think the chickens must have lived with the other birds.

The men were apart; they ate the fruits of the forest, but often, too, they killed animals and ate their flesh, and then there were palavers without end. The animals came and complained to the elephant. The elephant ordered the men to appear, but they never came, and they continued to kill the animals.

There were so many complaints against the men that the elephant said at last, "Since they will not come here, I must go to their village."

He made preparations for his journey and set off for the men's village. But first he had to find this village, and that was quite difficult, for the men had hidden it very well. The elephant set out. On his way he came first of all to the leopard village.

"Where are you going, Father Elephant?"

"I am going to the men's village, to judge their palaver with you."

"That's a good idea. We'll go with you."

"No, they would be too frightened. I would rather go alone."

And the elephant said that because he knew very well that Nzame had created the men, and that the chief of the men was the son of Nzame, like himself.

"Very well, go alone, Father Elephant, but first rest a day in our village."

The elephant agreed, because they treated him very well, and he stayed two whole days in the leopard village. He would have stayed three days, and even longer, but there was nothing left to eat. So he continued his journey and came to the antelope village.

"And where are you going, Father Elephant?"

"I am going to the men's village to judge their palavers, for I am getting tired of them."

"That's a very good idea. We'll go with you."

"No, I would rather go alone, for perhaps they might kill you in the night."

And the antelopes answered, "Very well, but at least stay two days with us."

And the father elephant willingly agreed, for the antelopes treated him very well, and he stayed two whole days in their village. He would have stayed three days, and even longer, but there was nothing left to eat and he was very hungry.

Father Elephant then went to the boars' village. And so, from village to village, the elephant continued on his way.

For some time past, however, the chief of the men, who often consulted his fetish (an antelope with a mirror imbedded in it), had known of the elephant's journey. That he did not want at all. And so in all the paths which led to his village from far, far away, he, together with the other men and with women who carried the earth, dug deep pits, with pointed stakes at the bottom; three, four, five traps one after another, at one hour's, two hours', three hours' march distant. And when the farthest pit was finished he said to his men, "Go and cut me some manioc stems."

And the men went and cut some manioc.

"Throw the stems down so that they cover the pit."

And the men laid the stems carefully, and some days after they began to sprout, so one no longer saw the bare wood. And at an hour's march from there, on the same path, the chief of the men had another pit dug. And he said to his men, "Go and fetch some potato stalks."

And they went, and came back with a lot of potato stalks. And their chief said, "Lay these stalks over the pit."

And they laid them well, so that the pit could not be seen.

And so he had five different pits dug along the path, each with a different plant. And on each path leading to the village he had five pits dug like this. The chief of the men was very cunning! He thought to himself, "If the elephant sees a heap of manioc in his path he will suspect something, for he is very clever." And so on the path, a long, long way off, at four or five different places, he had manioc thrown down; but underneath this there was no pit; and farther on still, after the first pit, he put more manioc again, and then potatoes, and then other plants. He put them all along the road!

Father Elephant was then well on his way to the men's village. And there on the road he came upon a heap of manioc. He turned it over and over with his trunk, for he was very wily, but he found nothing at all suspicious. "It is a present from my children," he said. "They wanted to leave food for me along the road; they are very good." But as he was still a little suspicious he ate only a tiny piece of the manioc.

It was good; he ate a second piece, and then the whole heap of it; there was not very much, and Father Elephant was very big, much bigger than the elephants nowadays. A little farther on there was a fresh heap of manioc. Father Elephant drew near cautiously, then he bit a little piece—nothing suspicious. "Ah," he said. "What good children!" And he ate the whole heap, for Father Elephant was big and the heap was very little. And Father Elephant had walked a long, long way! And when evening came, there in the path he saw a fresh heap of manioc, and as he was very hungry again he rushed toward it.

Plop! This time it was the pit! And as Father Elephant ran very fast he fell headfirst onto the pointed stakes. And that was lucky for him! For otherwise the stake would have pierced his belly and he would have been killed. But his head broke the stake. And all night Father Elephant stayed in the bottom of the pit, crying and groaning, "I am dead!" But in the morning the chief of the men, who was nearby with all his warriors, came to the edge of the pit.

"Why, what is this!" he exclaimed. "What? It is Father Elephant! Oh, how could he have fallen down there!" And at once he began to throw earth and branches into the hole, but as soon as he saw that the pit was nearly filled and the elephant just about to climb out, he scuttled away with all his men as fast as he could.

Father Elephant, however, climbed out of the pit, and, all bruised and smarting, very angry, went on his way. But his head ached very much, his eyes were all full of earth, and he could hardly manage to walk. At last, after many adventures, and many appeals both to his great fetishes and to all the other elephants, Father Elephant overcame all the obstacles and reached the men's village.

But when he arrived there was no one there! At his command, all the other animals gathered together and went in pursuit of the men, to bring them back. The monkeys pursued them in the trees, the boars and leopards in the forests, the birds called out when they found their hiding places, the snakes bit them from the grass, and at last they were brought back to judgment.

The men were then brought before Father Elephant, and the chief of the men was very much afraid in his heart, for he saw death before him. He went cold all over, for who has seen what lies beyond death? Death is like the moon; no one has seen the other side of it.

The chief of the men was cold. He shivered. But Father Elephant said, "Do you confess your sin?" And the chief of the men said, "I confess it."

"Then you now look upon death."

"Oh, Father Elephant, I am so small and you are so strong! Oh, pardon, pardon!"

And Father Elephant replied, "It is true; I am strong and you are weak, but Nzame has made you chief. Therefore I pardon you."

And the chief of the men cried, "Thank you! Thank you!" And his heart was content.

But the chief of the leopards came forth, furious. "Father Elephant, you have not spoken well! These men have killed my brother. I want vengeance!"

And so the man paid gifts to the leopard. And then Father Elephant said, "Now you shall 'make brothers' and the quarrel will be over."

The chief of the men called his brother and said to him, "Make the blood exchange with the leopard." And the leopard chief said to his brother, "Make the blood exchange with the men." The man made the blood exchange and the leopard made the blood exchange, and they dwelt as brothers in the same village.

Then the eagle chief came forward in his turn and made the same palaver, and the boar chief, and the gorilla chief, and many others, but they exchanged blood, and the palaver was ended.

And when the palavers were all decided, the elephant chief said in his turn, "I want to make brother with the man chief." So they killed a kid, for these had not made brother; he was the slave of man. They killed a big male kid, and Father Elephant and Father Man made brothers. Father Elephant recognized the fetishes of Father Man, and Father Man recognized the fetishes of Father Elephant. And ever since that time Father Elephant has become the *ototore* of men, and that is why they honor him very much. Those who do not honor him are savages.

Amanda. That is the end.

The Caribou Man

INUIT, ALASKA

A man and his wife lived alone. He always hunted caribou and they had meat all the time. In the wintertime they put snares all along the water running from open springs to catch caribou. After a few years they had a baby boy. One time when the boy was big enough to play out, his father went to hunt caribou and found a few. When he saw them he didn't try to kill them, but followed them from behind. When they stopped to eat he sat close and watched them. When they went to sleep he went to sleep too.

One time when they went to sleep the man who was sitting close by was going to sleep too, when one of the caribou got up. It came to him, put its nose to the ground, and opened its hood. It was a middle-aged female. The caribou gave the man a pair of mukluks because she knew his mukluk bottoms were torn. She said, "You can wear these if you go walking," and so he put them on.

When the caribou went again the man followed from behind. Pretty soon he started walking like a caribou, and so he went around with them. One time the caribou that had talked to him said, "If we stop and are going to eat, you think of what you'd like to eat and it will come so that you can eat it." When he was digging in the snow he thought of what he'd like to eat and that food was there.

The caribou came to him again and said, "The wolves always bother us. And when one of us is slow they catch him and eat him. We are going to test you and see if you are slow." The caribou started running fast and the man tried to run like them, but he started falling. He kept falling when they were running so when they stopped the caribou said, "Next time they start running, put your head up and look at the sky. Then you'll learn how to run like us." When the caribou started running again he looked up to the clouds. He started running better and caught up with them. Then the wolves started running after the caribou and they ran, scattering all over. He followed the caribou that talked to him. The wolves didn't catch them.

One time when he was walking he got caught in one of his own snares and couldn't come out. After awhile a boy came. When he got close he got his spear ready to kill the caribou. The caribou recognized his son so he took his hood off and said, "When you were a small boy I followed the caribou far and that's why I never came home. Take the snare off and take my parka off." The boy did and then led his father home. When he went into the house it was so smelly he couldn't stand it. He couldn't eat the food that he used to. He didn't sleep with his wife, but another place in the same house. His lips were big, just like a caribou's lips. Because the man couldn't eat human food he got skinny and died.

Momotaro,
the Peach Boy

*T*his was long ago. In a certain place lived an old man and his wife. One day the old man went to the mountains to cut wood, and the old woman went to the river to do her washing. As she was doing the washing, a peach came floating, *tsunbura tsunbura*, down the river. The old woman plucked it from the water and when she tasted it, found it to be delicious.

"This peach is so good, I'd like to take one to the old man too," she thought and called out, "Good peaches come this way; bad peaches go that way," and soon a large, delicious looking peach floated to where the old woman was. "This one looks good," she cried and picking it up, carried it home and put it in a cabinet.

When evening came, the old man returned home from the mountains with a load of wood on his back. "Old woman, old woman, I am home," he called.

"Old man, old man, I brought you a delicious peach today from the river; here I've saved it for you to eat," and she brought the peach from the cabinet.

Just as they put it on the cutting board to cut it open, it suddenly split apart; inside was a beautiful baby boy who began crying lustily, *hoogea hoogea*, waa waa.

The old man and his wife were overcome with surprise and made a great to-do, crying, "Oh, oh, what shall we do?"

"Since he was born from the peach, let us name him Momotaro, 'Peach Boy,'" they said, and so they did. They raised him very carefully, feeding him rice gruel and fish. He would eat one bowlful and grow that much bigger, and if he ate two bowlfuls, he would grow that much bigger. If he were taught to count to one, he could remember all the numbers up to ten. He grew to be a strong and intelligent boy. The old man and his wife loved him and took great pleasure in caring for him.

One day Momotaro went to the old man and his wife. He sat down on the floor in the formal style, with his hands on the floor before him, and said, "Grandfather and grandmother, I am grown now; I should like to go to the *Oni* Island and conquer the *oni*. Please make some of Japan's number one *kibi dango* (pounded rice and millet dough) for me."

The old man and his wife replied, "Why do you ask to do this? You are not old enough; you could not defeat the *oni*." And they tried to dissuade him.

Momotaro, however, said, "I will defeat them," and would not be dissuaded; so the old man and the old woman could do nothing but agree. "Then you may go and do it," they said and made a great number of Japan's number one *kibi dango*. They tied a new towel about his head and gave him new *hakama* (wide trousers). They gave him a sword and a flag upon which was written, "Japan's Number One Momotaro." Giving him a bag of the *kibi dango* to tie at his waist, they said: "Be careful. Go and return. We will wait for you until you have conquered the *oni*," and so dispatched by the old man and his wife, Momotaro departed.

He went as far as the edge of the village when a dog came barking up to him, *wan wan*, bow wow. "Momotaro, Momotaro, where are you going?"

"I am going to the *Oni* Island to conquer the *oni*."

"Then I shall go to the *Oni* Island with you. Please give me one of those Japan's number one *kibi dango*."

"You shall become my retainer. If you eat one of these, you will be as powerful as ten men," and he took one of the *dango* from the bag at his waist and gave it to the dog.

So the dog became his retainer, and they set off toward the mountains. Next a pheasant came flying, *ken ken*, up to them. He was given a *kibi dango* and became a retainer in the same way as the dog. Momotaro continued on to the mountains with his two retainers. Next a monkey came chattering up to them, *kya kya*, and he too became a retainer.

Momotaro became the general, the dog carried the flag, and they all hurried on to the *Oni* Island.

When they got to the *Oni* Island they could see a huge black gate. The monkey rapped, *don don*, on the door. From inside came a voice, "Who is there?" and a red *oni* came out.

Momotaro said, "I am Japan's number one Momotaro. I have come to conquer *Oni* Island; you had all better get ready," and pulling out his sword, he made ready to attack. The monkey took his long spear, the dog and the pheasant their swords, and all prepared to attack. The little *oni* at the gate set up an alarm and fled to the rear of the island. There all the *oni* were having a drinking party. When they heard that Momotaro was coming, they shouted, "Who is Momotaro, anyway?" and came out to fight.

Since the four had eaten Japan's number one *kibi dango*, they had the strength of thousands of men, and so they defeated the whole *oni* force. The black *oni* general fell down in front of Momotaro, his hands on the ground and, with tears falling, *boro boro*, from his huge eyes, begged forgiveness, crying: "We are no match for you; please at least spare our lives. We will never do anything wrong again."

"Then from now on you must never do evil again. If you promise that, I shall spare your lives," said Momotaro.

"We will give you all our treasure," said the *oni* general and surrendered all the treasure that they had to Momotaro. Momotaro put the treasure in a cart and with the dog, monkey, and pheasant pulling, *enyara enyara*, heave ho, heave ho, he returned with it as a present for his grandfather and grandmother.

The old man and his wife were overjoyed and praised Momotaro greatly. The emperor heard of it, and Momotaro was given a great reward, with which he cared for the old man and his wife the rest of their days.

The Crane Wife

Once there was a man named Karoku. He lived with his seventy-year-old mother far back in the mountains, where he made charcoal for a living. One winter, as he was going to the village to buy some *futon* (bedding), he saw a crane struggling in a trap where it had been caught.

Just as Karoku was stooping to release the poor crane, the man who had set the trap came running up. "What are you doing, interfering with other people's business?" he cried.

"I felt so sorry for the crane I thought I would let it go. Will you sell it to me? Here, I have the money I was going to use to buy *futon*. Please take the money, and let me have the crane." The man agreed, and Karoku took the crane and immediately let it fly away free.

"Well," thought Karoku, returning home, "we may get cold tonight, but it can't be helped." When he got home, his mother asked what he had done with the *futon*. He replied, "I saw a crane caught in a trap. I felt so sorry for it that I used all the money to buy it and set it free."

"Well," his mother said, "since you have done it, I suppose that it is all right."

The next evening, just as night was falling, a beautiful young lady such as they had never seen before came to Karoku's house. "Please let me spend the night here," she asked, but Karoku refused, saying, "My little hut is too poor." She replied, "No, I do not mind; please, I implore you, let me stay," until finally he consented, and she was allowed to spend the night.

During the evening she said, "I have something I should like to discuss with you," and when Karoku asked what it was, she replied, "I beg of you, please make me your wife."

Karoku, greatly surprised, said: "This is the first time in my life that I have seen such a beautiful woman as you. I am a very poor man; I do not even know where my next meal is coming from; how could I ever take you as my wife?"

"Please do not refuse," she pleaded; "please take me as your wife."

"Well, you beg me so much, I don't know what to do," he replied. When his mother heard this, she said to her, "Since you insist, you may become my son's bride. Please stay here and work hard." Soon preparations were made, and they were married.

Some time after this his wife said, "Please put me in a cabinet and leave me there for three days. Close the door tightly and be sure not to open it and look at me." Her husband put her in a cabinet, and on the fourth day, she came out. "It must have been very unpleasant in there," he said. "I was worried about you. Hurry and have something to eat."

"All right," she said. After she finished eating she said, "Karoku, Karoku, please take the cloth that I wove while in the cabinet and sell it for two thousand *ryo*." Saying this, she took a bolt of cloth from the cabinet and gave it to her husband. He took it to the lord of the province, who, when he saw it, said, "This is very beautiful material, I will pay you two or even three thousand *ryo* for it. Can you bring me another bolt like it?"

"I must ask my wife if she can weave another," Karoku replied.

"Oh, you need not ask her; it is all right if only you agree. I will give you the money for it now," the lord said.

Karoku returned home and told his wife what the lord had said. "Just give me time and I'll weave another bolt," she said. "This time please shut me in the cabinet for one week. During that time you must be sure not to open the door and look at me." And so he shut her in the cabinet again.

By the time the week was nearly over, Karoku became very worried about his wife. On the last day of the week, he opened the door to see if she were all right. There inside the cabinet was a crane, naked after having pulled out all her beautiful long feathers. She was using her feathers to weave the cloth and was just at the point of finishing it.

The crane cried out, "I have finished the cloth, but since you have seen who I really am, I am afraid that you can no longer love me. I must return to my home. I am not a person but the crane whom you rescued. Please take the cloth to the lord as you promised."

After she had said this, the crane silently turned toward the west. When she did this, thousands of cranes appeared, and taking her with them, they all flew out of sight.

Karoku had become a rich man, but he wanted to see his beloved wife so badly that he could not bear it. He searched for her throughout Japan until he was exhausted. One day as he was sitting on the seashore resting, he saw an old man alone in a rowboat, approaching from the open ocean. "How strange," thought Karoku. "Where could he be coming from; there are no islands near here." As he sat in bewilderment, the boat landed on the beach. Karoku called out, "Grandfather, where did you come from?"

"I came from an island called 'The Robe of Crane Feathers,'" the old man replied.

"Would you please take me to that island?" asked Karoku.

The old man quickly agreed, and Karoku climbed into the boat. The boat sped over the water, and in no time they had arrived at a beautiful white beach. They landed, and when Karoku got out of the boat and turned around, the boat and the old man had vanished from sight.

Karoku walked up the beach and soon came to a beautiful pond. In the middle of the pond was an island, and there on the island was the naked crane. She was surrounded by a myriad of cranes, for she was the queen of cranes.

Karoku stayed a short while and was given a feast. Afterward the old man with the boat returned, and Karoku was taken back to his home.

Jataka Tales:
The Woodpecker

*E*ven when provoked, a good person cannot turn to evil, it being alien to him.

According to tradition, the Bodhisattva once lived in a forest, as a woodpecker with brightly colored plumage of striking beauty. Although born in that state, he was deeply imbued with compassion and so did not follow the woodpecker's usual diet, which bore the stigma attached to harming living things. Instead he was entirely content with the tender shoots of trees, with the sweet and delicious fragrance of flowers, and with fruits of varying taste, scent, and color. He showed his concern for the good of others by preaching the Law to them when appropriate, by rescuing those in distress as far as he was able, and by preventing those who knew no better from misbehaving. With the Great Being to look after them like this, all the creatures in the forest throve and were happy. It was as though they had a teacher, a kinsman, a doctor, and a king, all in one. Sustained by his great sympathy, he grew in goodness, and that host of creatures, sustained by his protection, also increased their goodness.

One day, as the Great Being roamed through the forest, feeling sympathy for all creatures, he saw in a certain part of the wood a lion, writhing in acute pain, as though he had been hit by a poisoned arrow. His mane was dirty and matted with dust. The Bodhisattva went up to him and, prompted by pity, asked, "What is it, O king of beasts? I can see that you are in a very bad way. Are you suffering from exhaustion after overindulging in feats of pride against elephants or chasing eagerly after deer? Or have you been hit by a hunter's arrow? Or is it some disease? If you can tell me what it is, then do so.

Or at least say what can be done about it. Whatever help I can offer my friends is at your service, if it has power to restore you."

"You good and precious bird, it is not exhaustion that is making me suffer, nor disease, nor a hunter's arrow. It is a splinter of bone that has got caught in the middle of my throat and, like the tip of an arrow, is causing me acute pain. I can neither swallow it down nor cough it up. So this is the moment for a friend to help. If you know how, then make me well again."

The Bodhisattva with his keen intellect thought out a way of extracting the splinter of bone. Taking a stick large enough to prop open the lion's mouth, he told him to open his mouth as wide as he could. The lion did so. The Bodhisattva then duly wedged the stick between the two rows of teeth and went down to the bottom of his throat. With his beak he took hold of the splinter of bone that had stuck crosswise. Loosening it on one side, he grasped it by the other and drew it out. On his way out he let fall the stick that was propping open the lion's mouth. No surgeon, however skillful and practiced, could have extracted that splinter, hard though he tried. But the Bodhisattva managed to do so thanks to his intelligence, which was not something achieved by taking pains but had become an integral part of him in the course of hundreds of existences. Together with the splinter, he removed the pain and misery it caused. He was as happy to have relieved a sufferer as the lion was to have had his suffering relieved. For this is a characteristic of good people: they get more pleasure out of assuring someone else's happiness or averting someone else's misfortune—even though it may be with difficulty—than they do at their own good fortune, however easily come by.

So it was that the Great Being, well pleased at having relieved his distress, said good-bye to the lion, who in turn wished him farewell. Then he went on his way.

Now some time after this the woodpecker was flying around, his brightly colored plumage outspread, without finding any food of the right kind anywhere. As the pangs of hunger began to afflict him, he caught sight of that very same lion feasting on the flesh of a young fawn, not long killed. Its blood, tingeing his mouth, claws, and the tips of his mane, made him look like part of an autumn cloud catching the glow of twilight. Yet, though he had once given help, he could not bring himself to address the lion with anything so disagreeable as a request. Adept though he was, embarrassment imposed a temporary vow of silence on him. Even so, he was forced by need to hover about bashfully within sight of him. But although that scoundrel noticed the woodpecker, he did not invite him over. A seed sown on a rock face, an offering poured onto a heap of cinders that have gone cold—when the moment comes for some return, both are as productive as a favor done to an ungrateful person. And so is the flower on the vidula reed.

The Bodhisattva, thinking he must obviously not have recognized him, went up to the lion with greater boldness and asked him for a share, after first pronouncing a suitable blessing in the manner of a beggar: "May you find it wholesome, O lord of beasts, who earn your livelihood by your prowess! I ask you to treat a beggar kindly—it will ensure you fame and merit." But despite having this kind blessing pronounced on him, the lion, whose habitual cruelty and selfishness made him unused to behaving decently, looked askance at the Bodhisattva and, as though he wanted to burn him up with his bloodshot eyes that were blazing with anger, said, "Stop that. Is it not enough that you are still alive after entering the mouth of the likes of me? I know nothing of a weakling's pity as I devour deer who still twitch with life. Is it to insult me that you come back like this to beg favors? Are you tired of life? Perhaps you want to see what the next world is like?'

This rebuff, expressed so rudely, made the Bodhisattva feel embarrassed, and he immediately flew up into the sky. With the sound of his flapping wings he said to the lion, in effect, "Look! I am a bird," then flew away.

Now there was a wood sprite who either could not bear that the woodpecker should be so ill-treated or else wanted to discover the extent of his patience. She approached the Great Being and said, "Excellent bird, why do you put up with this ill treatment from that wicked creature whom you once helped, even though you have the power to do otherwise? What is the point in being so indulgent toward that ungrateful beast? Strong as he is, you could blind him if you suddenly swooped down on his face. And you could snatch the meat from between his teeth. So why do you suffer his insolence?"

Now although the Bodhisattva was hurt by being so illtreated, and although the wood sprite was provoking him, he showed his innate kindness by saying, "Enough. Do not go on like that. This is not the way people like us behave. Good people devote themselves to someone in distress out of pity, not in the hopes of getting something out of it. The other person may or may not realize this, but what is the use of getting angry about it? Anyone who does not acknowledge a favor done is only cheating himself, for no one who wants a return for his favors will help him again. On the other hand, the benefactor, by his restraint, acquires merit and its rewards in the life hereafter—and a fine reputation already in this life. If one does a kindness because it seems the right thing to do, what is there to be regretful about afterward? But if one does it for the sake of getting some return, then it isn't a kindness but a loan. He who decides to harm his neighbor because he is apparently ungrateful for services rendered, first earns a spotless reputation thanks to his good qualities, then behaves just like an elephant. If one's neighbor is too feeble to acknowledge a favor, no more will he attain that grace whose beauty comes from virtue. But that is no reason for an intelligent person to destroy his own lofty reputation. This is what seems right to me in such a case. Anyone who does not behave in a friendly manner even after he has received help from a kind person should be left quietly alone, without anger or recrimination."

The wood sprite was very pleased by the woodpecker's wise words and praised him repeatedly, saying "Excellent! excellent!" and then added these kind words, "Without the trouble of having clothes of bark and matted hair, you are a sage—you are an ascetic who knows the future. It is not merely one's appearance that makes one a saint. In this case the true saint is he who shows goodness." With this observation she commended him and forthwith vanished.

So, then—even when provoked, a good person cannot turn to evil, it being alien to him.

Jataka Tales:
The Lion

INDIA

Once upon a time when Brahmadatta was reigning in Benares, the Bodhisattva was a maned lion and dwelt at Gold Den in the Himalayas. Bounding forth one day from his lair, he looked North and West, South and East, and roared aloud as he went in quest of prey. Slaying a large buffalo, he devoured the prime of the carcass, after which he went down to a pool, and having drunk his fill of crystal water turned to go toward his den. Now a hungry jackal, suddenly meeting the lion, and being unable to make his escape, threw himself at the lion's feet. Being asked what he wanted, the jackal replied, "Lord, let me be thy servant." "Very well," said the lion; "serve me and you shall feed on prime meat." So saying, he went with the jackal following to Gold Den.

Lying one day in his den, the lion told the jackal to scan the valleys from the mountaintop, to see whether there were any elephants or horses or buffaloes about, or any other animals of which he, the jackal, was fond. If any such were in sight, the jackal was to report and say with due obeisance, "Shine forth in thy might, Lord." Then the lion promised to kill and eat, giving a part to the jackal. From that time on, the jackal used to climb the heights, and whenever he espied below beasts to his taste, he would report it to the lion, and falling at his feet, say, "Shine forth in thy might, Lord." Hereon the lion would nimbly bound forth and slay the beast, even if it were a rutting elephant, and share the prime of the carcass with the jackal. Glutted with his meal, the jackal would then retire to his den and sleep. Thenceforth the lion's leavings fell to the jackal, and he grew fat.

Now as time went on, the jackal grew bigger and bigger until he grew haughty. "Have not I too four legs?" he asked himself. "Why am I a pensioner day by day on others' bounty? Henceforth *I* will kill elephants and other beasts, for my own eating. The lion, king of beasts, only kills them because of the formula, 'Shine forth in thy might, Lord.' I'll make the lion call out to me, 'Shine forth in thy might, jackal,' and then I'll kill an elephant for myself." Accordingly he went to the lion, and pointing out that he had long lived on what the lion had killed, told his desire to eat an elephant of his own killing, ending with a request to the lion to let him, the jackal, couch in the lion's corner in Gold Den whilst the lion was to climb the mountain to look out for an elephant. The quarry found, he asked that the lion should come to him in the den and say, "Shine forth in thy might, jackal." He begged the lion not to grudge him this much. Said the lion, "Jackal, only lions can kill elephants, nor has the world ever seen a jackal able to cope with them. Give up this fancy, and continue to feed on what I kill." But say what the lion could, the jackal would not give way, and still pressed his request. So at last the lion gave way, and bidding the jackal couch in the den, climbed the peak and thence espied an elephant in rut. Returning to the mouth of the cave, he said, "Shine forth in thy might, jackal." Then from Gold Den the jackal nimbly bounded forth, looked around him on all four sides, and thrice raising its howl, sprang at the elephant, meaning to fasten on its head. But missing his aim, he alighted at the elephant's feet. The infuriated brute raised its right foot and crushed the jackal's head, trampling the bones into powder. Then pounding the carcass into a mass, and dunging upon it, the elephant dashed trumpeting into the forest. Seeing all this, the Bodhisattva observed, "Now shine forth in thy might, jackal," and uttered this stanza:

> Your mangled corpse, your brains mashed into clay,
> Prove how you've shone forth in your might today.

Thus spake the Bodhisattva, and living to a good old age he passed away in the fullness of time to fare according to his deserts.

Jataka Tales:
The Quail and
the Falcon

INDIA

Once upon a time, when Brahmadatta was king in Benares, the Bodhisattva came into the world as a young Quail. He got his food in hopping about over the clods left after ploughing.

One day he thought he would leave his feeding ground and try another; so off he flew to the edge of a forest. As he picked up his food there, a Falcon spied him, and attacking him fiercely, he caught him fast.

Held prisoner by this Falcon, our Quail made his moan: "Ah! how very unlucky I am! How little sense I have! I'm poaching on someone else's preserves! O that I had kept to my own place, where my fathers were before me! Then this Falcon would have been no match for me, I mean if he had come to fight!"

"Why, Qualie," says the Falcon, "what's your own ground, where your fathers fed before you?"

"A ploughed field all covered with clods!"

At this the Falcon, relaxing his strength, let go. "Off with you, Quail! You won't escape me, even there!"

The Quail flew back and perched on an immense clod, and there he stood calling—"Come along now, Falcon!"

Straining every nerve, poising both wings, down swooped the Falcon fiercely upon our Quail. "Here he comes with a vengeance!" thought the Quail; and as soon as he saw him in full career, just turned over and let him strike full against the clod of earth. The Falcon could not stop himself, and struck his breast against the earth; this broke his heart, and he fell dead with his eyes starting out of his head.

Jataka Tales:
The Antelope

Once upon a time, when Brahmadatta was king of Benares, the Bodhisattva became an Antelope, and lived within a forest, in a thicket near a certain lake. Not far from the same lake sat a Woodpecker perched at the top of a tree; and in the lake dwelt a Tortoise. And the three became friends, and lived together in amity.

A hunter, wandering about in the wood, observed the Bodhisattva's footprint at the going down into the water; and he set a trap of leather, strong, like an iron chain, and went his way. In the first watch of the night the Bodhisattva went down to drink, and got caught in the noose whereat he cried loud and long. Thereupon the Woodpecker flew down from her treetop, and the Tortoise came out of the water, and consulted what was to be done.

Said the Woodpecker to the Tortoise, "Friend, you have teeth—bite this snare through; I will go and see to it that the hunter keeps away; and if we both do our best, our friend will not lose his life." To make this clear he uttered the first stanza:

Come, Tortoise, tear the leathern snare, and bite it through and through,
And of the hunter I'll take care, and keep him off from you.

The Tortoise began to gnaw the leather thong; the Woodpecker made his way to the hunter's dwelling. At dawn of day the hunter went out, knife in hand. As soon as the bird saw him start, he uttered a cry, flapped his wings, and struck him in the face as he left the front door. "Some bird of ill omen has struck me!" thought the hunter; he turned back, and lay down for a little while. Then he rose up again, and took his knife. The bird reasoned within himself, "The first time he went out by the front door, so now he will leave by the back," and he sat him down behind the house. The hunter, too, reasoned in the same way, "When I went out by the front door, I saw a bad omen, now will I go out by the back!" And so he did. But the bird cried out again and struck him in the face. Finding that he was again struck by a bird of ill omen, the hunger exclaimed, "This creature will not let me go!" and turning back he lay down until sunrise, and when the sun was risen, he took his knife and started.

The Woodpecker made all haste back to his friends. "Here comes the hunter!" he cried. By this time the Tortoise had gnawed through all the thongs but one tough thong: his teeth seemed as though they would fall out, and his mouth was all smeared with blood. The Bodhisattva saw the young hunter coming on like lightning, knife in hand; he burst the thong and fled into the woods. The Woodpecker perched upon his treetop. But the Tortoise was so weak that he lay where he was. The hunter threw him into a bag, and tied it to a tree.

The Bodhisattva observed that the Tortoise was taken and determined to save his friend's life. So he let the hunter see him and made as though he were weak. The hunter saw him, and thinking him to be weak, seized his knife and set out in pursuit. The Bodhisattva, keeping just out of his reach, led him into the forest; and when he saw that they had come far away, gave him the slip and returned swift as the wind by another way. He lifted the bag with his horns, threw it upon the ground, ripped it open and let the Tortoise out. And the Woodpecker came down from the tree.

Then the Bodhisattva thus addressed them both: "My life has been saved by you, and you have done a friend's part to me. Now the hunter will come and take you; so do you, friend Woodpecker, migrate elsewhere with your brood, and you, friend Tortoise, dive into the water." They did so.

The Master, becoming perfectly enlightened, uttered the second stanza:

> *The Tortoise went into the pond, the Deer into the wood,*
> *And from the tree the Woodpecker carried away his brood.*

The hunter returned and saw none of them. He found his bag torn, picked it up, and went home sorrowful. And the three friends lived all their life long in unbroken amity, and then passed away to fare according to their deeds.

Jataka Tales:
The Tiger

INDIA

Once upon a time, when Brahmadatta was king of Benares, the Bodhisattva was a tree-spirit living in a wood. Not far from his abode lived another tree-spirit, in a great monarch of the forest. In the same forest dwelt a lion and a tiger. For fear of them no one dared till the earth, or cut down a tree, no one could even pause to look at it. And the lion and tiger used to kill and eat all manner of creatures; and what remained after eating, they left on the spot and departed, so that the forest was full of foul decaying stench.

The other spirit, being foolish and knowing neither reason nor unreason, one day bespoke thus the Bodhisattva:

"Good friend, the forest is full of foul stench all because of this lion and this tiger. I will drive them away."

Said he, "Good friend, it is just these two creatures that protect our homes. Once they are driven off, our homes will be made desolate. If men see not the lion and the tiger tracks, they will cut all the forest down, make it all one open space, and till the land. Please do not do this thing!" and then he uttered the first two stanzas:

> *What time the nearness of a bosom friend*
> *Threatens your peace to end,*
> *If you are wise, guard your supremacy*
> *Like the apple of your eye.*
>
> *But when your bosom friend does more increase*
> *The measure of your peace,*

Let your friend's life in everything right through
Be dear as yours to you.

When the Bodhisattva had thus explained the matter, the foolish sprite notwithstanding did not lay it to heart, but one day assumed an awful shape, and drove away the lion and tiger. The people, no longer seeing the footmarks of these, divined that the lion and tiger must have gone to another wood, and cut down one side of this wood. Then the sprite came up to the Bodhisattva and said to him,

"Ah, friend, I did not do as you said, but drove the creatures away; and now men have found out that they are gone, and they are cutting down the wood! What is to be done?" The reply was that they were gone to live in such and such a wood; the sprite must go and fetch them back. This the sprite did; and, standing in front of them, repeated the third stánza, with a respectful salute:

Come back, O Tigers! to the wood again,
And let it not be leveled with the plain;
For, without you, the ax will lay it low;
You, without it, for ever homeless go.

This request they refused, saying, "Go away! we will not come." The sprite returned to the forest alone. And the men after a very few days cut down all the wood, made fields, and brought them under cultivation.

The Frog-King, or Iron Henry

BROTHERS GRIMM, GERMANY

In olden times when wishing still helped one, there lived a king whose daughters were all beautiful, but the youngest was so beautiful that the sun itself, which has seen so much, was astonished whenever it shone in her face. Close by the King's castle lay a great dark forest, and under an old lime-tree in the forest was a well, and when the day was very warm, the King's child went out into the forest and sat down by the side of the cool fountain; and when she was bored she took a golden ball, and threw it up on high and caught it; and this ball was her favorite plaything.

Now it so happened that on one occasion the princess's golden ball did not fall into the little hand which she was holding up for it, but onto the ground beyond, and rolled straight into the water. The King's daughter followed it with her eyes, but it vanished, and the well was deep, so deep that the bottom could not be seen. At this she began to cry, and cried louder and louder, and could not be comforted. And as she thus lamented, someone said to her, "What ails you, King's daughter? You weep so that even a stone would show pity." She looked round to the side from whence the voice came, and saw a frog stretching forth its big, ugly head from the water. "Ah! old croaker, is it you?" said she; "I am weeping for my golden ball, which has fallen into the well."

"Be quiet, and do not weep," answered the frog. "I can help you, but what will you give me if I bring your plaything up again?" "Whatever you will have, dear frog," said she—"my clothes, my pearls and jewels, and even the golden crown which I am wearing."

The frog answered, "I do not care for your clothes, your pearls and jewels, nor for your golden crown; but if you will love me and let me be your companion and play-fellow, and sit by you at your little table, and eat off your little golden plate, and drink out of your little cup, and sleep in your little bed—if you will promise me this I will go down below, and bring you your golden ball up again."

"Oh, yes," said she, "I promise you all you wish, if you will but bring me my ball back again." But she thought: "How the silly frog does talk! All he does is to sit in the water with the other frogs, and croak! He can be no companion to a human being!"

But the frog when he had received this promise, put his head into the water and sank down, and in a short while came swimming up again with the ball in his mouth, and threw it on the grass. The King's daughter was delighted to see her pretty plaything once more, and picking it up, ran away with it. "Wait, wait," said the frog. "Take me with you. I can't run as you can." But what did it avail him to scream his croak, croak, after her, as loudly as he could? She did not listen to it, but ran home and soon forgot the poor frog, who was forced to go back into his well again.

The next day when she had seated herself at table with the King and all the courtiers, and was eating from her little golden plate, something came creeping splish splash, splish splash, up the marble staircase, and when it had got to the top, it knocked at the door and cried, "Princess, youngest princess, open the door for me." She ran to see who was outside, but when she opened the door, there sat the frog in front of it. Then she slammed the door to, in great haste, sat down to dinner again, and was quite frightened. The King saw plainly that her heart was beating violently and said, "My child, what are you so afraid of? Is there perchance a giant outside who wants to carry you away?" "Ah, no," replied she, "it is no giant, but a disgusting frog."

"What does the frog want with you?"

"Ah, dear father, yesterday as I was in the forest playing by the well, my golden ball fell into the water. And because I cried so, the frog brought it out again for me; and because he so insisted, I promised him he should be my companion, but I never thought he would be able to come out of his water! And now he is outside there, and wants to come in to me."

In the meantime it knocked a second time, and cried:

> *Princess! youngest princess!*
> *Open the door for me!*
> *Do you not know what you said to me*

Yesterday by the cool waters of the well?
Princess, youngest princess!
Open the door for me!

Then said the King, "That which you have promised must you perform. Go and let him in." She went and opened the door, and the frog hopped in and followed her, step by step, to her chair. There he sat and cried, "Lift me up beside you." She delayed, until at last the King commanded her to do it. Once the frog was on the chair he wanted to be on the table, and when he was on the table he said, "Now, push your little golden plate nearer to me that we may eat together." She did this, but it was easy to see that she did not do it willingly. The frog enjoyed what he ate, but almost every mouthful she took choked her. At length he said, "I have eaten and am satisfied; now I am tired. Carry me into your little room and make your little silken bed ready, and we will both lie down and go to sleep."

The King's daughter began to cry, for she was afraid of the cold frog which she did not like to touch, and which was now to sleep in her pretty, clean little bed. But the King grew angry and said, "He who helped you when you were in trouble ought not afterwards to be despised by you." So she took hold of the frog with two fingers, carried him upstairs, and put him in a corner. But when she was in bed he crept to her and said, "I am tired, I want to sleep as well as you; lift me up or I will tell your father." At this she was terribly angry, and took him up and threw him with all her might against the wall. "Now, will you be quiet, odious frog," said she. But when he fell down he was no frog but a king's son with kind and beautiful eyes. He by her father's will was now her dear companion and husband. Then he told her how he had been bewitched by a wicked witch, and how no one could have delivered him from the well but herself, and that tomorrow they would ride together to his kingdom. Then they went to sleep, and next morning when the sun awoke them, a carriage came driving up with eight white horses, which had white ostrich feathers on their heads, and were harnessed with golden chains, and behind stood the young King's servant, faithful Henry. Faithful Henry had been so unhappy when his master was changed into a frog, that he had caused three iron bands to be laid round his heart, lest it should burst with grief and sadness. The carriage was to conduct the young King into his kingdom. Faithful Henry helped them both in, and placed himself behind again, and was full of joy because of this deliverance. And when they had driven a part of the way, the King's son heard a cracking behind him as if something had broken. So he turned round and cried, "Henry, the carriage is breaking."

"No, master, it is not the carriage. It is a band from my heart, which was put there in my great pain when you were a frog and imprisoned in the well." Again and once again while they were on their way something cracked, and each time the King's son thought the carriage was breaking; but it was only the bands which were springing from the heart of faithful Henry because his master was set free and was happy.

The Serpent Mother

GUJERATI, INDIA

An old couple had seven married sons. All the sons and their wives lived with their old parents. The six senior daughters-in-law were well regarded because they had rich relatives. But the seventh one was ignored and despised, for she had no relatives at her father's place. She was an orphan. Everyone in her father-in-law's house took to calling her "the one who has no one at her father's place."

Every day the whole family would eat their meals joyously. The youngest daughter-in-law had to wait till everyone else was finished and then collect the scraps of food left in the bottom of the earthen pots and eat them. Then she had to clean the whole heap of pots.

Things went on this way till the season came for offering food to dead ancestors. They made sweet *khir* (rice pudding) with the milk of buffaloes. The youngest wife was pregnant and had a craving for the *khir*, but who would give her any? The others ate it with relish and left her nothing but half-burned crusts at the bottom of the earthen pot. She looked at them and said, "Half-burned crusts of *khir*—well, that'll do for me." She carefully scraped the crusts into a piece of cloth and decided to eat them somewhere where no one would see her. It was time to fetch water from the well. The well site was overcrowded with the women of the village. The young daughter-in-law thought she would eat her *khir* crusts after everyone else was gone. When her turn came to fetch water, she put her little bundle of *khir* near a snake-hole. She drew her pitcher of water from the well. She thought she would eat her *khir* after a bath.

While she was bathing, a female serpent came out of the hole unseen. She too was pregnant, and the smell of *khir* drew her. She craved to eat it, and she ate it all up and went back to her hole. She had decided that she would bite the owner of the *khir* if he or she used abusive language and cursed the thief who had taken it.

The young daughter-in-law returned eagerly after her bath to pick up her bundle. She found that the cloth was there but all the crusts of *khir* were gone. Not even a crumb was left.

"Oh," she cried, almost aloud, "I didn't get to eat any *khir* in the house and I didn't get to eat it even here. Maybe there's another unhappy woman like me somewhere around, and she may have eaten it. Whoever she is, let her be satisfied, as I would have been."

On hearing this, the female serpent came out of the hole and asked her, "Who are you, young woman?"

"Mother, I'm just an unhappy woman. I'm pregnant, and I craved to eat *khir*. I had some crusts here, but when I went for my bath, someone ate them up. Well, she must be someone unhappy like myself and may have been hungry. I'm glad that someone was made happy by my *khir*."

"Oh, I was the one who ate your *khir*," said the serpent. "If you had cursed me and abused me, I'd have bitten you. But you have blessed me. Now tell me why you're so miserable."

"Mother, I've no one to call mine in my father's place. The ceremony for my first pregnancy will be due soon. My parental relatives are supposed to perform it, and there's no one to do it," she said. As she spoke, her eyes filled with tears.

The serpent said, "Daughter, do not worry. From today on, just think of me and my kin as your parental relatives. We all live in this hole. When it's time to celebrate your first pregnancy, just put an invitation near the hole. It's a happy, auspicious occasion and should not go uncelebrated." Thus she became the young woman's foster mother. The young daughter-in-law went home, astonished at the turn of events.

When the auspicious day for celebrating the first pregnancy was near, the mother-in-law said, "This last daughter-in-law of mine has no brothers, nobody. Who's going to celebrate her first pregnancy?" The young wife said, "Mother-in-law, give me a letter of invitation for the ceremony."

"You brotherless woman, whom do you have at your father's or mother's place? Nobody! To whom will you give the letter of invitation?"

"I have a distant relative. Please give me a letter for her."

"Look, everybody! Our brotherless lady is out of her mind. She has suddenly found a relative."

At that point, a neighbor woman spoke up: "Oh, come along! Give the poor thing a piece of paper. What do you have to lose?"

The young daughter-in-law went to the snake-hole at the outskirts of the village, put the letter near it, and came back home.

The day for celebrating the first pregnancy came. The wives of the elder brothers and the mother-in-law ganged up on the young woman and began to mock her: "Just wait. Our daughter-in-law's relatives will come now from her father's place, her mother's place, from everywhere. They'll bring her presents and trunks full of clothes. Put pots of water on the stove to boil and bring wheat to make *lapasi*. Hurry, they'll all be here any minute!"

Even as they were teasing her and making jokes, guests arrived wearing festive red turbans. They looked like Moghul grandees. A noblewoman, looking like a Rajput, was among them. The young daughter-in-law knew at once that the noblewoman was none other than the serpent mother. Her mother-in-law and sisters-in-law were all astonished at the sight and began to mutter, "Where did these people come from? She has no one, not even a father or a mother or a brother. Where did all these relatives come from? And so rich!"

Then they began to welcome the guests: "Welcome, make yourselves at home. We have been waiting all this time for our young daughter-in-law's relatives." The pots for cooking *lapasi* for the festive occasion were actually placed on the stoves and preparations began.

Now the serpent mother called the young woman aside and whispered in her ear, "Daughter, tell them not to cook anything. Just put pots of spiced and boiled milk in this room. We'll drink it after we shut the door. We belong to the serpent community, as you know, and we can't eat ordinary food."

The young woman went to her mother-in-law and told her not to cook anything because her paternal relatives belonged to a caste that drank only spiced milk—that was their prescribed food.

It was time for the meal. Vessels full of milk boiled with spices were put in the room. As soon as the door was shut, the guests resumed their original form as snakes, put their mouths to the vessels, and drank up the milk in no time at all.

The first pregnancy of the daughter was celebrated with all due cere-

mony. The guests gave gold and silver and silk to the husband and his relatives, who were wonder-struck and said, "Oh, look how much they've
brought! They've given her such a rich dowry!"

The guests said at the end of it all, "Now give all of us leave to go and take
our sister to our house for the delivery."

"Oh surely, surely! Please. After all, this is the daughter of your house.
How can we refuse?" said the mother-in-law.

"And you don't have to send anyone to bring her back. We will come and
bring our sister back to you," said the guests.

All the husband's relatives came out to bid good-bye to the young
daughter-in-law and her relatives. The guests said, with great courtesy,
"Now please go back in. We'll find our way." When all of them had gone back
into the house, the serpents led the young woman to the hole on the outskirts
of the village. There they said to her, "Sister, don't be afraid. We'll now assume our original forms. And we'll take you into the hole." The girl said, "I'm
not afraid." Then they all entered the hole, taking the young woman with
them.

As they went inside, she found spacious rooms. They were as beautiful as
the datura flower. There were beautiful beds and swings. The serpent
mother, the matron of the family, sat on a swinging bed that made noises like
kikaduka, kikaduka. The snake god had jewels on his head and a big mustache.
He was sitting on a soft, satin-cushioned seat.

The snake god treated the young woman as his daughter and looked after
her every need in that underground world. She enjoyed the swinging bed
made of gold and silver. Her new parents and the entire clan treated her with
love and care.

Now the serpent mother was also ready to deliver. She told the young
daughter-in-law, "Look here, Daughter, I want to tell you something, and
don't be shocked. We are a community of snakes. We know that if all our babies survived, then we would disturb the balance in the world. There would
be no place for any other creature, no place for people to walk, even. Therefore we eat our babies as they are born, and only those that escape will live
on. Don't be upset when you see me doing this."

When the time came, the young woman stood near the serpent mother
with an earthen lamp in her hand. The serpent went on devouring the eggs
as they were laid. Seeing this, the young mother-to-be was filled with dis-

gust. Her hands shook and the lamp dropped from her hand. In the darkness two eggs hatched and escaped. The serpent mother could bite off only the tails of the two babies before they got away. So there were two tailless snakes.

When the young daughter-in-law was nine months pregnant, she went into labor and delivered a son, beautiful as the ring on the finger of a god. The son grew bigger day by day. When he began to crawl on his knees, she told her serpent mother, "Mother, you've done a lot for me. Now please take me to my house."

The serpent mother gave her mattresses, a cradle, necklaces, anklets, all sorts of ornaments, and overwhelmed her with gifts. Then she said, "Daughter, I want you to do something. Put your hand into the mouth of your grandfather sitting here. Don't be afraid. He won't bite you."

The young woman shook with fear but put her hand into the old snake's mouth. The hand and the whole arm went into his mouth, and when she took it out, shaking all the while, the arm was covered with bracelets of gold.

"Now put in the other hand, all the way," said the serpent mother. The young woman, less afraid this time, put her other arm all the way into the mouth of the snake, and when she withdrew it, it too was covered with bracelets of gold. Then two brothers in human form went with her and left her at the outskirts of her husband's village. When she arrived at her door, both mother and son, surrounded by all the relatives, shouted with joy, "The young daughter-in-law has come! The young daughter-in-law has come! She has brought a big dowry. But nobody knows where her relatives' village is."

The young woman said nothing.

Her son grew. One day the wife of the eldest son of the family was cleaning grain and getting it ready for grinding. The little boy picked up fistfuls of the grain and began scattering it. The eldest daughter-in-law shouted, "Son, don't do that. Why do you want to scatter the grain? We are poor people and can't afford to waste it." This was meant to taunt the young daughter-in-law about her dowry. She was hurt by the taunt. She went to the outskirts of the village, stood near the snake-hole, and wept. When she came back, a number of bulls arrived, carrying bags full of grain to her husband's house. The husband's relatives were put to shame.

Once her son spilled some milk. The eldest daughter-in-law threw him a taunt: "Son, don't do that. Your mother's relatives are rich. They will send you a herd of buffalo. But we are poor people. Don't spill our milk."

Again, the young daughter-in-law went to the snake-hole and wept there. The serpent mother came out and said to her, "We'll take care of it. Go home now, but when you go, do not look behind you. Do not give buttermilk to a juggler. Say *nagel, nagel* and a herd of buffalo will come to your house." The woman returned to her house, saying *nagel, nagel* all the way, and a herd of buffalo followed her. When she reached home, she called out to her in-laws and said, "We must clean the buffalo shed." All the relatives came out and were amazed to see countless buffalo-with white marks on their foreheads.

Now what was happening in the snake-hole? The two young snakes without tails were unhappy because no one wanted to play with them. Their playmates said:

> *Go away, Tailless, I won't let you play!*
> *Go away, Minus-Tail, I won't let you play!*

The two young snakes went to their mother and asked her, "Mother, Mother, tell us. Who made us without tails?"

She said, "Sons, you have a sister who lives out there on the earth. When you were born, the earthen lamp accidentally fell from her hand. So, you have no tails."

"Then we'll both go and bite her for doing this to us."

"No, no! How can you bite your sister? She is a good girl. She'll bless you."

"If she blesses us, we'll give her a sari and a blouse for a gift and come back. But if she says nasty things about us, we'll bite her."

Before the mother could say anything, the two tailless snakes crept away and went to the sister's house. It was evening. One hid himself near the threshold, the other one lay hidden in the watershed. They thought, "If she comes here, we'll bite her."

When the sister came to the threshold, she stumbled and her foot struck something. She said, "I'm the one without a parent. May my paternal relatives be pleased to forgive me if I've struck something. The serpent god is my father and the serpent mother is my mother. They've given me silk and jewels for my dowry."

When he heard these words, the tailless snake thought, "Oh, this sister is blessing me. How can I bite her?"

The sister went then to the watershed. There also, she stumbled and her foot hit something. Again she said, "I'm the one without parents. May my paternal relatives be pleased to forgive me if I've struck something. The serpent god is my father and the serpent mother is my mother. They've given me silk and jewels for my dowry."

The second tailless snake also thought, "This sister is blessing me. How can I bite her?"

Then both the brothers assumed human form, met their sister, gave her a sari and a blouse, gave her son golden anklets, and went home to their hole.

May the Serpent Mother be good to us all as she was good to her!

The Deer and the Snake

L ong long ago there was a great deluge, such as had never been seen before. The River Dědong overflowed its banks and washed away many houses. All the fields became a vast lake, and all the inhabitants and their animals were drowned.

An old man in Pyŏngyang went rowing on the flood in a boat. He found a deer almost exhausted and drowning, and he rescued it. Then he found a snake floating on the waters, and he rescued it too. Before long a boy came floating by, and the old man saved him also. He carried them to the shore in his boat. There he released the deer and the snake. The boy however would not leave the old man, since both his parents had been drowned and his home destroyed by the flood. So the old man gave him food to eat and adopted him as his son.

One day the deer came back and tugged at the old man's sleeve, swinging his tail from side to side. The old man guessed that it was trying to tell him something and so he followed it. Before long they came to a rock in the mountains. The deer pawed the ground nearby, and the old man guessed that something must lie hidden there. He began to dig, and lo and behold, he found a jar buried there full of gold and silver. He took the treasure home with him and was now a rich man.

His foster-son became very conceited and began to spend money extravagantly. His father would chide him for his recklessness, but he often answered him rudely and took no notice of his admonitions. In the end he decided that he would go away and live by himself, but his father refused to let him go. So the boy became angry and abusive, and brought a false charge against him. He went secretly to the local authorities and said, "My foster-father stole a lot of money, and he has some story that he got it from a deer." The official who was responsible for such matters went and arrested the old man, and would not listen to him when he told the true explanation of his wealth. He was cast into prison, but confidently expected that some day he would be released, for he was indeed innocent of any crime.

One night the snake came to him in his cell. It bit him on the arm and went away. His arm immediately swelled up from the effects of the poison and the pain became unbearable. "The snake returns evil for good," he said to himself, "How absurd that is!" But a little later the snake came back holding a small glass bottle in its mouth. It applied the bottle to the painful swelling on his arm, and at once the swelling subsided and the pain ceased, so that he was completely cured. Then the snake disappeared once more.

In the morning he heard a great commotion outside. He heard that the magistrate's wife had been bitten by a snake during the night and seemed likely to die from the poison. He guessed that it must have been the same snake as had bitten him, and so he had word taken to the magistrate that he could cure his wife's hurt. The magistrate sent for him immediately and he took the rest of the magic ointment the snake had brought him and applied it to the lady's wound. At once she was cured completely.

The magistrate was at last convinced of his innocence, and he was released at once. Then his wicked foster-son was arrested and punished for his crime.

The Pheasants and the Bell

Once upon a time there lived a woodcutter. One day he went into the mountains to cut firewood, and there he saw two pheasants flying up and down in a distracted manner. When he came nearer he saw a snake on the point of devouring their eggs, which were lying under a bush. So he took the stick that supported his pack-carrier and beat the snake to death with it.

Some ten years afterwards he went on a journey to Yŏngwŏl in the Province of Gangwŏn. One night he lost his way in a forest and at last came upon a house with a light in the window. He thought that perhaps he might stay the night there, and so he went and knocked at the door. A young girl came out and received him kindly, and took him in and gave him a good supper.

After a little while the woodcutter asked, "Are you living here alone, or are you expecting the rest of your family to return?" As he said this the girl changed colour and snarled viciously at him, "Ten years ago you killed a snake with your stick. I am that snake. I bid you welcome, my enemy! Now I shall savor my revenge to the full. I am going to eat you up!"

The woodcutter was very frightened at her menacing words, and begged her to spare his life. "You were trying to eat the pheasants' eggs," he pleaded. "I took pity on them and so I made up my mind to save them. So I beat you with my stick, but I did not mean to kill you. If I did kill you, it was quite by accident, and I apologize most humbly for my deed. Do spare my life, I beseech you!"

The girl considered for a moment and replied, "If you wish to live, there is one thing you must do for me. Near the summit of this mountain there stands an old deserted temple, and in it hangs a great bell. If you can sit here in this room and make that bell ring, then I shall let you go free and un-harmed. Can you do that for me?"

The woodcutter answered in great embarrassment, "How can I ring that bell if I am sitting here? It is quite impossible. You are just toying with me, are you not?"

"You mean you cannot do it?" said the girl. "Then you shall die this very minute."

So the girl transformed herself into a big snake to kill him, but no sooner had she done so than the solemn boom of the bell came clearly to their ears through the night. The snake immediately became a girl again, and sighed, "You must be under Heaven's protection. I cannot hurt you now." With these words she vanished.

In the morning the woodcutter climbed to the top of the mountain. There he found the temple standing desolate. Under the great bell he found two pheasants lying dead, their heads battered and their wings broken, and on the surface of the bell itself were great dark stains of blood. He realized then that the two pheasants he had helped so long ago had sacrificed their lives to repay his kindness. They had dashed their heads against the bell, so that its sound might save their benefactor.

The Centipede Girl

KOREA

*T*here was once a poor man who lived on the outskirts of Seoul. He was so poor that he could neither provide food for his family, nor keep a roof over their heads. His dire poverty reduced him to the uttermost depths of despair, and at last in the extremity of his misery he resolved to put an end to his life.

One day he left his wife without telling her where he was going. He went down to the banks of the Han River and walked along until he came to a towering rocky cliff. He climbed to the top, closed his eyes, and hurled himself over the precipice into the deep water below. He imagined that he must be killed instantly. Half an hour later, however, a beautiful woman who was washing clothes by the riverside found him lying on a sandbank. He was unconscious, but otherwise completely unhurt. Before long he came to his senses, and she asked him what had happened. He told her of his poverty and his resolve to end his life. So she said to him, "Happily you are safe. I hope you will never try to do such a terrible thing again. You are still young, and sometime Fortune will smile on you. If you like you can come home with me and rest a while at my house."

Thereupon she led him away, and soon they came to her house. It was very large and built of brick, and stood alone in the valley. Altogether it gave an impression of great wealth. The man stayed there as a guest and very soon fell in love with the girl. He forgot his family completely. In any case he was sure he must be dead, for had he not thrown himself in the river to put an end to his life? Never in his wildest dreams had he imagined that any such delights could exist in the world as the life he was now leading with this mysterious girl. She was of the most ethereal beauty, and gave him the finest clothes to wear, and the richest food to eat. Moreover the house itself was luxurious beyond his wildest imaginings, and he was completely over-whelmed by it all.

They lived together happily for a few months. Then, however, his new life began to pall a little, and he thought wistfully of his helpless family in Seoul. So he told his mistress that he would like to go away for a while, though he did not tell her that he wanted to visit his family. But she had al-ready guessed his intention, and said, "If you leave me now, I am afraid that you will forget me and never come back."

The man too thought that it was quite possible that he might stay with his family and not return to her, but he answered vehemently, "How could I ever forget you? Have no fear. I will come back to you without fail."

"On your way back, then," said the girl, "take no notice of anyone who may try to deter you. Come straight back, and I shall be waiting for you."

So he left her, and set out for his own house, where he had left his own family. When he reached the village he was astounded to see a magnificent new house built where his old home had stood. When he came closer he saw his own name on the gate. A sudden suspicion flashed into his mind that his wife might have been unfaithful in his absence. This thought made him rather angry, but then he reflected that he had no right to blame her, for he had neglected her for a long time.

He knocked at the gate, and his son came and opened it. He looked at his long-lost father with joyous tears in his eyes. "Welcome home, Father," he cried, and then called to his mother, "Mother, Father is home!" She imme-diately rushed out into the garden, wearing the most beautiful clothes.

Her husband looked sternly at her and asked, "Who built this house? Where did you get the money?"

His wife looked at him questioningly. "Wasn't it you who sent me money every day? I thought it was you who sent us all these wonderful presents. Am I mistaken, then?"

The truth slowly dawned on her husband. It must have been none other than the rich woman he had stayed with, for there could be no one else who would help his family. So he pretended he had just been joking and changed the subject. He said nothing of his suicide, nor of the mysterious woman he had met.

He was very happy to be reunited with his family after his long absence, but as the months went by he began to think longingly of the beautiful woman he had left in the country. At last his desire to see her once again became so strong that he could bear to wait no longer. Once again he left his wife and family and set out for his mistress's house.

On the way he had to pass by a big hollow tree. Just as he came to it he was surprised to hear a voice calling him by name. "My dear grandson," it said, "I am the spirit of your grandfather. Listen to me. You must not visit that woman again. I give you this warning for your own good. She is no woman, but a centipede a thousand years old."

It certainly sounded like his grandfather's voice, but he refused to believe what it had told him, for he trusted the woman implicitly. He would not have been deterred even if the warning had been true, for having once attempted suicide he was no longer afraid of death. So he answered, "Grandfather, I must see her again. I promised her I would return, and nothing will prevent me from keeping my promise. Death is nothing to me, for I believe that I have died once already. And even though it meant death I would see her, for it was she who saved my family when starvation stared them in the face."

The disembodied voice spoke solemnly to him. "I see that you are determined to go," it said. "There is one way for you to escape death. Go and buy the strongest tobacco you can, smoke it, and keep the juices in your mouth. As soon as you see her, spit them in her face. If you fail to do this you will surely die. Poor man, she has cast a spell on you with her beauty."

So he went to the market and bought the strongest tobacco he could find. Then he set out again and smoked hard all the way to his mistress's house. He carefully stored the tobacco juices in his mouth. When he got to her house he peeped in through a crack in the gate, and there he saw the tail of a great centipede in the house. Nothing daunted he determined to see her once again, whatever the outcome. So he boldly knocked at the door. His mistress came out and opened the gate and received him gladly. But he spoke not a word, for he was still holding the poisonous tobacco juices in his mouth. Seeing his clenched mouth and the strange expression of his eyes, she guessed that something must have happened, and she turned pale in her alarm.

He came into the room and gazed at her. She was as beautiful as ever, just as he remembered her. Her raven hair, her eyes clear as crystal, the curve of her brow, her nose and mouth—all were just as they had been before. He was torn between his love for her and the dire warning his grandfather's spirit had given him. He was on the point of spitting the poisonous tobacco juice in her face, when she suddenly gave a sob. She bowed her head and wept. He stared at her, undecided, and it seemed that she became twice as beautiful as before. As he looked he relented and turning to the window spat out the tobacco juices.

Her anxiety passed and she smiled. "Thank you for sparing me," she said. "The voice that you heard is not your grandfather's. It was the accursed snake that lives in the hollow tree. I am a daughter of the Heavenly King, and the snake was one of the servants in the palace. He fell in love with me and seduced me. The matter came to the ears of my Heavenly Father and he punished us both. Me he ordered to live for three years in the world of men as a centipede, and my seducer he condemned to live eternally as a snake. Ever resentful of his fate he has always tried to do me further harm. Today is the last day of my sentence, and tomorrow I return to my father. Had you spat in my face I should have had to suffer three long years more."

So they had just one more day of happiness together, and that night they dreamed the sweetest of dreams. When the man awoke in the morning he found himself lying on a rock. There was no sign of the house, and he was quite alone.

The Youth and
His Eagle

*I*n forgotten times, in the days of our ancients, at the Middle Place, or
what is now Shiwina (Zuñi), there lived a youth who was well grown, or perfect in manhood. He had a pet Eagle which he kept in a cage down on the roof
of the first terrace of the house of his family. He loved this Eagle so dearly
that he could not endure to be separated from it; not only this, but he spent
nearly all his time in caring for and fondling his pet. Morning, noon, and evening, yea, and even between those times, you would see him going down to
the eagle cage with meat and other kinds of delicate food. Day after day, there
you would find him sitting beside the Eagle, petting it and making affection-
ate speeches, to all of which treatment the bird responded with a most satisfied air and seemed equally fond of his owner.

Whenever a storm came the youth would hasten out of the house, as
though the safety of the crops depended upon it, to protect the Eagle. So,
winter and summer, no other care occupied his attention. Cornfield and
melon garden was this bird to this youth; so much so that his brothers, elder
and younger, and his male relatives generally, looked down upon him as neg-
ligent of all manly duties, and wasteful of their substance, which he helped
not to earn in his excessive care of the bird. Naturally, therefore, they looked
with aversion upon the Eagle; and one evening, after a hard day's work, after
oft-repeated remonstrances with the youth for not joining in their labors,
they returned home tired and out of humor, and, climbing the ladder of the
lower terrace, passed the great cage on their way into the upper house. They
stopped a moment before entering, and one of the eldest of the party exclaimed, "We have remonstrated in vain with the younger brother; we have

represented his duties to him in every possible light, yet without effect. What remains to be done? What plans can we devise to alienate him from this miserable Eagle?"

"Why not kill the wretched bird?" asked one of them. "That, I should say, would be the most simple means of curing him of his infatuation."

"That is an excellent plan," exclaimed all of the brothers as they went on into the house. "We must adopt it."

The Eagle, apparently so unconscious, heard all this and pondered over it. Presently came the youth with meat and other delicate food for his beloved bird, and, opening the wicket of the gate, placed it within and bade the Eagle eat. But the bird looked at him and at the food with no apparent interest, and, lowering its head on its breast, sat moody and silent.

"Are you ill, my beloved Eagle?" asked the youth. "Or why is it that you do not eat?"

"I do not care to eat," said the Eagle, speaking for the first time. "I am oppressed with much anxiety."

"Do eat, my beloved Eagle," said the youth. "Why should you be sad? Have I neglected you?"

"No, indeed, you have not," said the Eagle. "For this reason I love you as you love me; for this reason I prize and cherish you as you cherish me; and yet it is for this very reason that I am sad. Look you! Your brothers and relatives have often remonstrated with you for your neglect of their fields and your care for me. They have often been angered with you for not bearing your part in the duties of the household. Therefore it is that they look with reproach upon you and with aversion upon me, so much so that they have at last determined to destroy me in order to do away with your affection for me and to withdraw your attention. For this reason I am sad—not that they can harm me, for I need but spread my wings when the wicket is opened, and what can they do? But I would not part from you, for I love you. I would not that you should part with me, for you love me. Therefore am I sad, for I must go tomorrow to my home in the skies," said the Eagle, again relapsing into moody silence.

"Oh, my beloved bird! My own dear Eagle, how could I live without you? How could I remain behind when you went forward, below when you went upward?" exclaimed the youth, already beginning to weep. "No! Go, go, if it need be, alas! But let me go with you," said the youth.

"My friend! My poor, poor youth!" said the Eagle. "You cannot go with me. You have not wings to fly, nor have you knowledge to guide your course through the high skies into other worlds that you know not of."

"Let me go with you," cried the youth, falling on his knees by the side of the cage. "I will comfort you. I will care for you, even as I have done here, but live without you I cannot!"

"Ah, my youth," said the Eagle, "I would that you could go with me, but the end would not be well. You know not how little you love me that you wish to do this thing. Think for a moment! The foods that my people eat are not the foods of your people; they are not ripened by fire for our consumption, but whatever we capture abroad on our measureless hunts we devour as it is, asking no fire to render it palatable or wholesome. You could not exist thus."

"My Eagle! My Eagle!" cried the youth. "If I were to remain behind when you went forward, or below when you went upward, food would be as nothing to me; and were it not better that I should eat raw food, or no food, than that I should stay here, excessively and sadly thinking of you, and thus never eat at all, even of the food of my own people? No, let me go with you!"

"Once more I implore you, my youth," said the Eagle, "not to go with me, for to your own undoing and to my sadness will such a journey be undertaken."

"Let me go, let me go! Only let me go!" implored the youth.

"It is said," replied the Eagle calmly. "Even as you wish, so be it. Now go unto your own home for the last time. Gather large quantities of sustaining food, as for a long journey. Place this food in strong pouches, and make them all into a package which you can sling upon your shoulder or back. Then come to me tomorrow morning, after the people have begun to descend to their fields."

The youth bade good-night to his Eagle and went into the house. He took of parched flour a great quantity, of dried and pulverized wafer-bread a large bag, and of other foods, such as hunters carry and on which they sustain themselves long, he took a good supply, and made them all into a firm package. Then, with high hopes and much thought of the morrow, he laid himself to rest. He slept late into the morning, and it was not until his brothers had departed for their fields of corn that he arose, and, eating a hasty breakfast, slung the package of foods over his shoulders and descended to the cage of the Eagle. The great bird was waiting for him. With a smile in its eyes it came

forth when he opened the wicket, and, settling down on the ground, spread
out its wings and bade the youth mount.

"Sit on my back, for it is strong, oh youth! Grasp the base of my wings, and
rest your feet above my thighs, that you may not fall off. Are you ready? Ah,
well. And have you all needful things in the way of food? Good. Let us start
on our journey."

Saying this, the Eagle rose slowly, circling wider and wider as it went up,
and higher and higher, until it had risen far above the town, going slowly.
Presently it said, "My youth, I will sing a farewell song to your people for you
and for me, that they may know of our final departure." Then, as with great
sweeps of its wings it circled round and round, going higher and higher, it
sang this song:

> *Huli-i-i—Huli-i-i—*
> *Pa shish lakwa-a-a—*
> *U-u-u-u—*
> *U-u-u-u-a!*
>
> *Pa shish lakwa-a-a—*
> *U-u-u-u—*
> *U-u-u-u-a!*

As the song floated down from on high, "Save us! By our eyes!" exclaimed
the people. "The Eagle and the youth! They are escaping; they are leaving
us!"

And so the word went from mouth to mouth, and from ear to ear, until the
whole town was gazing at the Eagle and the youth, and the song died away in
the distance, and the Eagle became smaller and smaller, winding its way upward until it was a mere speck, and finally vanished in the very zenith.

The people shook their heads and resumed their work, but the Eagle and
the youth went on until at last they came to the great opening in the zenith
of the sky. In passing upward by its endless cliffs they came out on the other
side into the sky-world; and still upward soared the Eagle, until it alighted
with its beloved burden on the summit of the Mountain of Turquoises, so
blue that the light shining on it paints the sky blue.

"*Huhua!*" said the Eagle, with the weariness that comes at the end of a
long journey. "We have reached our journey's end for a time. Let us rest ourselves on this mountain height of my beloved world."

The youth descended and sat by the Eagle's side, and the Eagle, raising its wings until the tips touched above, lowered its head, and catching hold of its crown, shook it from side to side, and then drew upon it, and then gradually the eagle-coat parted, and while the youth looked and wondered in love and joy, a beautiful maiden was uncovered before him, in garments of dazzling whiteness, softness, and beauty. No more beautiful maiden could be conceived than this one—bright of face, clear and clean, with eyes so dark and large and deep, and yet sharp, that it was bewildering to look into them. Such eyes have never been seen in this world.

"Come with me, my youth—you who have loved me so well," said she, approaching him and reaching out her hand. "Let us wander for a while on this mountainside and seek the home of my people."

They descended the mountain and wound round its foot until, looking up in the clear light of the sky-world, they beheld a city such as no man has ever seen. Lofty were its walls—smooth, gleaming, clean, and white—no ladders, no smoke, no filth in any part whatsoever.

"Yonder is the home of my people," said the maiden, and resuming her eagle-dress she took the youth on her back again, and, circling upward, hovered for a moment over this home of the Eagles, then, through one of the wide entrances which were in the roof, slowly descended. No ladders were there, inside or outside; no need of them with a people winged like the Eagles, for a people they were, like ourselves—more a people, indeed, than we, for in one guise or the other they might appear at will.

No sooner had the Eagle-maiden and the youth entered this great building than those who were assembled there greeted them with welcome assurances of joy at their coming. "Sit ye down and rest," said they.

The youth looked around. The great room into which they had descended was high and broad and long, and lighted from many windows in its roof and upon its walls, which were beautifully white and clean and finished, as no walls in this world are, with many devices pleasing to the eye. Starting out from these walls were many hooks or pegs, suspended from which were the dresses of the Eagles who lived there, the forms of which we know.

"Yea, sit ye down and rest and be happy," said an old man. Wonderfully fine he was as he arose and approached the couple and said, spreading abroad his wings, "Be ye always one to the other wife and husband. Shall it be so?"

And they both, smiling, said, "Yes." And so the youth married the Eagle-maiden.

After a few days of rest they found him an eagle-coat, fine as the finest, with broad, strong wings, and beautiful plumage, and they taught him how to conform himself to it and it to himself. And as Eagles would teach a young Eagle here in this world of ours, so they taught the youth gradually to fly. At first they would bid him poise himself in his eagle-form on the floor of their great room, and, laying all over it soft things, bid him open his wings and leap into the air. Anxious to learn, he would spread his great wings and with a powerful effort send himself high up toward the ceiling, but untaught to sustain himself there, would fall with many a flap and tumble to the floor. Again and again this was tried, but after a while he learned to sustain and guide himself almost wholly round the room without once touching anything; and his wife in her eagle-form would fly around him, watching and helping, and whenever his flight wavered would fan a strong wind up against his wings with her own that he might not falter, until he had at last learned wholly to support himself in the air. Then she bade him one day come out with her to the roof of the house, and from there they sailed away, away, and away over the great valleys and plains below, ever keeping to the northward and eastward; and whenever he faltered in his flight she bore his wings up with her own wings, teaching him how, this way and that, until, when they returned to the roof, those who watched them said, "Now, indeed, is he learned in the ways of our people. How good it is that this is so!" And they were very happy, the youth and the Eagle-maiden and their people.

One day the maiden took the youth out again into the surrounding country, and as they flew along she said to him, "You may wonder that we never fly toward the southward. Oh, my youth, my husband! Never go yonder, for over that low range of mountains is a fearful world, where no mortal can venture. If you love me, oh, if you truly love me, never venture yonder!" And he listened to her advice and promised that he would not go there. Then they went home.

One day there was a grand hunt, and he was invited to join in it. Over the wide world flew this band of Eagle-hunters to faraway plains. Whatsoever they would hunt, behold! below them somewhere or other might the game be seen, were it rabbit, mountain sheep, antelope, or deer, and each according to his wish captured the kind of game he would, the youth bringing home with the rest his quarry. Of all the game they captured he could eat none, for in that great house of the Eagles, so beautiful, so perfect, no fire ever burned, no cooking was ever done. And after many days the food which the youth brought with him was diminished so that his wife took him out to a high mountain one day, and said, "As I have told you before, the region beyond those low mountains is fearful and deadly; but yonder in the east are other kinds of people than those whom you should dread. Not far away is the home of the Pelicans and Storks, who, as you know, eat food that has been cooked, even as your people do. When you grow hungry, my husband, go to them, and as they are your grandparents they will feed you and give you of their abundance of food, that you may bring it here, and thus we shall do well and be happy."

The youth assented, and, guided part of the way by his faithful, loving wife, he went to the home of the Storks. No sooner had he appeared than they greeted him with loud assurances of welcome and pleasure at his coming, and bade him eat. And they set before him bean-bread, bean-stews, beans which were baked, as it were, and mushes of beans with meat intermixed, which seemed as well cooked as the foods of our own people here on this mortal earth. And the youth ate part of them, and with many thanks returned to his home among the Eagles. And thus, as his wife had said before, it was all well, and they continued to live there happily.

Between the villages of the Eagles and the Storks the youth lived; so that by and by the Storks became almost as fond of him as were the Eagles, addressing him as their beloved grandchild. And in consequence of this fondness, his old grandfather and grandmother among the Storks especially called his attention to the fearful region lying beyond the range of mountains to the south, and they implored him, as his wife had done, not to go thither. "For the love of us, do not go there, oh, grandchild!" said they one day, when he was about to leave.

He seemed to agree with them, and spread his wings and flew away. But when he had gone a long distance, he turned southward, with this exclamation: "Why should I not see what this is? Who can harm me, floating on these strong wings of mine? Who can harm an Eagle in the sky?" So he flew over the edge of the mountains, and behold! rising up on the plains beyond them was a great city, fine and perfect, with walls of stone built as are the towns of our dead ancients. And the smoke was wreathing forth from its chimneys, and in the hazy distance it seemed teeming with life at the moment when the youth saw it, which was at evening time.

The inhabitants of that city saw him and sent messages forth to the town of the Eagles that they would make a grand festival and dance, and invited the Eagles to come with their friends to witness this dance. And when the youth returned to the home of his Eagle-people, behold! already had this message been delivered there, and his wife in sorrow was awaiting him at the doorway.

"Alas! Alas! My youth! My husband!" said she. "And so, regarding more your own curiosity than the love of your wife, you have been into that fearful country, and as might have been expected, you were observed. We are now invited to visit the city you saw and to witness a dance of the inhabitants thereof, which invitation we cannot refuse, and you must go with us. It remains to be seen, oh my youth, whom I trusted, if your love for me be so great that you may stand the test of this which you have brought upon yourself, by heedlessness of my advice and that of your grandparents, the Storks. Oh, my husband, I despair of you, and thus despairing, I implore you to heed me once more, and all may be well with you even yet. Go with us tonight to the city you saw, the most fearful of all cities, for it is the city of the damned, and wonderful things you will see; but do not laugh or even smile once. I will sit by your side and look at you. Oh, think of me as I do of you, and thus thinking you will not smile. If you truly love me, and would remain with me always, and be happy as I would be happy, do this one thing for me."

The youth promised over and over, and when night came he went with the Eagle-people to that city. A beautiful place it was, large and fine, with high walls of stone and many a little window out of which the red firelight was shining. The smoke was going up from its chimneys, the sparks winding up through it, and, with beacon fires burning on the roofs, it was a happy, bustling scene that met the gaze of the youth as he approached the town. There were sounds and cries of life everywhere. Lights shone and merriment echoed from every street and room, and they were ushered into a great dance hall, or *kiwitsin*, where the audience was already assembled.

By and by the sounds of the coming dance were heard, and all was expectation. The fires blazed up and the lights shone all round the room, making it bright as day. In came the dancers, maidens mostly, beautiful, and clad in the richest of ancient garments; their eyes were bright, their hair black and soft, their faces gleaming with merriment and pleasure. And they came joking down the ladders into the room before the place where the youth sat, and as they danced down the middle of the floor they cried out in shrill, yet not unpleasant voices, as they jostled each other, playing grotesque pranks and assuming the most laughter-stirring attitudes:

"*Hapa! hapa! is! is! is!*" ("Dead! dead! this! this! this!")—pointing at one another, and repeating this baleful expression, although so beautiful, and full of life and joy and merriment.

Now, the youth looked at them all through this long dance, and though he thought it strange that they should exclaim thus one to another, so lively and pretty and jolly they were, he was nevertheless filled with amusement at their strange antics and wordless jokes. Still he never smiled.

Then they filed in again and there were more dancers, merrier than before, and among them were two or three girls of surpassing beauty even in that throng of lovely women, and one of them looked in a coquettish manner constantly toward the youth, directing all her smiles and merriment to him as she pointed round to her companions, exclaiming, "*Hapa! hapa! is! is! is!*"

The youth grew forgetful of everything else as he leaned forward, absorbed in watching this girl with her bright eyes and merry smiles. When, finally, in a more amusing manner than before, she jostled some merry dancer, he laughed outright and the girl ran forward toward him, with two others following, and reaching out, grasped his hands and dragged him into the dance. The Eagle-maiden lifted her wings and with a cry of woe flew away with her people. But ah, ah! The youth minded nothing, he was so wild with merriment, like the beautiful maidens by his side, and up and down the great lighted hall he danced with them, joining in their uncouth postures and their exclamations, of which he did not yet understand the true meaning—"*Hapa! hapa! is! is! is!*"

By and by the fire began to burn low, and the maidens said to him, "Come and pass the night with us all here. Why go back to your home? Are we not merry companions? Ha! ha! ha! ha! *Hapa! hapa! is! is! is!*" They began to laugh and jostle one another again. Thus they led the youth, not unwillingly on his part, away into a far-off room, large and fine like the others, and there on soft blankets he lay himself down, and these maidens gathered round him, one pillowing his head on her arm, another smiling down into his face, another sitting by his side, and soon he fell asleep. All became silent, and the youth slept on.

In the morning, when broad daylight had come, the youth opened his eyes and started. It seemed as though there were more light than there should be in the house. He looked up, and the room which had been so fine and finished the night before was tottering over his head; the winds shrieked through great crevices in the walls; the windows were broken and wide open; sand sifted through on the wind and eddied down into the old, barren room. The rafters, dried and warped with age, were bending and breaking, and pieces of the roof fell now and then when the wind blew more strongly. He raised himself, and clammy bones fell from around him; and when he cast his eyes about him, there on the floor were strewn bones and skulls. Here and there a face half buried in the sand, with eyes sunken and dried and patches of skin clinging to it, seemed to glare at him. Fingers and feet, as of mummies, were strewn about, and it was as if the youth had entered a great cemetery, where the remains of the dead of all ages were littered about. He lifted himself still farther, and where the head of one maiden had lain or the arms of another had entwined with his, bones were clinging to him. One by one he picked them off stealthily and laid them down, until at last he freed himself, and, rising, cautiously stepped between the bones which were lying around, making no noise until he came to the broken-down doorway of the place. There, as he passed out, his foot tripped against a splinter of bone which was embedded in the debris of the ruin, and as a sliver sings in the wind, so this sang out. The youth, startled and terrorized, sprang forth and ran for his life in the direction of the home of the Storks. Shrieking, howling, and singing like a slivered stick in the wind, like creaking boughs in the forest, with groans and howls and whistlings that seemed to freeze the youth as he ran, these bones and fragments of the dead arose and, like a flock of vampires, pursued him noisily.

He ran and ran, and the great cloud of the dead were coming nearer and nearer and pressing round him, when he beheld one of his grandparents, a Badger, near its hole. The Badger, followed by others, was fast approaching him, having heard this fearful clamor, and cried out, "Our grandson! Let's save him!" So they ran forward and, catching him up, cast him down into one of their holes. Then, turning toward the uncanny crowd and bristling up, with sudden emotion and mighty effort they cast off that odor by which, as you know, they may defile the very winds. *Thlitchiii!* It met the crowd of ghosts. *Thliwooo!* The whole host of them turned with wails and howls and gnashings of teeth back toward the City of the Dead, whence they had come. And the Badgers ran into the hole where lay the youth, lifted him up, and scolded him most vigorously for his folly.

Then they said, "Sit up, you fool, for you are not yet saved! Hurry!" said they, one to another. "Heat water!" And, the water being heated, nauseating herbs and other medicines were mingled with it, and the youth was directed to drink of that. He drank, not once, but four times. *Ukch, usa*! And after he had been thus treated the old Badgers asked him if he felt relieved or well, and the youth said he was very well compared with what he had been.

Then they stood him up in their midst and said to him, "You fool and faithless lout, why did you go and become enamored of Death, however beautiful? It is only a wonder that with all our skill and power we have saved you thus far. It will be a still greater wonder, O foolish one, if she who loved you still loves you enough after this faithlessness to save the life which you have forfeited. Who would dance and take joy in Death? Go now to the home of your grandparents, the Storks, and there live. Your plumage gone, your love given up, what remains? You can neither descend to your own people below without wings, nor can you live with the people of the Eagles without love. Go, therefore, to your grandparents!"

And the youth got up and dragged himself away to the home of the Storks; but when he arrived there they looked at him with downcast faces and reproached him over and over, saying, "There is small possibility of your regaining what you have forfeited—the love and affection of your wife."

"But I will go to her and plead with her," said the youth. "How should I know what I was doing?"

"We told you not to do it, and you heeded not our telling."

So the youth lagged away to the home of the Eagles, where, outside that great house with high walls, he lingered, moping and moaning. The Eagles came and went, or they gathered and talked on the housetop, but no word of greeting did they offer him; and his wife, at last, with a shiver of disgust, appeared above him and said, "Go back! Go back to your grandparents. Their love you may not have forfeited; mine you have. Go back! For we never can receive you again amongst us. Oh, folly and faithlessness, in you they have an example!"

So the youth sadly returned to the home of the Storks. There he lingered, returning ever and anon to the home of the Eagles; but it was as though he were not there, until at last the elder Eagles, during one of his absences, implored the Eagle-maid to take the youth back to his own home.

"Would you ask me, his wife, who loved him, now to touch him who has been polluted by being enamored of Death?" asked she.

But they implored, and she acquiesced. So, when the youth appeared again at the home of the Eagles, she had found an old, old Eagle dress, many of the feathers in it broken; ragged and disreputable it was, and the wing-feathers were so thin that the wind whistled through them. Descending with this, she bade him put it on, and when he had done so, she said, "Come with me now, according to the knowledge in which we have instructed you."

And they flew away to the summit of that blue mountain, and, after resting there, they began to descend into the sky which we see, and from that downward and downward in very narrow circles.

Whenever the youth, with his worn-out wings, faltered, the wife bore him up, until, growing weary in a moment of remembrance of his faithlessness, she caught in her talons the Eagle-dress which sustained him and drew it off, bade him farewell forever, and sailed away out of sight in the sky. And the youth, with one gasp and shriek, tumbled over and over and over, fell into the very center of the town in which he had lived when he loved his Eagle, and utterly perished.

�◫ ◫ ◫

Thus it was in the times of the ancients; and for this reason by no means whatsoever may a mortal man, by any alliances under the sun, avoid Death. But if one would live as long as possible, one should never, in any manner whatsoever, remembering this youth's experience, become enamored of Death.

Thus shortens my story.

PART THREE

Tricksters

Found frequently throughout Africa, Asia, and the Americas, and usually but not always a male, Trickster is a Transformer, a Bungler, a Buffoon, an Overreacher, a Culture Hero, a sometimes Creator, a consistent Survivor. In Coyote Was Going There, *Jarold Ramsey describes Trickster as a quintessential mediator—negotiating between the human and nonhuman worlds, human society and nature, social collectivity and individuality, Id and Superego, childhood and adulthood, past and present, and what might have been and what is. Lévi-Strauss characterizes Trickster as a* bricoleur, *one who patches creation together, while Barre Toelken says simply that Trickster, with his exuberant excesses, is the "exponent of all possibilities."*

Protean, Trickster takes on many forms and names. In different parts of the world he appears as Fox, Raven, Spider, Hare, Bluejay, Man, or the ubiquitous Coyote. Among the Ashanti in West Africa and the Caribbean, the Trickster Spider is known as Anansi, while in some African American communities of the southeastern United States, he is referred to as Aunt Nancy or Miss Nancy. The Tortoise Trickster of the Yoruba is called Ijapa, but in North America, in the form of an amorphous man, he is known as Wakdjunkaga to the Winnebago; Nanabush, the Hare, to the Ojibway; the Spider Iktomi to the Lakota; Br'er Rabbit and many other names in various other regions.

In whatever form he appears and by whatever names he is called, Trickster's character is predictable. He has a voracious appetite that drives his actions. He is greedy for food, drink, sex, experience of every kind. (Some would say he is the embodiment of unrestrained human desire.) Shunning

*responsibility and work, he wanders about attempting to dupe others in order
to obtain what he wants. Trickster, with his great knowledge of human nature,
uses his victims' weaknesses against them, and is able to trick others by
appealing to their greed or their vanity or their insecurity.*

*Trickster is ever on the lookout for someone to trick. Trickster attempts to
outwit animals, humans, and occasionally even the deities themselves.
Anansi becomes "the owner of all stories that are told" by using his intelligence to trick the hornets, the python, and the leopard, all mightier animals
than he; Coyote must outsmart the old woman to get close enough to the sun to
steal him. Sometimes Trickster's plots backfire, though, as when Anansi (later
Br'er Rabbit) gets stuck to the gum-man or tarbaby, or when Ijapa loses all his
horses because he cannot control his greed, or when Wakdjunkaga burns himself in his eagerness to punish the culprit who ate his roasted ducks, or when
Coyote loses his eyes because he is so eager to borrow another's perception.*

*Despite himself, Trickster is sometimes inadvertently responsible for the
creation of something helpful to humankind: part of nature such as the sun or
the moon in the Juruna tale, for instance; or particular animals like the two
men who turned into crocodile and heron in the Murinbata tale from northern
Australia; or specific body parts such as the shape of the human anus as nar-
rated in the sections of the Winnebago Trickster cycle excerpted here; or certain cultural institutions or practices. Be assured, though, that Trickster has
no intention of doing good, just as (usually) he has no malevolent intentions.
Just as Trickster can transform others, he can change himself—into human or
animal, male or female—reflecting and enacting the ever-changing dynamics
of the world. Part deity, yet quite recognizably human, Trickster is the manifestation of pure energy infused with desire and curiosity and an enduring
sense of humor.*

*In West Africa Trickster tales often begin with an account of a particular
hardship in the natural world—a famine or drought, for instance. But when
the tales were retold in new and desperate contexts by Africans forcibly
removed from their homelands and sold into slavery in the so-called New
World, they were transformed mightily. The Trickster Spider using his wits to
overcome natural adversity becomes, in many instances, the Rabbit, often perceived to be a weak animal, using his wits to outsmart the powerful Br'er Bear
or the sly Br'er Fox, both representative of enslavers. Many Trickster tales in
North America have been adapted to include white people among the power-*

ful forces who may be brought low by the ever inventive and resourceful Trickster.

Trickster tales educate and entertain. Granted, Trickster teaches by negative example; he teaches us what not to do. Listeners and readers of Trickster's shenanigans enjoy his forbidden behavior vicariously, while, at the same time, the tales reaffirm necessary social constraints. If everyone acted as selfishly as Trickster, anarchy would result. Thus the stories teach the value of cooperation and comically relieve the strain of subduing individual desire, serving as a societal safety valve and offering a unifying web of story.

Anansi Owns All Tales
That Are Told

A S H A N T I ,   G H A N A

*I*n the beginning, all tales and stories belonged to Nyame, the Sky God. But Kwaku Anansi, the spider, yearned to be the owner of all the stories known in the world, and he went to Nyame and offered to buy them.

The Sky God said, "I am willing to sell the stories, but the price is high. Many people have come to me offering to buy, but the price was too high for them. Rich and powerful families have not been able to pay. Do you think you can do it?"

Anansi replied to the Sky God, "I can do it. What is the price?"

"My price is three things," the Sky God said. "I must first have Mmoboro, the hornets. I must then have Onini, the great python. I must then have Osebo, the leopard. For these things I will sell you the right to tell all stories."

Anansi said, "I will bring them."

He went home and made his plans. He first cut a gourd from a vine and made a small hole in it. He took a large calabash and filled it with water. He went to the tree where the hornets lived. He poured some of the water over himself, so that he was dripping. He threw some water over the hornets, so that they too were dripping. Then he put the calabash on his head, as though to protect himself from a storm, and called out to the hornets, "Are you foolish people? Why do you stay in the rain that is falling?"

The hornets answered, "Where shall we go?"

"Go here, in this dry gourd," Anansi told them.

The hornets thanked him and flew into the gourd through the small hole. When the last of them had entered, Anansi plugged the hole with a ball of grass, saying, "Oh, yes, but you are really foolish people!"

He took his gourd full of hornets to Nyame, the Sky God. The Sky God accepted them. He said, "There are two more things."

Anansi returned to the forest and cut a long bamboo pole and some strong vines. Then he walked toward the house of Onini, the python, talking to himself. He said, "My wife is stupid. I say he is longer and stronger. My wife says he is shorter and weaker. I give him more respect. She gives him less respect. Is she right or am I right? I am right, he is longer. I am right, he is stronger."

When Onini, the python, heard Anansi talking to himself, he said, "Why are you arguing this way with yourself?"

The spider replied, "Ah, I have had a dispute with my wife. She says you are shorter and weaker than this bamboo pole. I say you are longer and stronger."

Onini said, "It's useless and silly to argue when you can find out the truth. Bring the pole and we will measure."

So Anansi laid the pole on the ground, and the python came and stretched himself out beside it.

"You seem a little short," Anansi said.

The python stretched farther.

"A little more," Anansi said.

"I can stretch no more," Onini said.

"When you stretch at one end, you get shorter at the other end," Anansi said. "Let me tie you at the front so you don't slip."

He tied Onini's head to the pole. Then he went to the other end and tied the tail to the pole. He wrapped the vine all around Onini, until the python couldn't move.

"Onini," Anansi said, "it turns out that my wife was right and I was wrong. You are shorter than the pole and weaker. My opinion wasn't as good as my wife's. But you were even more foolish than I, and you are now my prisoner."

Anansi carried the python to Nyame, the Sky God, who said, "There is one thing more."

Osebo, the leopard, was next. Anansi went into the forest and dug a deep pit where the leopard was accustomed to walk. He covered it with small branches and leaves and put dust on it, so that it was impossible to tell where the pit was. Anansi went away and hid. When Osebo came prowling in the black of night, he stepped into the trap Anansi had prepared and fell to the bottom. Anansi heard the sound of the leopard falling, and he said, "Ah, Osebo, you are half-foolish!"

When morning came, Anansi went to the pit and saw the leopard there.

"Osebo," he asked, "what are you doing in this hole?"

"I have fallen into a trap," Osebo said. "Help me out."

"I would gladly help you," Anansi said. "But I'm sure that if I bring you out, I will have no thanks for it. You will get hungry, and later on you will be wanting to eat me and my children."

"I swear it won't happen!" Osebo said.

"Very well. Since you swear it, I will take you out," Anansi said.

He bent a tall green tree toward the ground, so that its top was over the pit, and he tied it that way. Then he tied a rope to the top of the tree and dropped the other end of it into the pit.

"Tie this to your tail," he said.

Osebo tied the rope to his tail.

"Is it well tied?" Anansi asked.

"Yes, it is well tied," the leopard said.

"In that case," Anansi said, "you are not merely half-foolish, you are all-foolish."

And he took his knife and cut the other rope, the one that held the tree bowed to the ground. The tree straightened up with a snap, pulling Osebo out of the hole. He hung in the air head downward, twisting and turning. And while he hung this way, Anansi killed him with his weapons.

Then he took the body of the leopard and carried it to Nyame, the Sky God, saying, "Here is the third thing. Now I have paid the price."

Nyame said to him, "Kwaku Anansi, great warriors and chiefs have tried, but they have been unable to do it. You have done it. Therefore, I will give you the stories. From this day onward, all stories belong to you. Whenever a man tells a story, he must acknowledge that it is Anansi's tale."

In this way Anansi, the spider, became the owner of all stories that are told. To Anansi all tales belong.

Anansi's Rescue
from the River

ASHANTI, GHANA

When the first of Anansi's sons was born, Anansi prepared to give him a name. But the baby spoke up and said, "You needn't bother to name me. I have brought my own name. I am called Akakai." This name signified "Able to See Trouble."

When the second of Anansi's sons was born, he too announced that he had brought his own name. "I am called Twa Akwan," he said. This name signified "Road Builder."

When the third son was born, he said, "My name is Hwe Nsuo." That meant "Able to Dry Up Rivers."

When the fourth was born, he announced, "I am Adwafo." That meant "The Skinner of Game."

The fifth son said when he was born, "I have been named already. I am known as Toto Abuo." His name signified "Stone Thrower."

The sixth son told Anansi, "I am called Da Yi Ya." That meant "Lie on the Ground Like a Cushion."

One day Kwaku Anansi went on a long journey. Several weeks passed, and he failed to return. Akakai, the son who had the ability to see trouble, announced that Anansi had fallen into a distant river in the middle of a dense jungle.

Two Akwan, the builder of roads, constructed a highway through the jungle, and the brothers passed through it to the edge of the river.

Hwe Nsuo, who had the power to dry up rivers, dried up the river, and they found there a great fish which had swallowed Anansi.

Adwafo, the skinner of game, cut into the fish and released his father.

But as soon as they brought Anansi to the edge of the river, a large hawk swooped down out of the sky, caught Anansi in his mouth, and soared into the air with him.

Toto Abuo, the stone thrower, threw a rock into the sky and hit the hawk, which let go of Anansi.

And as Anansi dropped towards the earth, Da Yi Ya threw himself on the ground like a cushion to soften his father's fall.

Thus Kwaku Anansi was saved by his six sons and brought home to his village.

Then one day when he was in the forest, Anansi found a bright and beautiful object called Moon. Nothing like it had ever been seen before. It was the most magnificent object he had ever seen. He resolved to give it to one of his children.

He sent a message to Nyame, the Sky God, telling him about his discovery. He asked Nyame to come and hold the Moon, and to award it as a prize to one of Anansi's sons—the one who had done the most to rescue him when he was lost in the river.

The Sky God came and held the Moon. Anansi sent for his sons. When they saw the Moon, each of them wanted it. They argued. The one who had located Anansi in the jungle river said he deserved the prize. The one who had built the road said he deserved it. The one who had dried up the river said he deserved it. The one who had cut Anansi out of the fish said he deserved it. The one who had hit the hawk with the stone said he deserved it. The one who had cushioned Anansi's fall to earth said he deserved it.

They argued back and forth, and no one listened to anybody else. The argument went on and on and became a violent squabble. Nyame, the Sky God, didn't know who should have the prize. He listened to the arguments for a long time. Then he became impatient. He got up from where he sat and went back to the sky, taking the Moon along with him.

And that is why the Moon is always seen in the heavens, where Nyame took it, and not on the earth where Anansi found it.

Anansi Plays Dead

One year there was a famine in the land. But Anansi and his wife Aso and his sons had a farm, and there was food enough for all of them. Still the thought of famine throughout the country made Anansi hungry. He began to plot how he could have the best part of the crops for himself. He devised a clever scheme.

One day he told his wife that he was not feeling well and that he was going to see a sorcerer. He went away and didn't return until night. Then he announced that he had received very bad news. The sorcerer had informed him, he said, that he was about to die. Also, Anansi said, the sorcerer had prescribed that he was to be buried at the far end of the farm, next to the yam patch. When they heard this news, Aso, Kweku Tsin, and Intikuma were very sad. But Anansi had more instructions. Aso was to place in his coffin a pestle and mortar, dishes, spoons, and cooking pots, so that Anansi could take care of himself in the Other World.

In a few days, Anansi lay on his sleeping mat as though he were sick, and in a short time he pretended to be dead. So Aso had him buried at the far end of the farm, next to the yam patch, and they put in his coffin all of the cooking pots and other things he had asked for.

But Anansi stayed in the grave only while the sun shone. As soon as it grew dark, he came out of the coffin and dug up some yams and cooked them. He ate until he was stuffed. Then he returned to his place in the coffin. Every night he came out to select the best part of the crops and eat them, and during the day he hid in his grave.

Aso and her sons began to observe that their best yams and corn and cassava were being stolen from the fields. So they went to Anansi's grave and held a special service there. They asked Anansi's soul to protect the farm from thieves.

That night Anansi again came out, and once more he took the best crops and ate them. When Aso and her sons found out that Anansi's soul was not protecting them, they devised a plan to catch the person who was stealing their food. They made a figure out of sticky gum. It looked like a man. They set it up in the yam patch.

That night Anansi crawled out of his coffin to eat. He saw the figure standing there in the moonlight.

"Why are you standing in my fields?" Anansi asked.

The gum-man didn't answer.

"If you don't get out of my fields, I will give you a thrashing," Anansi said.

The gum-man was silent.

"If you don't go quickly, I will have to beat you," Anansi said.

There was no reply. The gum-man just stood there. Anansi lost his temper. He gave the gum-man a hard blow with his right hand. It stuck fast to the gum-man. Anansi couldn't take it away.

"Let go of my right hand," Anansi said. "You are making me angry!"

But the gum-man didn't let go.

"Perhaps you don't know my strength," Anansi said fiercely. "There is more power in my left hand than in my right. Do you want to try it?"

As there was no response from the gum-man, Anansi struck him with his left hand. Now both his hands were stuck.

"You miserable creature," Anansi said, "so you don't listen to me! Let go at once and get out of my fields or I will really give you something to remember! Have you ever heard of my right foot?"

There was no sound from the gum-man, so Anansi gave him a kick with his right foot. It, too, stuck.

"Oh, you like it, do you?" Anansi shouted. "Then try this one, too!"

He gave a tremendous kick with his left foot, and now he was stuck by both hands and both feet.

"Oh, are you the stubborn kind?" Anansi cried. "Have you ever heard of my head?"

And he butted the gum-man with his head, and that stuck as well.

"I'm giving you your last chance now," Anansi said sternly. "If you leave quietly, I won't complain to the chief. If you don't, I'll give you a squeeze you will remember!"

The gum-man was still silent. So Anansi took a deep breath and gave a mighty squeeze. Now he was completely stuck. He couldn't move this way or that. He couldn't move at all.

In the morning when Aso, Kweku Tsin, and Initkuma came out to the fields, they found Anansi stuck helplessly to the gum-man. They understood everything. They took him off the gum-man and led him toward the village to be judged by the chief. People came to the edge of the trail and saw Anansi all stuck up with gum. They laughed and jeered and sang songs about him. He was deeply shamed and covered his face with his headcloth. And when Aso, Kweku Tsin, the Intikuma stopped at a spring to drink, Anansi broke away and fled. He ran into the nearest house, crawled into the rafters, and hid in the darkest corner he could find.

From that day until now, Anansi has not wanted to face people because of their scoffing and jeering, and that is why he is often found hiding in dark corners.

The Jackal and the Hen

KABYLE, ALGERIA

A hen and her chicks lived on a high rock. One day the jackal came and called up to her, "Throw me down one of your chicks or I'll climb up there and eat all your chicks and you, too." The hen was afraid and threw him a chick. And the jackal, pleased, took it home with him. For him, it was a perfect situation. He came to the rock every day and called up to the hen, "Throw me down a chick or I'll climb up there and eat all your chicks and you, too." And every day the hen threw him down a chick.

One day the eagle passed that way and asked the hen, "Hen, what have you done with your chicks?" The hen said, "Every day the jackal comes and calls, 'Hen, throw me down one of your chicks or I'll climb up there and eat all your chicks and you, too.' What can I do? So every morning I throw him down a chick." The eagle said, "Listen, hen, don't do that any more. It is not necessary. The jackal cannot climb up there and so you don't have to throw away your chicks to satisfy his greed." The hen said, "I will try to take your advice."

The next morning the jackal came again and said to the hen, "Throw me down one of your chicks or I'll climb up there and eat all your chicks and you, too." The hen said, "Just try it." The jackal tried it. But as soon as he had scrambled half-way up the rock his feet slipped out from under him and he fell down to the ground.

The eagle came by. The eagle saw the jackal's exertions and asked, "Jackal, what are you trying to do?" The jackal said, "The hen used to give me a chick every morning. But today she won't and now I'm trying to get what I want by myself." The eagle said, "My dear jackal, if it is chicks you want, then I can show you a country where there are so many chicks that not even you and your whole family could eat them all." The jackal said, "Dear eagle, just show me that country right away. For young chicks are our favorite food." The eagle said, "In that case you'll have to climb on my back." The jackal said, "Then come a bit lower."

The eagle flew down. The jackal climbed on the eagle's back. The eagle went into a steep climb and when he had reached a good height he asked the jackal, "Now, jackal, what does the earth look like to you?" The jackal said, "The earth looks green to me. I see green trees and green fields." The eagle climbed steeply and then asked again: "Well, jackal, what does the earth look like now?" The jackal said, "I can no longer see the trees, I can no longer see the fields. The earth is no longer green. It seems to be black."

The eagle said, "Then you are high enough to be able to see thousands of chicks. So pick out your chick for today." The eagle side-slipped and the jackal slid from his back. The jackal fell. The jackal prayed to God, "Let me fall in water or on a pile of straw." But the jackal fell on a rock and died.

The Jackal and the Lion

KABYLE, ALGERIA

One day the lion's foot was sore and he limped. The lion met the jackal, and the jackal saw that the lion limped. The jackal said, "Lion, what's the matter with you?" The lion said, "I've got such a sore foot that I cannot put my weight on it and can scarcely walk." The jackal said, "I know a splendid cure for that. Let's go and kill a cow. Then we'll drag the cow into the woods and I'll make you a cowhide bandage that will fix you up in no time." The lion agreed.

The jackal brought the lion to a place where there were many cows. The lion killed one of them and, limping painfully, dragged it into the woods. The lion and the jackal skinned the cow. The jackal said to the lion, "Wouldn't you rather eat first, before I bandage you?" The lion said, "Catching and killing the cow hurt my foot so badly that I've completely lost my appetite."

The jackal said, "Then I'll bandage you right away." He made the lion lie on his back and put his four feet up in the air. Then he threw the damp hide over the four paws, tied the hide around each paw and all four paws together with the sinews of the dead cow. He said to the lion, "Now you had better stay in this position till the bandage dries a bit and is really firm. And after a while you'll feel much better." The lion lay with all four feet in the air. Meanwhile the jackal dragged the cow, piece by piece, to his lair.

When the jackal had taken away all the cow meat he said to the other animals, "Go and visit the lion. He has sore feet. I've made him a bandage but I'm going to be busy for the next few days and will not be able to trouble myself about him any longer."

The other animals called on the lion to ask him about his health. They found him in a miserable condition. The cowhide had dried and was as stiff as iron and, with the now chainlike sinews, it held his legs stiffly in the air. The lion could not move. They took pity on the lion.

At that time the hedgehog and the heron were deadly enemies. And as the heron visited the lion he said, "I know a splendid cure for sore feet. That is hedgehog's blood." The lion said, "I'll think about it." After a time the hedgehog came to pay the lion a visit. The lion said, "The heron told me that your blood was the best possible medicine for my sore feet." The hedgehog said, "The heron spoke the truth. Five drops of my blood are quite enough to heal you completely. On the other hand my blood is not the least bit effective if it is not mixed with heron's brains." The lion said, "Will you come again as soon as I'm rid of this bandage and give me some of your blood?" The hedgehog said, "I'll come any day at any hour. You have only to call me." The hedgehog left.

The lion said to the animals, "Now take off this bandage." Many animals came and they all tried to remove the bandage. But it had become much too dry and hard. Then came the partridge. The partridge, flying back and forth, moistened the cowhide with drops of water carried in its beak. The hide became soft. The animals could remove it. The lion said, "Now I'll try the heron's medicine. Call me the heron and the hedgehog." The heron and the hedgehog came. The lion struck off the heron's head and took out the brain. The hedgehog stepped forward, stuck one of his own barbs in his foot so that a few drops of blood appeared. These he gave to the lion. The lion thanked him and the hedgehog went his way.

The lion wanted to revenge himself on the jackal, the jackal who had tied him up so that he couldn't move for eight days. One day he met the jackal in the woods and sprang at him. But the jackal ducked to one side and fled so that the lion got only his tail. The lion looked at the tail in his paw and said, "The tail will enable me to pick out the jackal who hurt me." The lion ordered all the jackals to be summoned. When the jackal heard that he went to his cousins, his relatives, and all the other jackals and said, "The lion is looking for a jackal with a long tail. So you must all cut your tails off as I have done. Then, when you go to the lion in the morning you can be sure that, if you are tailless, nothing will happen to you."

All the jackals cut off their tails. The next morning they obeyed the lion's command. All the jackals came to the lion. The lion saw that he was unable to distinguish the jackal whose tail he had from all the other tailless jackals. And so the jackal was saved.

How Ijapa,
Who Was Short,
Became Long

YORUBA, NIGERIA

*I*japa the tortoise was on a journey. He was tired and hungry, for he had been walking a long time. He came to the village where Ojola the boa lived, and he stopped there, thinking, "Ojola will surely feed me for I am famished."

Ijapa went to Ojola's house. Ojola greeted him, saying, "Enter my house and cool yourself in the shade, for I can see you have been on the trail."

Ijapa entered. They sat and talked. Ijapa smelled food cooking over the fire. He groaned with hunger, for when Ijapa was hungry he was more hungry than anyone else. Ojola said politely, "Surely the smell of my food does not cause you pain?"

Ijapa said, "Surely not, my friend. It only made me think that if I were at home now, my wife would be cooking likewise."

Ojola said, "Let us prepare ourselves. Then we shall eat together."

Ijapa went outside. He washed himself in a bowl of water. When he came in again he saw the food in the middle of the room and smelled its odors. But Ojola the boa was coiled around the food. There was no way to get to it. Ijapa walked around and around, trying to find an opening through which he could approach the waiting meal. But Ojola's body was long, and his coils lay one atop the other, and there was no entrance through them. Ijapa's hunger was intense.

Ojola said, "Come, do not be restless. Sit down. Let us eat."

Ijapa said, "I would be glad to sit with you. But you, why do you surround the dinner?"

Ojola said, "This is our custom. When my people eat, they always sit this way. Do not hesitate any longer." The boa went on eating while Ijapa again went around and around trying to find a way to the food. At last he gave up. Ojola finished eating. He said, "What a pleasure it is to eat dinner with a friend."

Ijapa left Ojola's house hungrier than he had come. He returned to his own village. There he ate. He brooded on his experience with Ojola. He decided that he would return the courtesy by inviting Ojola to his house to eat with him. He told his wife to prepare a meal for a certain festival day. And he began to weave a long tail out of grass. He spent many days weaving the tail. When it was finished, he fastened it to himself with tree gum.

On the festival day, Ojola arrived. They greeted each other at the door, Ijapa saying, "You have been on a long journey. You are hungry. You are tired. Refresh yourself at the spring. Then we shall eat."

Ojola was glad. He went to the spring to wash. When he returned, he found Ijapa already eating. Ijapa's grass tail was coiled several times around the food. Ojola could not get close to the dinner. Ijapa ate with enthusiasm. He stopped sometimes to say, "Do not hesitate, friend Ojola. Do not be shy. Good food does not last forever."

Ojola went around and around. It was useless. At last he said, "Ijapa, how did it happen that once you were quite short but now you are very long?"

Ijapa said, "One person learns from another about such things." Ojola then remembered the time Ijapa had been his guest. He was ashamed. He went away. It was from Ijapa that came the proverb:

> *The lesson that a man should be short came*
> *from his fellowman.*
> *The lesson that a man should be tall also came*
> *from his fellowman.*

Ijapa Cries for His Horse

*I*t happened one time that Ijapa the tortoise owned a fine white horse with beautiful trappings. When Ijapa sat on his horse, he felt proud and vain because he was the center of all eyes. Instead of working his garden, he rode from place to place so that everyone could see him. If he came to a town on market day, he rode his horse through the crowded market so that he might hear people say, "What a distinguished stranger! What an important person!" If he came to a village in the evening, he rode before the headman's house so that his presence would be properly noted. And because Ijapa appeared so distinguished on his white horse, the headman would provide him with food and a place to sleep and then send him on his way with dignity. Never had life been so good for Ijapa.

One day Ijapa arrived at the city of Wasimi. As he rode through the streets, he attracted great attention. People said, "He appears to be an important merchant," or, "He looks like a hero returning from battle." Word went to the compound of the *oba*, or king, that an important personage had arrived. When Ijapa appeared at the *oba*'s palace, he was welcomed with courtesy and dignity. The *oba*'s family took him to the guesthouse and brought him food. When night fell and it was time to sleep, they said, "We shall take care of the horse."

But Ijapa said, "Oh, no, I will keep him here with me in the guesthouse."

People said, "A horse has never before slept in the guesthouse."

Ijapa said, "My horse and I are like brothers. Therefore he always shares my sleeping quarters." So the horse was left in the guesthouse with Ijapa, and the *oba*'s household slept.

In the middle of the night, Ijapa heard his horse groan. He arose, lighted a torch, and went to see what was the matter. His horse was dead.

Ijapa cried out, "My horse! My horse!" Ijapa's cries awakened everyone. The *oba's* servants came. They tried to console Ijapa and quiet him. But he would not be consoled. He kept crying out, "My horse! My fine white horse! He is dead! He is dead!"

Members of the *oba's* family came. They said, "Do not cry out so. In their time, all horses die. Be consoled."

But Ijapa went on mourning the death of his horse in a loud voice that was heard everywhere. At last the *oba* himself came to the guesthouse. He listened to Ijapa's cries, and he said, "Do not cry anymore. To soothe your misery, I will give you one of my own horses."

One of the *oba's* best horses was brought into the guesthouse. Ijapa stopped crying. He thanked the *oba.* People went back to their beds. Once more, the night was quiet. Ijapa kept the torch burning so that he could see his new horse. Then, suddenly, he began to cry again, "Oh, misfortune! Oh, how awful it is! See how I am suffering! Who has brought this terrible thing to happen!"

The servants came back. The *oba's* family came back. They couldn't quiet Ijapa. Then the *oba* appeared. He said, "Why do you continue this way? Your lost horse has been replaced."

Ijapa said, "Sir, I cannot help crying out when I think of my bad fortune. The horse you gave me is a fine one. So was my own white horse that died. If he had not died, how lucky I would have been, for I now would have two fine horses instead of one." And again Ijapa broke into loud cries, "Oh, misery! Oh, misfortune! How awful it is!"

They could not stop him. So the *oba* said, "Very well, if it is only your need for two horses that keeps the city awake, think no more about it. I will give you another horse." The servants brought another horse. Ijapa stopped crying. He thanked the *oba* for his kindness. Everyone went back to bed. They slept. Only Ijapa couldn't sleep. He kept thinking about his good fortune. He had come with one horse. Now he had two.

Then his eyes fell upon the dead horse. He began to cry, "Oh, great misfortune! Oh, terrible thing! How awful it is! Bad luck falls on my head! Oh, misery!" He went on crying.

Again the household was awakened. Again they came and tried to console him. Again the *oba* himself had to come. The *oba* said, "This grief for a dead horse is too much. Many men have horses. Their horses die. But men cannot grieve forever."

Ijapa said, "Sir, I cannot help it. I looked at my dead white horse. I realized that only a few hours ago he was alive. Had he not died, I would own three fine horses and be the most fortunate of men!"

The *oba* was tired. He was cross. But he ordered another horse be brought for Ijapa. "You are now the most fortunate of men," the *oba* said. "You own three fine horses. Now let us all sleep." The family and the servants returned to their beds. They slept.

And then, just when everything had become quiet. Ijapa began crying out in grief again, "Oh, misery! Oh, misfortune! What a terrible thing has happened!" It went on and on. The *oba* called his servants. He gave them instructions. They went to the guesthouse and took the *oba*'s three horses away. They took Ijapa to the gate and pushed him out.

He had no horse at all now, and he went on foot like ordinary people. He returned to his own village in shame, for he had ridden away like a distinguished person and now his legs were covered with dust.

T'appin
(Terrapin)

It was famine time an' T'appin had six chillun. Eagle hide behin' cloud an' he went crossed de ocean an' go gittin' de palm oil; got de seed to feed his chillun wid it. T'appin see it, say "hol' on, it har' time. Where you git all dat to feed your t'ree chillun? I got six chillun, can't you show me wha' you git all dat food?" Eagle say, "No, I had to fly 'cross de ocean to git dat." T'appin say, "Well, gimme some o' you wings an' I'll go wid you." Eagle say, "A' right. When shall we go?" T'appin say, "Morrow mornin' by de firs' cock crow." So 'morrow came but T'appin didn' wait till mornin'. T'ree 'clock in de mornin' T'appin came in fron' Eagle's house say, "Cuckoo—cuckoo—coo." Eagle say, "Oh, you go home. Lay down. 'Taint day yit." But he kep' on, "Cuckoo—cuckoo—coo." An bless de Lor' Eagle got out, say, "Wha' you do now?" T'appin say, "You put t'ree wings on this side an' t'ree on udda side." Eagle pull out six feathers an' put t'ree on one side an' t'ree on de udda. Say, "Fly, le's see." So T'appin commence to fly. One o' de wings fall out. But T'appin said, "Da's all right, I got de udda wings. Le's go." So dey flew an' flew; but when dey got over de ocean all de eagle wings fell out. T'appin about to fall in de water. Eagle went out an' ketch him. Put him under his wings. T'appin say, "Gee it stink here." Eagle let him drop in ocean. So he went down, down, down to de underworl'. De king o' de underworl' meet him. He say, "Why you come here? Wha' you doin' here?" T'appin say, "King, we in te'bul condition on de earth. We can't git nothin' to eat. I got six chillun an' I can't git nothin' to eat for dem. Eagle he on'y got t'ree an' he go 'cross de ocean an' git all de food he need. Please gimme sumpin' so I kin feed my chillun." King say, "A' right, a'right," so he go an' give T'appin a dipper. He say to T'appin, "Take dis dipper. When you want food for your chillun say:

Bakon coleh
Bakon cawbey
Bakon cawhubo lebe lebe.

So, T'appin carry it home an' go to de chillun. He say to dem, "Come here." When dey all come he say:

Bakon coleh
Bakon cawbey
Bakon cawhubo lebe lebe.

Gravy, meat, biscuit, ever'ting in de dipper. Chillun got plenty now. So one time he say to de chillun, "Come here. Dis will make my fortune. I'll sell dis to de King." So he showed de dipper to de King. He say:

Bakon coleh
Bakon cawbey
Bakon cawhubo lebe lebe.

Dey got somet'ing. He feed ev'ryone. So de King went off, he call ev'ryboda. Pretty soon ev'ryboda eatin'. So dey ate an' ate, ev'ryt'ing, meats, fruits, all like dat. So he took his dipper an' went back home. He say, "Come, chillun." He try to feed his chillun; nothin' came. When it's out it's out. So T'appin say, "Aw right, I'm going back to de King an' git him to fixa dis up." So he went down to de underworl' an' say to de King, "King, wha' de matter? I can't feeda my chillun no mora." So de King say to him, "You take dis cowhide an' when you want somepin' you say:

Sheet n oun
n-jacko
nou o quaako.

So T'appin went off an' he came to crossroads. Den he said de magic:

Sheet n oun
n-jacko
nou o quaako.

De cowhide commence to beat um. It beat, beat. Cowide said, "Drop, drop."
So T'appin droup an' de cowhide stop beatin'. So he went home. He called his
chillun in. He gim um de cowhide an' tell dem what to say, den he went out.
De chillun say:

> *Sheet n oun*
> *n-jacko*
> *nou o quaako.*

De cowhide beat de chillun. It say, "Drop, drop." Two chillun dead an' de
others sick. So T'appin say, "I will go to de King." He calls de King, he call all
de people. All de people came. So before he have de cowhide beat, he has a
mortar made an' gits in dere an' gits all covered up. Den de King say:

> *Sheet n oun*
> *n-jacko*
> *nou o quaako.*

So de cowhide beat, beat. It beat everyboda, beat de King too. Dat cowhide
beat, beat, beat right t'roo de mortar wha' was T'appin an' beat marks on his
back, an' da's why you never fin' T'appin in a clean place, on'y under leaves
or a log.

Sheer Crops

*B*r'er Bear en Br'er Rabbit dey wuz farmers. Br'er Bear he has acres en acres uf good bottomland, en Br'er Rabbit has des' er small sandy-land farm. Br'er Bear wuz allus er "raisin' Cain" wid his neighbors, but Br'er Rabbit was er most engenerally raisin' chillun.

Arter while Br'er Rabbit's boys 'gun to git grown, en Br'er Rabbit 'lows he's gwine to have to git more land if he makes buckle en tongue meet.

So he goes ober to Br'er Bear's house, he did, en he say, sez he, "Mo'nin', Br'er Bear. I craves ter rent yer bottom field nex' year."

Br'er Bear he hum en he haw, en den he sez, "I don't spec I kin 'commodate yer, Br'er Rabbit, but I moughten consider hit, bein's hit's yer."

"How does you rent yer land, Br'er Bear?"

"I kin onliest rent by der sheers."

"What is yer sheer, Br'er Bear?"

"Well," said Br'er Bear, "I takes der top of de crop fer my sheer, en yer takes de rest fer yer sheer."

Br'er Rabbit thinks erbout it rale hard, en he sez, "All right, Br'er Bear, I took it; we goes ter plowin' ober dare nex' week."

Den Br'er Bear goes back in der house des' er-laughin'. He sho is tickled ez to how he hez done put one by ole Br'er Rabbit dat time.

Well, 'long in May Br'er Rabbit done sont his oldest son to tell Br'er Bear to come down to the field to see erbout dat are sheer crop. Br'er Bear he comes er-pacin' down to de field en Br'er Rabbit wuz er-leanin' on de fence.

"Mo'nin', Br'er Bear. See what er fine crop we hez got. You is to hab de tops fer yer sheer. Whare is you gwine to put 'em? I wants ter git 'em off so I kin dig my 'taters."

Br'er Bear wuz sho hot. But he done made dat trade wid Br'er Rabbit, en he had to stick to hit. So he went off all huffed up, en didn't even tell Br'er Rabbit what to do wid de vines. But Br'er Rabbit perceeded to dig his 'taters.

'Long in de fall Br'er Rabbit 'lows he's gwine to see Br'er Bear ergin en try to rent der bottom field. So he goes down to Br'er Bear's house en after passin' de time of day en other pleasant sociabilities, he sez, sez he, "Br'er Bear, how erbout rentin' der bottom field nex' year? Is yer gwine ter rent hit to me ergin?"

Br'er Bear say, he did, "You cheat me out uf my eyes las' year, Br'er Rabbit. I don't think I kin let yer hab it dis year."

Den Br'er Rabbit scratch his head er long time, en he say, "Oh, now, Br'er Bear, yer know I ain't cheated yer. Yer jes' cheat yerself. Yer made de trade yerself en I done tuck yer at yer word. Yer sed yer wanted de tops fer yer sheer, en I gib um ter yer, didn't I? Now yer jes' think hit all ober ergin and see if yer can't make er new deal fer yerself."

Den Br'er Bear said, "Well, I rents to yer only on dese perditions: dat yer hab all de tops fer yer sheer en I hab all de rest fer my sheer."

Br'er Rabbit he twis' en he turn en he sez, "All right, Br'er Bear, I'se got ter hab more land fer my boys. I'll tuck hit. We go to plowin' in dare right erway."

Den Br'er Bear he amble back into de house. He wuz shore he'd made er good trade dat time.

Way 'long in nex' June Br'er Rabbit done sont his boy down to Br'er Bear's house ergin, to tell him to come down ter de field ter see erbout his rent. When he got dare, Br'er Rabbit say, he did:

"Mo'nin', Br'er Bear. See what er fine crop we hez got? I specks hit will make forty bushels to der acre. I'se gwine ter put my oats on der market. What duz yer want me ter do wid yer straw?"

Br'er Bear sho wuz mad, but hit wa'n't no use. He done saw whar Br'er Rabbit had 'im. So he lies low en 'lows to hisself how he's gwine to git eben wid Br'er Rabbit yit. So he smile en say, "Oh, der crop is all right, Br'er Rabbit. Jes' stack my straw anywheres eround dare. Dat's all right."

Den Br'er Bear smile en he say, "What erbout nex' year, Br'er Rabbit? Is yer cravin' ter rent dis field ergin?"

"I ain't er-doin nothin' else but wantin' ter rent hit, Br'er Bear," sez Br'er Rabbit.

"All right, all right, yer kin rent her ergin. But dis time I'se gwine ter hab der tops fer my sheer, en I'se gwine ter hab de bottoms fer my sheer too."

Br'er Rabbit wuz stumped. He didn't know whatter do nex'. But he finally managed to ask, "Br'er Bear, ef yer gits der tops en der bottoms fer yer sheer, what will I git fer my sheer?"

Den ole Br'er Bear laff en say, "Well, yer would git de middles."

Br'er Rabbit he worry en he fret, he plead en he argy, but hit do no good.

Br'er Bear sez, "Take hit er leave hit," en jes' stand pat.

Br'er Rabbit took hit.

Way 'long nex' summer ole Br'er Bear 'cided he would go down to der bottom field en see erbout dat dare sheer crop he had wid Br'er Rabbit. While he wuz er-passin' through de woods on hiz way, he sez to himself, he did:

"De fust year I rents to de ole Rabbit, I makes de tops my sheer, en ole Rabbit planted 'taters; so I gits nothin' but vines. Den I rents ergin, en der Rabbit is to hab de tops, en I de bottoms, en ole Rabbit plants oats; so I gits nothin' but de straw. But I sho is got dat ole Rabbit dis time. I gits both de tops en de bottoms, en de ole Rabbit gits only de middles. I'se bound ter git 'im dis time."

Jes' den de old Bear come ter de field. He stopped. He look at hit. He shet up his fist. He cuss en he say, "Dat derned little scoundrel! He done went en planted dat fiel' in corn."

The Crocodile Man
and the Heron Man

MURINBATA, NORTHERN AUSTRALIA

*T*wo old men, Muntungun and Walgutkut, were wading about in a billabong, feeling with their hands and feet in the mud for lily bulbs. One old man threw all the tucker (food) he found out onto the bank on one side. The other old man threw all the tucker he found onto another side of the billabong.

The old man Walgutkut had found that billabong, called Tumunga, the first time, but these two old men always hunted about for tucker together.

At last the two old men had thrown out a lot of lily-tucker in two different piles onto the banks. They came out of the water and each gathered up the lily-bulbs he had thrown out. They tied up the lily bulbs in paperbark. Walgutkut had found some good lily-tucker but Muntungun had found some that were a little bit better.

"Which place are we going to cook this tucker?" asked one old man. "We'll roast 'em about here," said the other old man.

These two old men sat down and made a fire and put all their lily bulbs onto the coals to roast. Then they raked the roasted bulbs out of the coals and shared them out between them.

Now Muntungun found out that Walgutkut was giving him all the bitter lily bulbs, so, as they shared out the tucker, Muntungun passed these bitter lily bulbs round his back and put them in Walgutkut's pile. The old man Walgutkut saw what Muntungun was doing, so he passed the bitter lily bulbs round his back and gave them to Muntungun again.

All right. Those two old men each took half of that lily-tucker. They each tied up their share in paperbark again. "Which way do you want to go?" asked

Muntungun. "I go to Ngarrai. I camp there," said Walgutkut. "Well, I go along Punintunga. I've got fresh water there," said Muntungun.

"*Battai!*" "*Yo!*" The two old men called as they left each other. "Bye and bye you come here again." "*Yo!*" "You and I will meet along this tucker-place another time." The two old men still called to each other as they both started out, carrying their lily-tucker, tied up in paperbark, on their heads.

Now the old man Muntungun sat down to eat some of his lily-tucker. It was bitter. Muntungun got up and began to hurry back. He called out, "*Coi!* Walgutkut, *Coi!* I want to talk along you." Walgutkut heard the old man calling. "Might be that old man has found out. I've got to cut a stick now," he said to himself. He cut himself a waddy (a hardwood club).

The old man Muntungun stopped and cut a waddy too. When he came up to the other old man he called. "What name? I'm going to talk to you. You bin give it back to me that tucker!" "Which one tucker I bin give you?" old man Walgutkut asked. "That one bitter tucker I bin give you," said Muntungun.

These two old men began to fight. One old man threw his waddy and the other old man ducked down and the waddy missed him. They fought all the way back to the billabong. Each caught hold of the other's paperbark bundle of lily-tucker and tugged at it. That lily-tucker fell out of the bundles all the way as they fought and shouted at each other. Walgutkut hit Muntungun on the neck with his waddy and Muntungun hit Walgutkut back.

At last those two old men were knocked up. "O, we go along water," they said. "We make ourselves cool fellows." The two old men waded into the billabong and sat down in the water together. They both called out "Oi! Oi!" as they sat down in the billabong. As they swam about in the cool water the old man Muntungun turned into the freshwater crocodile Yagpa. The old man Walgutkut, he turned into that big water bird. He has a big beak. He sings out "Kroak!" as he flies away.

All the lily-tucker, which fell out of the two old men's bundles when they had that row, all that tucker is in these water holes now. That lily-tucker has a purple flower.

We never kill the old man Yagpa. He has a long tail. We can see that old man. We can't spear him. If any man tries to spear him, bye and bye when that man goes into a water hole, old man Yagpa will come and take him away.

The Monkey-Son

TAMILNADU, INDIA

*T*here once were two brothers. The younger brother had no children. One day a man came to the village with a monkey tied in a bag. He kept it in the bag and pretended it was a child. The younger brother asked the price and the man answered, "It is worth one measure of maize plus one quarter of a rupee." So the younger brother bought the bag without even opening it. Afterwards, when he looked inside, he discovered a monkey. The monkey jumped up on a rafter and began to cry. The young man was very sad. His wife was sad as well.

The monkey turned to the couple and asked them why they were sad. The younger brother answered, "Can you operate an irrigation device at our well?" The monkey said, "Of course I can." He then went and assisted both brothers at their family well. For every single bag of water that the two men could lift the monkey managed to lift two more. After a time the monkey be-gan to call the younger brother his father. He then asked the elder brother what types of grain grew best in his field. The elder brother answered, "To-bacco grows well." The monkey continued and asked, "Do you want the up-per or the lower part?" The elder brother asked for the lower part. The mon-key boy agreed that he and his father would take what was left.

The monkey then began to harvest tobacco leaves and to take them home. Keeping to the bargain, he carried all the tobacco stalks to the elder brother's house, and all of the fine upper leaves to his own home. This started an ar-gument between the elder brother and his wife. Finally this man said, "Wait until the next harvest and we'll see what happens then." So after the harvest the monkey asked again, "What crop grows well in your field?" The elder brother now answered, "Onions grow best." So the monkey planted onions and when they were well grown he returned to the elder brother and asked, "Do you want the upper or lower part?" The elder brother remembered his previous experience and now said, "This time I'll take the upper part." So when the harvest came, the monkey took all the onions for himself and carried only the upper leaves and stems to his father's brother's home. Again this started an argument.

The elder brother was so angry at his monkey-nephew that he now killed the two cows that operated the irrigation device for his younger brother. But the monkey boy called two leather workers and asked them to cure the hides of these dead animals. The leather workers did their work. Then the monkey took the hides, went to a nearby field, and climbed a tree. He knew of a spot there where a group of thieves always met. Monkey-boy was ready. The thieves soon brought some money to that spot and began to divide it. One thief was blind. As the men were dividing their money, the blind man said to the others, "Divide it fairly, otherwise the sky will fall in." At that moment, monkey-boy let go of the hides that had been prepared. They fell on the thieves who quickly became frightened and ran away. The monkey then came down and picked up the money that they had left behind. He took it home and gave it to his father.

The next day the monkey's mother asked her husband to go to his elder brother's house to fetch a measuring basket. She wanted to count just how much money the boy had brought home. But the elder brother was puzzled as to why they suddenly needed to measure so much wealth. So the monkey explained that he had cut the tanned skins into pieces, and that he had sold these in the market for cash. When the elder brother learned about this he killed all four of his cows, had the leather cured, and then took the skins to market. But no one was willing to buy them. The elder brother returned home. Next he decided to burn down his younger brother's house. One day he did this and his younger brother's house was reduced to ashes. The monkey-boy however had already left it empty, having carried all of the family's belongings outside. Then the monkey-boy tied all the ashes left from the fire in a large sack. He put that sack in a place where he knew that thieves habitually met. When the thieves arrived the monkey-boy said to them, "Look at all the cash and jewels I have stolen. Let us sleep awhile. Then we can divide up the proceeds." When the thieves fell asleep, the monkey ex-

changed his bag for one the thieves had been carrying. After that he crept off
and returned home.

When the monkey-boy arrived with the big bag full of jewels his mother
again asked him to fetch a measuring basket from his father's brother's house.
Once more the father's brother wondered, "Where is all their money coming
from?" So this time he took a little tamarind and stuck it to the bottom of his
basket to make sure some trace of the measured contents would remain inside. Monkey-boy explained that he had sold the ashes from his burnt house
and obtained some money. The elder brother thought he would try this too.
So he burned down his own house. He then filled a huge sack with the ashes
and took it to market. No one would buy it. This caused another fight in his
house. He and his wife now decided that one way or another the monkey-boy
would have to be killed.

The elder brother soon caught the monkey and tied him in a sack. He took
the sack to a river and threw it in. But a young boy was grazing goats nearby,
and he heard the monkey crying out, "They brought me here to the river because I refused to marry my father's sister's daughter." The shepherd ran into
the water and grabbed the sack. He let the monkey out and pulled him from
the river. Meanwhile, the elder brother had returned home. He had gone to
get a stick to beat the sack with. But by the time he returned to the river the
monkey had tied the shepherd boy inside it instead. When the elder brother
began to beat this sack the boy cried out and tried to explain what had happened. But the elder brother did not believe him. Meanwhile the monkey-
boy took all of the shepherd's goats home. When the elder brother returned,
he found the monkey and asked how he had escaped. He replied, "I have lots
of relatives in this area. They gave me all these goats. Indeed, they have invited me to come back and get some more. Therefore, why don't you tie me in
a sack again?" But the elder brother said, "Put me in the sack instead. I would
like to have some goats too." So the monkey took his father's brother to the
river in that sack and drowned him.

The Raven and the Whale

*T*here was once a raven who by accident flew into the mouth of a big bow-headed whale. He flew right down the throat and ended up in the belly. There he saw a little house built of ribs and soft hides; a shabby little house, just like a human dwelling. Inside this house was a young woman minding a blubber lamp. "You may stay here as long as you like," she told him, "but you must never touch this lamp." For the lamp was the whale's heart.

The raven decided to stay there for quite awhile. The woman was very pleasant company. Likewise she did all the work. "Eat," she'd say, and offer him some fish, mussels, or crabs which the whale had swallowed. There would be more *mataq* than he could eat in a dozen lifetimes. Sometimes the raven would even sleep with the woman.

"Is there anything you would like?" the woman would ask him.

"Yes," said the raven. "I would like to touch the lamp."

"You must never, never touch the lamp," she told him.

But this made the raven all the more curious. More than anything else, he wanted to touch that lamp. He gazed at it for long hours. And once, while the woman's back was turned, he walked up and pecked at it. Instantly the lamp went out and the woman fell down dead.

Now the raven stumbled around in the dark. At last he found the throat-passage and crawled through it. Then he climbed on top of the whale, which was dead. He saw that they were floating toward a human village, so he turned himself into a man. "Behold!" he exclaimed. "I've just killed this enormous bow-headed whale without even using a harpoon . . ."

No one believed him. Perhaps he could show off his hunting prowess once again? Whenever you wish, he declared. And he went to live in that village, waiting for the opportunity to show off his ability. Then one day a herd of narwhals was sighted in the harbor. "Leave this to me," he said. He got into a kayak and paddled it toward the herd. Almost at once the kayak was knocked over and he was pierced by a narwhal's horn. Thus did the mighty hunter die. But as he died, he turned back into a raven, and was eaten by one of the narwhals.

The Raven and the Hunter

A hunter found an excellent run of seal breathing holes. Then he searched around for a good place to camp. Along flew a raven, which pointed to a certain plain beneath a mountain. "There," the raven said, "all the hunters who come here camp there."

The man made his house where the raven indicated. But in the night a big boulder rolled down the mountain and crushed him to death.

"I don't know why all these hunters believe my silly stories," said the raven, pecking out the man's eyes.

The Lustful Raven

INUIT, ALASKA AND NORTHWESTERN CANADA

Once there was a raven whose wife was killed by humans. Being very lustful, he needed a new wife right away. He happened upon a little sparrow whose husband had been killed by humans, too.

"Oh, my husband was so sweet," the sparrow said, "for he used to catch nice fat worms for me."

Replied the raven, "I'll be your husband now. We'll make love all night long. I'll give you lovely shit to eat."

"Unfortunately," said the sparrow, "that doesn't appeal to me."

So the raven flew away—again to seek a new wife. Soon he met a ptarmigan whose husband had left her.

"Yes," said the ptarmigan, "he left me because he wanted to exchange wives and I did not feel like sleeping with a fulmar."

The raven asked her to be his wife.

"I could never do that," she said. "You have such a high forehead and your beak is much too big for your face. You're really quite ugly, you know."

So the raven continued his search for a new wife. By now he was so lustful that he was unable to sleep. At last he came to a flock of wild geese, two of whom he picked out, saying: "Since that damned ptarmigan turned me down, I'm twice as lustful as before. I think I'll take the two of you to wife."

"But we're just getting ready to leave this place," the geese told him.

The raven said that he'd go with them.

"But you can neither swim nor rest on the water," they said.

"I'll manage . . ."

Whereupon the raven flew away with the geese. They flew for some distance over open water. Now the raven was getting rather tired. "Lie down on the sea, you two," he said to his wives.

The wives did as they were told. Soon the raven was making love to them, first the one, then the other. In the middle of his lovemaking, however, the wives saw their comrades flying farther and farther away. And they rose up to join them. The raven fell into the water, gasping:

"Come back here, you two! Come back and get together! I need something to sit on . . ."

But they had already flown away. The raven sank to the bottom of the sea where he was transformed into thousands of tiny black snails, each calling to the other: "Get together, get together . . ."

The Winnebago Trickster Cycle
(*Excerpts*)

Twelve

As he was walking along suddenly he came to a lake, and there in the lake he saw numerous ducks. Immediately he ran back quietly before they could see him and sought out a spot where there was a swamp. From it he gathered a large quantity of reed-grass and made himself a big pack. This he put on his back and carried it to the lake. He walked along the shore of the lake carrying it ostentatiously. Soon the ducks saw him and said, "Look, that is Trickster walking over there. I wonder what he is doing? Let us call and ask him." So they called to him, "Trickster, what are you carrying?" Thus they shouted at him, but he did not answer. Then, again they called to him. But it was only after the fourth call that he replied and said, "Well, are you calling me?" "What are you carrying on your back?" they asked. "My younger brothers, surely you do not know what it is you are asking. What am I carrying? Why, I am carrying songs. My stomach is full of bad songs. Some of these my stomach could not hold and that is why I am carrying them on my back. It is a long time since I sang any of them. Just now there are a large number in me. I have met no people on my journey who would dance for me and let me sing some for them. And I have, in consequence, not sung any for a long time." Then the ducks spoke to each other and said, "Come, what if we ask him to sing? Then we could dance, couldn't we?" So one of them called out, "Well, let it be so. I enjoy dancing very much and it has been a very long time since I last danced."

So they spoke to Trickster, "Older brother, yes, if you will sing to us we will dance. We have been yearning to dance for some time but could not do so because we had no songs." Thus spoke the ducks. "My younger brothers," replied Trickster, "you have spoken well and you shall have your desire granted. First, however, I will erect a dancing-lodge." In this they helped him and soon they had put up a a dancing-lodge, a grass-lodge. Then they made a drum. When this was finished he invited them all to come in and they did so. When he was ready to sing he said, "My younger brothers, this is the way in which you must act. When I sing, when I have people dance for me, the dancers must, from the very beginning, never open their eyes." "Good," they answered. Then when he began to sing he said, "Now remember, younger brothers, you are not to open your eyes. If you do they will become red." So, as soon as he began to sing, the ducks closed their eyes and danced.

After a while one of the ducks was heard to flap his wings as he came back to the entrance of the lodge, and cry, "Quack!" Again and again this happened. Sometimes it sounded as if the particular duck had somehow tightened its throat. Whenever any of the ducks cried out, then Trickster would tell the other ducks to dance faster and faster. Finally a duck whose name was Little-Red-Eyed-Duck secretly opened its eyes, just the least little bit it opened them. To its surprise, Trickster was wringing the necks of his fellow ducks! He would also bite them as he twisted their necks. It was while he was doing this that the noise which sounded like the tightening of the throat was heard. In this fashion Trickster killed as many as he could reach.

Little-Red-Eyed-Duck shouted, "Alas! He is killing us! Let those who can save themselves." He himself flew out quickly through the opening above. All the others likewise crowded toward this opening. They struck Trickster with their wings and scratched him with their feet. He went among them with his eyes closed and stuck out his hands to grab them. He grabbed one in each hand and choked them to death. His eyes were closed tightly. Then suddenly all of them escaped except the two he had in his grasp.

When he looked at these, to his annoyance, he was holding in each hand a scabby-mouthed duck. In no way perturbed, however, he shouted, "Ha, ha, this is the way a man acts! Indeed these ducks will make fine soup to drink!" Then he made a fire and cut some sharp-pointed sticks with which to roast them. Some he roasted in this manner, while others he roasted by covering them with ashes. "I will wait for them to be cooked," he said to himself. "I

had, however, better go to sleep now. By the time I awake they will unques-
tionably be thoroughly done. Now, you, my younger brother, must keep
watch for me while I go to sleep. If you notice any people, drive them off." He
was talking to his anus. Then, turning his anus toward the fire, he went to
sleep.

Thirteen

· · · · · · · · · · · · · · · · · · ·

When he was sleeping some small foxes approached and, as they ran
along, they scented something that seemed like fire. "Well, there must be
something around here," they said. So they turned their noses toward the
wind and looked and, after a while, truly enough, they saw the smoke of a
fire. So they peered around carefully and soon noticed many sharp-pointed
sticks arranged around a fire with meat on them. Stealthily they approached
nearer and nearer and, scrutinizing everything carefully, they noticed someone asleep there. "It is Trickster and he is asleep! Let us eat this meat. But
we must be very careful not to wake him up. Come, let us eat," they said to
one another. When they came close, much to their surprise, however, gas
was expelled from somewhere. "Pooh!" Such was the sound made. "Be careful! He must be awake." So they ran back. After a while one of them said,
"Well, I guess he is asleep now. That was only a bluff. He is always up to some
tricks." So again they approached the fire. Again gas was expelled and again
they ran back. Three times this happened. When they approached the fourth
time gas was again expelled. However, they did not run away. So Trickster's
anus, in rapid succession, began to expel more and more gas. Still they did
not run away. Once, twice, three times, it expelled gas in rapid succession.
"Pooh! Pooh!" Such was the sound it made. Yet they did not run away. Then
louder, still louder, was the sound of the gas expelled. "Pooh! Pooh! Pooh!"
Yet they did not run away. On the contrary, they now began to eat the roasted
pieces of duck. As they were eating, the Trickster's anus continued its "Pooh"
incessantly. There the foxes stayed until they had eaten up all the pieces that
were being roasted under ashes and, in spite of the fact that the anus was ex-
pelling gas, "Pooh! Pooh! Pooh! Pooh!" continuously, they ate these all up
too. Then they replaced the pieces with the meat eaten off, nicely under the
ashes. Only after that did they go away.

Fourteen
· · · · · · · · · · · · · · · · · · · ·

After a while Trickster awoke. "My, O my!" he exclaimed joyfully, "the things I had put on to roast must be cooked crisp by now." So he went over, felt around, and pulled out a leg. To his dismay it was but a bare bone, completely devoid of meat. "How terrible! But this is the way they generally are when they are cooked too much!" So he felt around again and pulled out another one. But this leg also had nothing on it. "How terrible! These, likewise, must have been roasted too much! However, I told my younger brother, anus, to watch the meat roasting. He is a good cook indeed!" He pulled out one piece after the other. They were all the same. Finally he sat up and looked around. To his astonishment, the pieces of meat on the roasting sticks were gone! "Ah, ha, now I understand! It must have been those covetous friends of mine who have done me this injury!" he exclaimed. Then he poked around the fire again and again but found only bones. "Alas! Alas! They have caused my appetite to be disappointed, those covetous fellows! And you, too, you despicable object, what about your behavior? Did I not tell you to watch this fire? You shall remember this! As a punishment for your remissness, I will burn your mouth so that you will not be able to use it!"

Thereupon he took a burning piece of wood and burnt the mouth of his anus. He was, of course, burning himself and, as he applied the fire, he exclaimed, "Ouch! Ouch! This is too much! I have made my skin smart. Is it not for such things that they call me Trickster? They have indeed talked me into doing this just as if I had been doing something wrong!"

Trickster had burnt his anus. He had applied a burning piece of wood to it. Then he went away.

As he walked along the road he felt certain that someone must have passed along it before for he was on what appeared to be a trail. Indeed, suddenly, he came upon a piece of fat that must have come from someone's body. "Someone has been packing an animal he had killed," he thought to himself. Then he picked up a piece of fat and ate it. It had a delicious taste. "My, my, how delicious it is to eat this!" As he proceeded however, much to his surprise, he discovered that it was a part of himself, part of his own intestines, that he was eating. After burning his anus, his intestines had contracted and fallen off, piece by piece, and these pieces were the things he was picking up. "My, my! Correctly, indeed, am I named Foolish One, Trickster! By their calling me thus, they have at last actually turned me into a Foolish One, a Trickster!" Then he tied his intestines together. A large part, however, had been lost. In tying it, he pulled it together so that wrinkles and ridges were formed. That is the reason why the anus of human beings has its present shape.

The Stealing of the Sun

*F*our times Coyote went to sleep. The first time he slept with his head toward the west, the second time to the north, the third time to the south, and the fourth and last time with his head to the east. As he lay sleeping with his head to the east his forehead grew very warm.

"I dreamed about the sun," he said when he awoke.

Then Coyote decided to get the sun and bring it back for the people. He set off. On the way he met three mice, and he took them with him for dogs.

"My heart is glad because I found you, my three dogs," he told them.

When they arrived at the house where Coyote knew the sun was, he instructed his dogs.

"The sun is covered with a blanket and tied down in the middle of this house. I am going in and shall sleep there tonight. When all are asleep you must come in and chew off the straps that hold the sun. Leave, however, the straps with which I am to carry the sun. When you are through, poke me with your noses."

Coyote then went into the house.

"I do not want food, grandmother," he said to the old woman of the house. "I will sleep."

"Yes," said the old woman, and give him a blanket.

Covering his head in it, Coyote began to sing: "You sleep, you sleep, you sleep." Soon the woman fell asleep. After a while the mice came and poked Coyote.

"We have finished," one of them said.

So Coyote got up, took the sun, and carried it off.

Mole saw him do this and he called out: "He is carrying off the sun," but no one heard him for his mouth was too small. Then Lizard saw him. He took up a stick and beat on the house of the old woman, calling: "He is carrying off the sun."

The old woman heard this time, and she got up and started to chase Coyote.

As she neared him she called out to him: "Why did you take it? I was fixing it."

"You were hiding it," Coyote called back. "Turn into a stone where you are standing."

At these words of Coyote the woman turned into a stone. Then Coyote took the sun and cut it up, and from it he made the moon, the stars, and the sun. As he made them he told them when they were to appear.

To the morning star he said: "You shall come up just before day." To the sun he said: "You shall come up in the east in the morning, and go down at night. You shall be hot." To the moon he said: "You shall travel at night. You shall be cold."

The people were very grateful to Coyote for what he had done, and they brought him many presents upon his return.

Sun's Arrival in the Sky

Hawk Chief was going around complaining because there was no sun in the world. Sun had shut herself up in her house, and no one could get to her, for the house she lived in was built of stone and she would not come out.

"I want the sun, grandfather. Why is there no sun? I want the sun," Hawk Chief kept crying.

So Coyote went to see the two doves. He took his walking stick and his little sack of beads, and started trotting along the trail.

"My grandson wants the sun," he said to the doves when he arrived. "He doesn't like it all dark."

"All right, grandfather," the doves replied. "We know where she lives. We have seen her house. We know how to catch her for you."

The doves then got ready and set out for Sun's house, Coyote accompanying them. When they spied Sun's house in the distance, they stopped where they were and waited, hoping that somebody would come out. But nobody came out.

The two doves then decided to shoot at Sun's house and thus make her rise up out of the smoke hole. Once out of her stone house they could easily catch her. But they started quarreling over who should do the shooting.

"You had better let me do the shooting," the older dove said. "You might miss."

"You? You are too old. You can hardly see any more," the younger one replied. "But my eye is good. I am young. My arm is strong."

"All right, shoot then, and don't talk so much," the older dove snapped at him.

The younger of the two doves took up his sling, put a stone in it, and started singing as he whirled it. Then he let fly. The stone sailed through the air toward Sun's house, striking it on one side, and breaking right through the stone.

Sun became frightened and started out of her smoke hole, rising in the air. She soon went back into her house when she saw that not much damage had been done; the stone had only broken the wall of one side of her house.

"There! Didn't I tell you. Didn't I tell you to let me shoot?" the older dove screamed. "Didn't I tell you you would miss? Now you watch me. Watch me, grandfather, and don't be afraid."

"Oh, I am not afraid," said Coyote.

Then the other dove took up his sling, and he sang the same kind of song while he was whirling it. Then he let fly! This time the stone hit the house of Sun right in the center. Sun rose through the smoke hole and went straight up into the sky, blazing light, and hung way up there in the middle of the sky.

Coyote got so scared when Sun went up that he jumped and fell over on his back, blinking and rolling his eyes with amazement.

"Well, well, well, well," he said. "Now my grandson will be happy."

Coyote Juggles His Eyes

As he was walking through the timber one morning, Coyote heard some-one say, "I throw you up and you come down in!"

Coyote thought that was strange talk. It made him curious. He wanted to learn who was saying that, and why. He followed the sound of the voice, and he came upon little *Zst-shaka'-na*—Chickadee—who was throwing his eyes into the air and catching them in his eye sockets. When he saw Coyote peering at him from behind a tree, Chickadee ran. He was afraid of Coyote.

"That is my way, not yours," Coyote yelled after him.

Now, it wasn't Coyote's way at all, but Coyote thought he could juggle his eyes just as easily as Chickadee juggled his, so he tried. He took out his eyes and tossed them up and repeated the words used by the little boy: "I throw you up and you come down in!" His eyes plopped back where they belonged. That was fun. He juggled the eyes again and again.

Two ravens happened to fly that way. They saw what Coyote was doing, and one of them said, "*Sin-ka-lip'* is mocking someone. Let us steal his eyes and take them to the Sun-dance. Perhaps then we can find out his medicine-power."

"Yes, we will do that," agreed the other raven. "We may learn something."

As Coyote tossed his eyes the next time, the ravens swooped, swift as ar-rows from a strong bow. One of them snatched one eye and the other raven caught the other eye.

"Quoh! Quoh! Quoh!" they laughed, and flew away to the Sun-dance camp.

Oh, but Coyote was mad! He was crazy with rage. When he could hear the ravens laughing no longer, he started in the direction they had gone. He hoped somehow to catch them and get back his eyes. He bumped into trees and bushes, fell into holes and gullies, and banged against boulders. He soon was bruised all over, but he kept on going, stumbling along. He became thirsty, and he kept asking the trees and bushes what kind they were, so that he could learn when he was getting close to water. The trees and bushes answered politely, giving their names. After awhile he found he was among the mountain bushes, and he knew he was near water. He came soon to a little stream and satisfied his thirst. Then he went on and presently he was in the pine timber. He heard someone laughing. It was *Kok'-qhi Ski'-kaka*—Bluebird. She was with her sister, *Kwas'-kay*—Bluejay.

"Look, sister," said Bluebird. "There is *Sin-ka-lip'* pretending to be blind. Isn't he funny?"

"Do not mind *Sin-ka-lip'*," advised Bluejay. "Do not pay any attention to him. He is full of mean tricks. He is bad."

Coyote purposely bumped into a tree and rolled over and over toward the voices. That made little Bluebird stop her laughing. She felt just a little bit afraid.

"Come, little girl," Coyote called. "Come and see the pretty star that I see!"

Bluebird naturally was very curious, and she wanted to see that pretty star, but she hung back, and her sister warned her again not to pay attention to Coyote. But Coyote used coaxing words, told her how bright the star looked.

"Where is the star?" asked Bluebird, hopping a few steps toward Coyote.

"I cannot show you while you are so far away," he replied. "See, where I am pointing my finger!'

Bluebird hopped close, and Coyote made one quick bound and caught her. He yanked out her eyes and threw them into the air, saying:

"I throw you up and you come down in!" and the eyes fell into his eye sockets.

Coyote could see again, and his heart was glad. "When did you ever see a star in the sunlight?" he asked Bluebird, and then ran off through the timber.

Bluebird cried, and Bluejay scolded her for being so foolish as to trust Coyote. Bluejay took two of the berries she had just picked and put them into her sister's eye sockets, and Bluebird could see as well as before. But, as the berries were small, her new eyes were small, too. That is why Bluebird has such berrylike eyes.

While his new eyes were better than none at all, Coyote was not satisfied. They were too little. They did not fit very well into his slant sockets. So he kept on hunting for the ravens and the Sun-dance camp. One day he came to a small tepee. He heard someone inside pounding rocks together. He went in and saw an old woman pounding meat and berries in a stone mortar. The old woman was *Su-see-wass*—Pheasant. Coyote asked her if she lived alone.

"No," she said, "I have two granddaughters. They are away at the Sun-dance. The people there are dancing with Coyote's eyes."

"Aren't you afraid to be here alone?" Coyote asked. "Isn't there anything that you fear?"

"I am afraid of nothing but the *stet'-chee-hunt*—stinging-bush," she said.

Laughing to himself, Coyote went out to find a stinging-bush. In a swamp not far away he found several bushes of that kind. He broke off one of those nettle bushes and carried it back to the tepee. Seeing it, Pheasant cried:

"Do not touch me with the *stet'-chee-hunt*! Do not touch me! It will kill me!"

But Coyote had no mercy in his heart, no pity. He whipped poor Pheasant with the stinging-bush until she died. Then, with his flint knife, he skinned her, and dressed himself in her skin. He looked almost exactly like the old woman. He hid her body and began to pound meat in the stone mortar. He was doing that when the granddaughters came home. They were laughing. They told how they had danced over Coyote's eyes. They did not recognize Coyote in their grandmother's skin, but Coyote knew them. One was little Bluebird and the other was Bluejay. Coyote smiled. "Take me with you to the Sun-dance, granddaughters," he said in his best old woman's voice.

The sisters looked at each other in surprise, and Bluejay answered, "Why, you did not want to go with us when the morning was young."

"Grandmother, how strange you talk!" said Bluebird.

"That is because I burned my mouth with hot soup," said Coyote.

"And, Grandmother, how odd your eyes look!" Bluejay exclaimed. "One eye is longer than the other!"

"My grandchild, I hurt that eye with my cane," explained Coyote.

The sisters did not find anything else wrong with their grandmother, and the next morning the three of them started for the Sun-dance camp. The sisters had to carry their supposed grandmother. They took turns. They had gone part way when Coyote made himself an awkward burden and almost caused Bluejay to fall. That made Bluejay angry, and she threw Coyote to the ground. Bluebird then picked him up and carried him. As they reached the edge of the Sun-dance camp, Coyote again made himself an awkward burden, and Bluebird let him fall. Many of the people in the camp saw that happen. They thought the sisters were cruel, and the women scolded Bluebird and Bluejay for treating such an old person so badly.

Some of the people came over and lifted Coyote to his feet and helped him into the Sun-dance lodge. There the people were dancing over Coyote's eyes, and the medicine-men were passing the eyes to one another and holding the eyes up high for everyone to see. After a little Coyote asked to hold the eyes, and they were handed to him.

He ran out of the lodge, threw his eyes into the air, and said, "I throw you up and you come down in!"

His eyes returned to their places, and Coyote ran to the top of a hill.

There he looked back and shouted, "Where are the maidens who had Coyote for a grandmother?"

Bluejay and Bluebird were full of shame. They went home, carrying Pheasant's skin, which Coyote had thrown aside. They searched and found their grandmother's body and put it back in the skin, and Pheasant's life was restored. She told them how Coyote had killed her with the stinging-bush.

PART FOUR

Tales to Live By

This final section contains meditations by contemporary writers from indigenous cultures who reflect about how their respective traditions might address the global environmental problems of our day. By closing the volume in this way we intend to emphasize that indigenous traditions and their oral literatures are by no means simply the past, to which modern, more transient and cosmopolitan societies can now look back wistfully. Rather, these are peoples and perspectives that have persisted around the world, though often in the face of persecution and adversity. Members of industrial societies have much to learn from indigenous cultures. Granted, serious difficulties will arise in this regard. For example, some stories may be difficult to understand for a reader who does not share a particular storyteller's landscape or community. There are similar concerns that outsiders who come for stories and instruction to indigenous peoples may deal further blows to the integrity of those communities. Dialogue at and about this turbulent confluence of cultures will intensify in coming years, and among the voices with a special authority will be those exemplified here: people standing in an oral tradition and at the same time drawing their own conclusions in writing about how the history and wisdom of their people might help to guide humanity at this time of environmental crisis.

Under the influence of writers such as John Muir, the environmental movement in the United States has often emphasized the protection and the special spiritual value of wilderness. There has been enormous benefit in this wilderness ethic and in the National Park system so closely associated with it. At the same time, it has sometimes been accompanied by a hermetic sense—

an assumption that inside the green line of federal preserves one may experience the sanctity of nature, while on the other side of the border modern civilization and its crassly applied technology hold sway. Each of the authors in this section, in their different ways, suggests the necessity for a broader and more integrated vision of the place of human beings in nature.

Rigoberta Menchú, a Nobel laureate and a member of the Quechua of Guatemala; Pablo Santos, whose people are the Aeta of the Philippines; and Kamoriongo Ole Aimerru Nkongoi, an elder of the Maasai in Kenya, all address the relationship between environmental damage and political oppression. They confirm and illustrate an understanding that has been gaining strength among Western environmentalists ever since Rachel Carson's Silent Spring was first published in 1962: that all environmental issues are finally global issues, and that they are all tied up with politics, economics, and issues of social justice. For prosperous residents of the Northern Hemisphere, there is a pressing need to curb inordinate appetites for diminishing resources, lest the less powerful and their lands suffer even more drastically. As is also true with regard to the creation myths and animal stories from around the world, beneath these political and ethical questions lies a fundamental issue of perception: those of us who have been isolated within our own affluence need to register the reality of other lives, both the nonhuman lives in the woods, fields, and waters around us and the human communities grounded in ancestral lands of which we've known little and have taken even less heed.

Leslie Marmon Silko (Laguna Pueblo), Joseph Bruchac (Abenaki), N. Scott Momaday (Kiowa), and Linda Hogan (Chickasaw) are inheritors of native traditions in North America. The indigenous cultures of this continent are often the traditions best known internationally, and have been accorded a classic, or representative, status by many outsiders who are interested in righting the imbalance between humanity and the rest of nature. One special value in the work of writers such as these four is to make concrete and specific what the outlook of their peoples has been, and what the implications of such visions are today. Silko and Bruchac help to dismantle the distinctions between nature and culture that have sometimes led to carelessness and waste. Landforms and animals are not outside the human circle for them, but are rather the tangible and vivid reminders of their people's history, literature, and religion. The essays in this section thus reinforce the discipline and sympathy upon which a harmoniously functioning culture depends. Momaday and

Hogan reflect specifically upon questions of cultural transmission. How may a solitary writer or reader tap into and perpetuate the mythic and oral legacies of an indigenous community? In a certain sense this is the most "literary" issue raised in the present section. At the same time, however, it points to the central intention of the entire collection of stories. Just as biodiversity contributes to the sustainability of a complex ecosystem, in the same way a diversity of stories may promote a more stable relationship between humanity and the rest of nature. As we cultivate the sensitivity to track the tales and testimony of indigenous peoples, we may begin to appreciate the inextricable wholeness of humanity within the natural world.

Landscape, History, and the Pueblo Imagination

•••

Leslie Marmon Silko
LAGUNA PUEBLO,
SOUTHWESTERN UNITED STATES

From a High Arid Plateau in New Mexico

••••••••••••••••••

You see that after a thing is dead, it dries up. It might take weeks or years, but eventually if you touch the thing, it crumbles under your fingers. It goes back to dust. The soul of the thing has long since departed. With the plants and wild game the soul may have already been borne back into bones and blood or thick green stalk and leaves. Nothing is wasted. What cannot be eaten by people or in some way used must then be left where other living creatures may benefit. What domestic animals or wild scavengers can't eat will be fed to the plants. The plants feed on the dust of these few remains.

The ancient Pueblo people buried the dead in vacant rooms or partially collapsed rooms adjacent to the main living quarters. Sand and clay used to construct the roof make layers many inches deep once the roof has collapsed. The layers of sand and clay make for easy gravedigging. The vacant room fills with cast-off objects and debris. When a vacant room has filled deep enough, a shallow but adequate grave can be scooped in a far corner. Archaeologists have remarked over formal burials complete with elaborate funerary objects excavated in trash middens of abandoned rooms. But the rocks and adobe mortar of collapsed walls were valued by the ancient people. Because each rock had been carefully selected for size and shape, then chiseled to an even face. Even the pink clay adobe melting with each rainstorm had to be prayed over, then dug and carried some distance. Corn cobs and husks, the rinds and stalks and animal bones were not regarded by the ancient people as filth or garbage. The remains were merely resting at a midpoint in their journey back to dust. Human remains are not so different. They should rest with the bones and rinds where they all may benefit living creatures—small rodents and insects—until their return is completed. The remains of things—animals and plants, the clay and the stones—were treated with respect. Because for the ancient people all these things had spirit and being. The antelope merely consents to return home with the hunter. All phases of the hunt are conducted with love. The love the hunter and the people have for the Antelope People. And the love of the antelope who agree to give up their meat and blood so that human beings will not starve. Waste of meat or even the thoughtless handling of bones cooked bare will offend the antelope spirits. Next year the hunters will vainly search the dry plains for antelope. Thus it is necessary to return carefully the bones and hair, and the stalks and leaves to the earth who first created them. The spirits remain close by. They do not leave us.

The dead become dust, and in this becoming they are once more joined with the Mother. The ancient Pueblo people called the earth the Mother Creator of all things in this world. Her sister, the Corn Mother, occasionally merges with her because all succulent green life rises out of the depths of the earth.

Rocks and clay are part of the Mother. They emerge in various forms, but at some time before, they were smaller particles or great boulders. At a later time they may again become what they once were. Dust.

A rock shares this fate with us and with animals and plants as well. A rock has being or spirit, although we may not understand it. The spirit may differ from the spirit we know in animals or plants or in ourselves. In the end we all originate from the depths of the earth. Perhaps this is how all beings share in the spirit of the Creator. We do not know.

From the Emergence Place

Pueblo potters, the creators of petroglyphs and oral narratives, never conceived of removing themselves from the earth and sky. So long as the human consciousness remains *within* the hills, canyons, cliffs, and the plants, clouds, and sky, the term *landscape*, as it has entered the English language, is misleading. "A portion of territory the eye can comprehend in a single view" does not correctly describe the relationship between the human being and his or her surroundings. This assumes the viewer is somehow *outside* or *sep-*

arate from the territory he or she surveys. Viewers are as much a part of the landscape as the boulders they stand on. There is no high mesa edge or mountain peak where one can stand and not immediately be part of all that surrounds. Human identity is linked with all the elements of Creation through the clan: you might belong to the Sun Clan or the Lizard Clan or the Corn Clan or the Clay Clan.[1] Standing deep within the natural world, the ancient Pueblo understood the thing as it was—the squash blossom, grasshopper, or rabbit itself could never be created by the human hand. Ancient Pueblos took the modest view that the thing itself (the landscape) could not be improved upon. The ancients did not presume to tamper with what had already been created. Thus *realism*, as we now recognize it in painting and sculpture, did not catch the imaginations of Pueblo people until recently.

The squash blossom itself is *one thing*: itself. So the ancient Pueblo potter abstracted what she saw to be the key elements of the squash blossom—the four symmetrical petals, with four symmetrical stamens in the center. These key elements, while suggesting the squash flower, also link it with the four cardinal directions. By representing only its intrinsic form, the squash flower is released from a limited meaning or restricted identity. Even in the most sophisticated abstract form, a squash flower or a cloud or a lightning bolt became intricately connected with a complex system of relationships which the ancient Pueblo people maintained with each other, and with the populous natural world they lived within. A bolt of lightning is itself, but at the same time it may mean much more. It may be a messenger of good fortune when summer rains are needed. It may deliver death, perhaps the result of manipulations by the Gunnadeyahs, destructive necromancers. Lightning may strike down an evil-doer. Or lightning may strike a person of good will. If the person survives, lightning endows him or her with heightened power.

Pictographs and petroglyphs of constellations or elk or antelope draw their magic in part from the process wherein the focus of all prayer and concentration is upon the thing itself, which, in its turn, guides the hunter's hand. Connection with the spirit dimensions requires a figure or form which is all-inclusive. A "lifelike" rendering of an elk is too restrictive. Only the elk *is* itself. A *realistic* rendering of an elk would be only one particular elk any-

---

1. Clan: A social unit composed of families sharing common ancestors who trace their lineage back to the Emergence where their ancestors allied themselves with certain plants or animals or elements [Silko's note].

way. The purpose of the hunt rituals and magic is to make contact with *all* the spirits of the Elk.

The land, the sky, and all that is within them—the landscape—includes human beings. Interrelationships in the Pueblo landscape are complex and fragile. The unpredictability of the weather, the aridity and harshness of much of the terrain in the high plateau country explain in large part the relentless attention the ancient Pueblo people gave the sky and the earth around them. Survival depended upon harmony and cooperation not only among human beings, but among all things—the animate and the less animate, since rocks and mountains were known to move, to travel occasionally.

The ancient Pueblos believed the Earth and the Sky were sisters (or sister and brother in the post-Christian version). As long as good family relations are maintained, then the Sky will continue to bless her sister, the Earth, with rain, and the Earth's children will continue to survive. But the old stories recall incidents in which troublesome spirits or beings threaten the earth. In one story, a malicious ka'tsina, called the Gambler, seizes the Shiwana, or Rainclouds, the Sun's beloved children.[2] The Shiwana are snared in magical power late one afternoon on a high mountaintop. The Gambler takes the Rainclouds to his mountain stronghold where he locks them in the north room of his house. What was his idea? The Shiwana were beyond value. They brought life to all things on earth. The Gambler wanted a big stake to wager in his games of chance. But such greed, even on the part of only one being, had the effect of threatening the survival of all life on earth. Sun Youth, aided by old Grandmother Spider, outsmarts the Gambler and the rigged game, and the Rainclouds are set free. The drought ends, and once more life thrives on earth.

Through the Stories
We Hear Who We Are
••••••••••••••••••

All summer the people watch the west horizon, scanning the sky from south to north for rainclouds. Corn must have moisture at the time the tassels form. Otherwise pollination will be incomplete, and the ears will be stunted

---

2. Ka'tsina: Ka'tsinas are spirit beings who roam the earth and who inhabit kachina masks worn in Pueblo ceremonial dances [Silko's note].

and shriveled. An inadequate harvest may bring disaster. Stories told at Hopi, Zuñi, and at Acoma and Laguna describe drought and starvation as recently as 1900. Precipitation in west-central New Mexico averages fourteen inches annually. The western pueblos are located at altitudes over 5,600 feet above sea level, where winter temperatures at night fall below freezing. Yet evidence of their presence in the high desert plateau country goes back ten thousand years. The ancient Pueblo people not only survived in this environment, but many years they thrived. In A.D. 1100 the people at Chaco Canyon had built cities with apartment buildings of stone five stories high. Their sophistication as sky-watchers was surpassed only by Mayan and Inca astronomers. Yet this vast complex of knowledge and belief, amassed for thousands of years, was never recorded in writing.

Instead, the ancient Pueblo people depended upon collective memory through successive generations to maintain and transmit an entire culture, a world-view complete with proven strategies for survival. The oral narrative, or "story," became the medium in which the complex of Pueblo knowledge and belief was maintained. Whatever the event or the subject, the ancient people perceived the world and themselves within that world as part of an ancient continuous story composed of innumerable bundles of other stories.

The ancient Pueblo vision of the world was inclusive. The impulse was to leave nothing out. Pueblo oral tradition necessarily embraced all levels of human experience. Otherwise, the collective knowledge and beliefs comprising ancient Pueblo culture would have been incomplete. Thus stories about the Creation and Emergence of human beings and animals into this World continue to be retold each year for four days and four nights during the winter solstice. The *humma-hah* stories related events from the time long ago when human beings were still able to communicate with animals and other living things. But, beyond these two preceding categories, the Pueblo oral tradition knew no boundaries. Accounts of the appearance of the first Europeans in Pueblo country or of the tragic encounters between Pueblo people and Apache raiders were no more and no less important than stories about the biggest mule deer ever taken or adulterous couples surprised in cornfields and chicken coops. Whatever happened, the ancient people instinctively sorted events and details into a loose narrative structure. Everything became a story.

◧ ◧ ◧

Traditionally everyone, from the youngest child to the oldest person, was expected to listen and to be able to recall or tell a portion, if only a small detail, from a narrative account or story. Thus the remembering and retelling were a communal process. Even if a key figure, an elder who knew much more than others, were to die unexpectedly, the system would remain intact. Through the efforts of a great many people, the community was able to piece together valuable accounts and crucial information that might otherwise have died with an individual.

Communal storytelling was a self-correcting process in which listeners were encouraged to speak up if they noted an important fact or detail omitted. The people were happy to listen to two or three different versions of the same event or the same *humma-hah* story. Even conflicting versions of an incident were welcomed for the entertainment they provided. Defenders of each version might joke and tease one another, but seldom were there any direct confrontations. Implicit in the Pueblo oral tradition was the awareness that loyalties, grudges, and kinship must always influence the narrator's choices as she emphasizes to listeners this is the way *she* has always heard the story told. The ancient Pueblo people sought a communal truth, not an absolute. For them this truth lived somewhere within the web of differing versions, disputes over minor points, outright contradictions tangling with old feuds and village rivalries.

A dinner-table conversation, recalling a deer hunt forty years ago when the largest mule deer ever was taken, inevitably stimulates similar memories in listeners. But hunting stories were not merely after-dinner entertainment. These accounts contained information of critical importance about behavior and migration patterns of mule deer. Hunting stories carefully described key landmarks and locations of fresh water. Thus a deer-hunt story might also serve as a "map." Lost travelers, and lost piñon-nut gatherers, have been saved by sighting a rock formation they recognize only because they once heard a hunting story describing this rock formation.

The importance of cliff formations and water holes does not end with hunting stories. As offspring of the Mother Earth, the ancient Pueblo people could not conceive of themselves except within a specific landscape. Location, or "place," nearly always plays a central role in the Pueblo oral narratives. Indeed, stories are most frequently recalled as people are passing by a specific geographical feature or the exact place where a story takes place. The precise date of the incident often is less important than the place or location of the happening. "Long, long ago," "a long time ago," "not too long ago," and "recently" are usually how stories are classified in terms of time. But the places where the stories occur are precisely located, and prominent geographical details recalled, even if the landscape is well-known to listeners. Often because the turning point in the narrative involved a peculiarity or special quality of a rock or tree or plant found only at that place. Thus, in the case of many of the Pueblo narratives, it is impossible to determine which came first: the incident or the geographical feature which begs to be brought alive in a story that features some unusual aspect of this location.

There is a giant sandstone boulder about a mile north of Old Laguna, on the road to Paguate. It is ten feet tall and twenty feet in circumference. When I was a child, and we would pass this boulder driving to Paguate village, someone usually made reference to the story about Kochininako, Yellow Woman, and the Estrucuyo, a monstrous giant who nearly ate her. The Twin Hero Brothers saved Kochininako, who had been out hunting rabbits to take home to feed her mother and sisters. The Hero Brothers had heard her cries just in time. The Estrucuyo had cornered her in a cave too small to fit its monstrous head. Kochininako had already thrown to the Estrucuyo all her rabbits, as well as her moccasins and most of her clothing. Still the creature had not been satisfied. After killing the Estrucuyo with their bows and arrows, the Twin Hero Brothers slit open the Estrucuyo and cut out its heart. They threw the heart as far as they could. The monster's heart landed there, beside the old trail to Paguate village, where the sandstone boulder rests now.

It may be argued that the existence of the boulder precipitated the creation of a story to explain it. But sandstone boulders and sandstone formations of strange shapes abound in the Laguna Pueblo area. Yet most of them do not have stories. Often the crucial element in a narrative is the terrain—some specific detail of the setting.

A high dark mesa rises dramatically from a grassy plain fifteen miles southeast of Laguna, in an area known as Swanee. On the grassy plain one hundred and forty years ago, my great-grandmother's uncle and his brother-in-law were grazing their herd of sheep. Because visibility on the plain extends for over twenty miles, it wasn't until the two sheepherders came near the high dark mesa that the Apaches were able to stalk them. Using the mesa to obscure their approach, the raiders swept around from both ends of the mesa. My great-grandmother's relatives were killed, and the herd lost. The high dark mesa played a critical role: the mesa had compromised the safety which the openness of the plains had seemed to assure. Pueblo and Apache alike relied upon the terrain, the very earth herself, to give them protection and aid. Human activities or needs were maneuvered to fit the existing surroundings and conditions. I imagine the last afternoon of my distant ancestors as warm and sunny for late September. They might have been traveling slowly, bringing the sheep closer to Laguna in preparation for the approach of colder weather. The grass was tall and only beginning to change from green to a yellow which matched the late-afternoon sun shining off it. There might have been comfort in the warmth and the sight of the sheep fattening on good pasture which lulled my ancestors into their fatal inattention. They might have had a rifle whereas the Apaches had only bows and arrows. But there would have been four or five Apache raiders, and the surprise attack would have canceled any advantage the rifles gave them.

Survival in any landscape comes down to making the best use of all available resources. On that particular September afternoon, the raiders made better use of the Swanee terrain than my poor ancestors did. Thus the high dark mesa and the story of the two lost Laguna herders became inextricably linked. The memory of them and their story resides in part with the high black mesa. For as long as the mesa stands, people within the family and clan will be reminded of the story of that afternoon long ago. Thus the continuity and accuracy of the oral narratives are reinforced by the landscape—and the Pueblo interpretation of that landscape is *maintained*.

The Migration Story: An Interior Journey

The Laguna Pueblo migration stories refer to specific places—mesas, springs, or cottonwood trees—not only locations which can be visited still, but also locations which lie directly on the state highway route linking Paguate village with Laguna village. In traveling this road as a child with older Laguna people I first heard a few of the stories from that much larger body of stories linked with the Emergence and Migration.[3] It may be coincidental that Laguna people continue to follow the same route which, according to the Migration story, the ancestors followed south from the Emergence Place. It

3. The Emergence: All the human beings, animals, and life which had been created emerged from the four worlds below when the earth became habitable. The Migration: The Pueblo people emerged into the Fifth World, but they had already been warned they would have to travel and search before they found the place they were meant to live [Silko's note].

may be that the route is merely the shortest and best route for car, horse, or foot traffic between Laguna and Paguate villages. But if the stories about boulders, springs, and hills are actually remnants from a ritual that retraces the creation and emergence of the Laguna Pueblo people as a culture, as the people they became, then continued use of that route creates a unique relationship between the ritual-mythic world and the actual, everyday world. A journey from Paguate to Laguna down the long incline of Paguate Hill retraces the original journey from the Emergence Place, which is located slightly north of the Paguate village. Thus the landscape between Paguate and Laguna takes on a deeper significance: the landscape resonates the spiritual or mythic dimension of the Pueblo world even today.

Although each Pueblo culture designates a specific Emergence Place— usually a small natural spring edged with mossy sandstone and full of cattails and wild watercress—it is clear that they do not agree on any single location or natural spring as the one and only true Emergence Place. Each Pueblo group recounts its own stories about Creation, Emergence, and Migration, although they all believe that all human beings, with all the animals and plants, emerged at the same place and at the same time.[4]

Natural springs are crucial sources of water for all life in the high desert plateau country. So the small spring near Paguate village is literally the source and continuance of life for the people in the area. The spring also functions on a spiritual level, recalling the original Emergence Place and linking the people and the spring water to all other people and to that moment when the Pueblo people became aware of themselves as they are even now. The Emergence was an emergence into a precise cultural identity. Thus the Pueblo stories about the Emergence and Migration are not to be taken as literally as the anthropologists might wish. Prominent geographical features and landmarks which are mentioned in the narratives exist for ritual purposes, not because the Laguna people actually journeyed south for hundreds of years from Chaco Canyon or Mesa Verde, as the archaeologists say, or eight miles from the site of the natural springs at Paguate to the sandstone hilltop at Laguna.

The eight miles, marked with boulders, mesas, springs, and river cross-

---

4. Creation: Tse'itsi'nako, Thought Woman, the Spider, thought about it, and everything she thought came into being. First she thought of three sisters for herself, and they helped her think of the rest of the Universe, including the Fifth World and the four worlds below. The Fifth World is the world we are living in today. There are four previous worlds below this world [Silko's note].

ings, are actually a ritual circuit or path which marks the interior journey the Laguna people made: a journey of awareness and imagination in which they emerged from being within the earth and from everything included in earth to the culture and people they became, differentiating themselves for the first time from all that had surrounded them; always aware that interior distances cannot be reckoned in physical miles or in calendar years.

The narratives linked with prominent features of the landscape between Paguate and Laguna delineate the complexities of the relationship which human beings must maintain with the surrounding natural world if they hope to survive in this place. Thus the journey was an interior process of the imagination, a growing awareness that being human is somehow different from all other life—animal, plant, and inanimate. Yet we are all from the same source: the awareness never deteriorated into Cartesian duality, cutting off the human from the natural world.

The people found the opening into the Fifth World too small to allow them or any of the animals to escape. They had sent a fly out through the small hole to tell them if it was the world which the Mother Creator had promised. It was, but there was the problem of getting out. The antelope tried to butt the opening to enlarge it, but the antelope enlarged it only a little. It was necessary for the badger with her long claws to assist the antelope, and at last the opening was enlarged enough so that all the people and animals were able to emerge up into the Fifth World. The human beings could not have emerged without the aid of antelope and badger. The human beings depended upon the aid and charity of the animals. Only through interdependence could the human beings survive. Families belonged to clans, and it was by clan that the human being joined with the animal and plant world. Life on the high arid plateau became viable when the human beings were able to imagine themselves as sisters and brothers to the badger, antelope, clay, yucca, and sun. Not until they could find a viable relationship to the terrain, the landscape they found themselves in, could they *emerge*. Only at the moment the requisite balance between human and *other* was realized could the Pueblo people become a culture, a distinct group whose population and survival remained stable despite the vicissitudes of climate and terrain.

Landscape thus has similarities with dreams. Both have the power to seize terrifying feelings and deep instincts and translate them into images— visual, aural, tactile—into the concrete where human beings may more readily confront and channel the terrifying instincts or powerful emotions into rituals and narratives which reassure the individual while reaffirming cherished values of the group. The identity of the individual as a part of the group and the greater Whole is strengthened, and the terror of facing the world alone is extinguished.

Even now, the people at Laguna Pueblo spend the greater portion of social occasions recounting recent incidents or events which have occurred in the Laguna area. Nearly always, the discussion will precipitate the retelling of older stories about similar incidents or other stories connected with a specific place. The stories often contain disturbing or provocative material, but are nonetheless told in the presence of children and women. The effect of these inter-family or inter-clan exchanges is the reassurance for each person that she or he will never be separated or apart from the clan, no matter what might happen. Neither the worst blunders or disasters nor the greatest financial prosperity and joy will ever be permitted to isolate anyone from the rest of the group. In the ancient times, cohesiveness was all that stood between extinction and survival, and, while the individual certainly was recognized, it was always as an individual simultaneously bonded to family and clan by a complex bundle of custom and ritual. You are never the first to suffer a grave loss or profound humiliation. You are never the first, and you understand that you will probably not be the last to commit or be victimized by a repugnant act. Your family and clan are able to go on at length about others now passed on, others older or more experienced than you who suffered similar losses.

The wide deep arroyo near the Kings Bar (located across the reservation borderline) has over the years claimed many vehicles. A few years ago, when a Viet Nam veteran's new red Volkswagen rolled backwards into the arroyo while he was inside buying a six-pack of beer, the story of his loss joined the lively and large collection of stories already connected with that big arroyo. I do not know whether the Viet Nam veteran was consoled when he was told the stories about the other cars claimed by the ravenous arroyo. All his savings of combat pay had gone for the red Volkswagen. But this man could not have felt any worse than the man who, some years before, had left his children and mother-in-law in his station wagon with the engine running. When he came out of the liquor store his station wagon was gone. He found it and its passengers upside down in the big arroyo. Broken bones, cuts and bruises, and a total wreck of the car. The big arroyo has a wide mouth. Its existence needs no explanation. People in the area regard the arroyo much as they might regard a living being, which has a certain character and personality. I seldom drive past that wide deep arroyo without feeling a familiarity with and even a strange affection for this arroyo. Because as treacherous as it may be, the arroyo maintains a strong connection between human beings and the earth. The arroyo demands from us the caution and attention that constitute respect. It is this sort of respect the old believers have in mind when they tell us we must respect and love the earth.

Hopi Pueblo elders have said that the austere and, to some eyes, barren plains and hills surrounding their mesa-top villages actually help to nurture the spirituality of the Hopi *way*. The Hopi elders say the Hopi people might have settled in locations far more lush where daily life would not have been so grueling. But there on the high silent sandstone mesas that overlook the sandy arid expanses stretching to all horizons, the Hopi elders say the Hopi people must "live by their prayers" if they are to survive. The Hopi way cherishes the intangible: the riches realized from interaction and interrelationships with all beings above all else. Great abundances of material things, even food, the Hopi elders believe, tend to lure human attention away from what is most valuable and important. The views of the Hopi elders are not much different from those elders in all the Pueblos.

The bare vastness of the Hopi landscape emphasizes the visual impact of every plant, every rock, every arroyo. Nothing is overlooked or taken for granted. Each ant, each lizard, each lark is imbued with great value simply because the creature is there, simply because the creature is alive in a place where any life at all is precious. Stand on the mesa edge at Walpai and look west over the bare distances toward the pale blue outlines of the San Francisco peaks where the ka'tsina spirits reside. So little lies between you and the sky. So little lies between you and the earth. One look and you know that simply to survive is a great triumph, that every possible resource is needed, every possible ally—even the most humble insect or reptile. You realize you will be speaking with all of them if you intend to last out the year. Thus it is that the Hopi elders are grateful to the landscape for aiding them in their quest as spiritual people.

The Circle Is the Way to See

···

Joseph Bruchac
ABENAKI, NORTHEASTERN UNITED STATES
AND SOUTHEASTERN CANADA

Waudjoset *nudatlokugan bizwakamigwi alnabe*. My story was out walking around, a wilderness lodge man. *Wawigit nudatlokugan*. Here lives my story. *Nudatlokugan Gluskabe*. It is a story of Gluskabe.

One day, Gluskabe went out to hunt. He tried hunting in the woods, but the game animals were not to be seen. Hunting is slow, he thought, and he returned to the wigwam where he lived with his grandmother, Woodchuck. He lay down on his bed and began to sing:

> *I wish for a game bag*
> *I wish for a game bag*
> *I wish for a game bag*
> *To make it easy to hunt*

He sang and sang until his grandmother could stand it no longer. She made him a game bag of deer hair and tossed it to him. But he did not stop singing:

> *I wish for a game bag*
> *I wish for a game bag*
> *I wish for a game bag*
> *To make it easy to hunt*

So she made him a game bag of caribou hair. She tossed it to him, but still he continued to sing:

I wish for a game bag
I wish for a game bag
I wish for a game bag
To make it easy to hunt

She tried making a game bag of moose hair, but Gluskabe ignored that as well. He sang:

I wish for a game bag
I wish for a game bag
I wish for a game bag
Of Woodchuck hair

Then Grandmother Woodchuck plucked the hair from her belly and made a game bag. Gluskabe sat up and stopped singing. "*Oleohneh, noh-kemes*," he said. "Thank you, Grandmother."

He went into the forest and called the animals. "Come," he said. "The world is going to end and all of you will die. Get into my game bag and you will not see the end of the world."

Then all of the animals came out of the forest and into his game bag. He carried it back to the wigwam of his grandmother and said, "Grandmother, I have brought game animals. Now we will not have a hard time hunting."

Grandmother Woodchuck saw all the animals in the game bag. "You have not done well, Grandson," she said. "In the future, our small ones, our children's children, will die of hunger. You must not do this. You must do what will help our children's children."

So Gluskabe went back into the forest with his game bag. He opened it. "Go, the danger is past," he said. Then the animals came out of the game bag and scattered throughout the forest. *Nedali medabegazu.*

There my story ends.

◧   ◧   ◧

The story of Gluskabe's game bag has been told many times. A version much like this one was given to the anthropologist Frank Speck in 1918 by an elderly Penobscot man named Newell Lion. This and other Gluskabe stories that illustrate the relationship of human beings to the natural order are told to this day among the Penobscot and Sokokl, the Passamaquoddy and the Mississquoi, the Micmac and the other Wabanaki peoples whose place on this continent is called Ndakinna in the Abenaki language. Ndakinna—Our Land. A land that owns us and a land we must respect.

Gluskabe's game bag is a story that is central for an understanding of the native view of the place of human beings in the natural order, and it is a story with many, many meanings. Gluskabe, the Trickster, is the ultimate human being and also an old one who was here before human beings came. He contains both the Good Mind, which can benefit the people and help the Earth, and that other Twisted Mind, a mind governed by selfish thoughts that can destroy the natural balance and bring disaster.

He is greater than we are, but his problems and his powers are those of human beings. Because of our cunning and our power—a magical power—to make things, we can affect the lives of all else that lives around us. Yet when we overuse that power, we do not do well.

We must listen to the older and wiser voices of the earth—like the voice of Grandmother Woodchuck—or our descendants will, quite literally, starve. It is not so much a mystical as a practical relationship. Common sense.

Though my own native ancestry is Abenaki, and I regard the teachings and traditions of my Abenaki friends and elders, like the tales of Gluskabe, as a central part of my existence, I have also spent much of the last thirty-two years of my life learning from the elders of the Haudenosaunee nations, the People of the Longhouse—those nations of the Mohawk, Oneida, Onondaga, Cayuga, Seneca, and Tuscarora—commonly referred to today as the Iroquois.

We share this endangered corner of our continent, the area referred to on European-made maps as New York and New England. In fact, I live within a few hours' drive of the place where a man regarded as a messenger from the Creator and known as the Peacemaker joined with Hiawatha—perhaps a thousand years ago—to bring together five warring tribal nations into a League of Peace and plant a great pine tree as the living symbol of that green and growing union of nations.

That Great League is now recognized by many historians as a direct influence on the formation of modern ideas of democracy and on the Constitution of the United States.

I think it right to recall here some of the environmental prophecies of the Haudenosaunee people, not as an official representative of any native nation, but simply as a humble storyteller. I repeat them not as a chief nor as an elder, but as one who has listened and who hopes to convey the messages he has heard with accuracy and honesty.

According to Iroquois traditions, some of which were voiced by the prophet Ganio-dai-yo in the early 1800s, a time would come when the elm trees would die. And then the maple, the leader of all the trees, would also begin to die, from the top down.

In my own early years, I saw the elms begin to die. I worked as a tree surgeon in my early twenties, cutting those great trees in the Finger Lakes area of New York State, the traditional lands of the Cayuga Nation of the Iroquois.

As I cut them, I remembered how their bark had once been used to cover the old longhouses and how the elm was a central tree for the old-time survival of the Iroquois. But an insect, introduced inadvertently, like the flus and measles and smallpox and the other diseases of humans that killed more than 90 percent of the natives of North America in the sixteenth and seventeenth centuries, brought with it Dutch elm disease and spelt the end of the great trees.

Those trees were so beautiful, their limbs so graceful, their small leaves a green fountain in the springtime, a message that it was time to plant the corn as soon as they were the size of a squirrel's ear. And now they are all gone because of the coming of the Europeans. Now, in the last few years, the maple trees of New York and New England have begun to die, from the top down—weakened, some say, by the acid rain that falls, acid blown into the clouds by the smokestacks of the industries of the Ohio Valley, smoke carried across the land to fall as poison.

Is the Earth sick? From a purely human perspective, the answer must certainly be yes. Things that humans count on for survival—basic things such as clean water and clean air—have been affected.

The Iroquois prophecies also said a time would come when the air would be harmful to breathe and the water harmful to drink. That time is now. The waters of the St. Lawrence River are so full of chemicals from industries, like Kaiser and Alcoa, on its shores that the turtles are covered with cancers. (In the story of Creation as told by the Haudenosaunee, it was the Great Turtle that floated up from the depths and offered its back as a place to support the Earth.)

Tom Porter, a Bear Clan chief of the Mohawks, used to catch fish from that same river to feed his family. The water that flowed around their island, part of the small piece of land still legally in the hands of the Mohawk people and called the St. Regis Reservation, that water brought them life. But a few years ago, he saw that the fish were no longer safe to eat. They would poison his children. He left his nets by the banks of the river. They are still there, rotting.

If we see "the Earth" as the web of life that sustains us, then there is no question that the web is weakened, that the Earth is sick. But if we look at it from another side, from the view of the living Earth itself, then the sickness is not that of the planet, the sickness is embodied in human beings, and, if carried to its illogical conclusion, the sickness will not kill the Earth, it will kill us.

Human self-importance is a big part of the problem. It is because we human beings have one power that no other creatures have—the power to upset the natural balance—that we are so dangerous to ourselves. Because we have that great power, we have been given ceremonies and lesson stories (which in many ways are ceremonies in and of themselves) to remind us of our proper place.

We are not the strongest of all the beings in Creation. In many ways, we are the weakest. We were given original instructions by the Creator. Those instructions, to put them as simply as possible, were to be kind to each other and to respect the Earth. It is because we human beings tend to forget those instructions that the Creator gave us stories like the tales of Gluskabe and sends teachers like the Peacemaker and Handsome Lake every now and then to help us remember and return us to the path of the Good Mind.

I am speaking now not of Europeans but of native people themselves. There are many stories in the native traditions of North America—like the Hopi tales of previous worlds being destroyed when human beings forgot those instructions—that explain what can happen when we lose sight of our proper place. Such stories and those teachers exist to keep human beings in balance, to keep our eyes focused, to help us recognize our place as part of the circle of Creation, not above it. When we follow our original instructions, we are equal to the smallest insects and the greatest whales, and if we take the

lives of any other being in this circle of Creation it must be for the right reason—to help the survival of our own people, not to threaten the survival of
the insect people or the whale people.

If we gather medicinal herbs, we must never take all that we find, only a
few. We should give thanks and offer something in exchange, perhaps a bit
of tobacco, and we should always loosen the earth and plant seeds so that
more will grow.

But we, as humans, are weak and can forget. So the stories and the teachers who have been given the message from Creation come to us and we listen
and we find the right path again.

That had been the way on this continent for tens of thousands of years
before the coming of the Europeans. Ten thousand years passed after the
deaths of the great beasts on this continent—those huge beings like the cave
bear and the mammoth and the giant sloth, animals that my Abenaki people
remember in some of our stories as monsters that threatened the lives of the
people—before another living being on this continent was brought to
extinction.

If it was native people who killed off those great animals ten thousand
years ago, then it seems they learned something from that experience. The
rattlesnake is deadly and dangerous, the grizzly and the polar bear have been
known to hunt and kill human beings, but in native traditions those creatures are honored even as they are feared; the great bear is seen as closely related to human beings, and the rattlesnake is sometimes called Grandfather.

Then, with the coming of the Europeans, that changed. In the five hundred years since the arrival of Columbus on the shores of Hispaniola, hundreds of species have been exterminated. It has been done largely for profit,
not for survival. And as the count goes higher, not only the survival of other
species is in question but also the survival of the human species.

Part of my own blood is European because, like many native Americans
today, many of my ancestors liked the new white people and the new black
people (some of whom escaped from slavery and formed alliances and even,
for a time, African/Indian maroon nations on the soils of the two American
continents—such as the republic of Palmares in northeastern Brazil, which
lasted most of the seventeenth century). I am not ashamed of any part of my
racial ancestry. I was taught that it is not what is in the blood but what is carried in the culture that makes human beings lose their balance and forget
their rightful place.

The culture of those human beings from Europe, however, had been at war with nature for a long time. They cut down most of their forests and killed most of the wild animals. For them, wildness was something to be tamed. To the native peoples of North America, wilderness was home, and it was not "wild" until the Europeans made it so. Still, I take heart at the thought that many of those who came to this hemisphere from Europe quickly learned to see with a native eye. So much so that the leaders of the new colonies (which were the first multinational corporations and had the express purpose of making money for the mother country—not of seeking true religious freedom, for they forbade any religions but their own) just as quickly passed laws to keep their white colonists from "going native."

If you do not trust my memory, then take a look at the words written by those colonizing Europeans themselves. You will find laws still on the books in Massachusetts that make it illegal for a man to have long hair. Why? Because it was a sign of sympathy with the Indians who wore their hair long. You will find direct references to colonists "consorting with the devil" by living like the "savages."

The native way of life, the native way of looking at the world and the way we humans live in that world, was attractive and meaningful. It was also more enjoyable. It is simple fact that the native people of New England, for example, were better fed, better clothed, and healthier than the European colonists. They also had more fun. European chroniclers of the time often wrote of the way in which the Indians made even work seem like play. They turned their work, such as planting a field or harvesting, into a communal activity with laughter and song.

Also, the lot of native women was drastically different from that of the colonial women. Native women had control over their own lives. They could decide who they would or would not marry, they owned their own land, they had true reproductive freedom (including herbal methods of birth control), and they had political power. In New England, women chiefs were not uncommon, and throughout the Northeast there were various arrangements giving women direct control in choosing chiefs. (To this day, among the Haudenosaunee, it is the women of each clan who choose the chiefs to represent them in the Grand Council of the League.)

In virtually every aspect of native life in North America—and I realize this is a huge generalization, for there were more than four hundred different cultures in North America alone in the fifteenth century and great differences between them—the idea of the circle, in one form or another, was a guiding principle. There was no clock time, but cyclical time. The seasons completed a circle, and so too did our human lives.

If we gather berries or hunt game in one place this year, then we may return to that place the following year to do the same. We must take care of that place properly—burning off the dry brush and dead berry bushes so that the ashes will fertilize the ground and new canes will grow, while at the same time ensuring that there will still be a clearing there in the forest with new green growth for the deer to eat.

The whole idea of wildlife conservation and ecology, in fact, was common practice among the native peoples of this continent. (There is also very sound documented evidence of the direct influence of native people and native ideas of a "land ethic" on people such as Henry David Thoreau, George Bird Grinnell, Ernest Thompson Seton, and others who were the founders of organizations like the Audubon Society, the Boy Scouts of America, and the whole modern conservation movement itself.) There was not, therefore, the European idea of devastating your own backyard and then moving on to fresh ground—to a new frontier (the backyard of your weaker neighbor).

If you see things in terms of circles and cycles, and if you care about the survival of your children, then you begin to engage in commonsense practices. By trial and error, over thousands of years, perhaps, you learn how to do things right. You learn to live in a way that keeps in mind, as native elders put it, seven generations. You ask yourself—as an individual and as a nation—how will the actions I take affect the seven generations to come? You do not think in terms of a four-year presidency or a yearly national budget, artificial creations that mean nothing positive in terms of the health of the Earth and the people. You say to yourself, what will happen if I cut these trees and the birds can no longer nest there? What will happen if I kill the female deer who has a fawn so that no animals survive to bring a new generation into the world? What will happen if I divert the course of this river or build a dam so that the fish and animals and plants downstream are deprived of water? What will happen if I put all the animals in my game bag?

And then, as the cycles of the seasons pass, you explain in the form of lesson stories what will happen when the wrong actions are taken. Then you will remember and your children's children will remember. There are thousands of such lesson stories still being kept by the native people of North America, and it is time for the world as a whole to listen.

The circle is the way to see. The circle is the way to live, always keeping in mind the seven generations to come, always asking: how will my deeds affect the lives of my children's children's children?

This is the message I have heard again and again. I give that message to you. My own "ethnic heritage" is a mixture of European and native, but the messages I have heard best and learned the most from spring from this native soil.

If someone as small and pitiful as I am can learn from those ancient messages and speak well enough to touch the lives of others, then it seems to me that any human being—native or nonnative—has the ability to listen and to learn. It is because of that belief that I share these words, for all the people of the Earth.

Excerpts from
I, Rigoberta Menchú:
An Indian Woman in Guatemala

Rigoberta Menchú
QUECHUA, GUATEMALA

The Nahual

*That night he spent howling like a coyote while he
slept as a person.
To become animal, without ceasing to be a person.
Animal and person coexist in them through the will
of their progenitors at birth.*
—Miguel Angel Asturias, *Men of Maize*

Every child is born with a *nahual*. The *nahual* is like a shadow, his protective spirit who will go through life with him. The *nahual* is the representative of the earth, the animal world, the sun and water, and in this way the child communicates with nature. The *nahual* is our double, something very important to us. We conjure up an image of what our *nahual* is like. It is usually an animal. The child is taught that if he kills an animal, that animal's human double will be very angry with him because he is killing his *nahual*. Every animal has its human counterpart and if you hurt him, you hurt the animal too.

Our days are divided into dogs, cats, bulls, birds, etc. There is a *nahual* for every day. If a child is born on a Wednesday, his *nahual* is a sheep. The day of his birth decides his *nahual*. So for a Wednesday child, every Wednesday is special. Parents know what a child's behavior will be from the day of the week he is born. Tuesday is a bad day to be born because the child will grow up bad-tempered. That is because Tuesday's *nahual* is a bull and bulls are always angry. The child whose *nahual* is a cat will like fighting with his brothers and sisters.

We have ten sacred days, as our ancestors have always had. These ten days have their *nahual*. They can be dogs, cats, horses, bulls, but they can also be wild animals, like lions. Trees can be *nahuals* too: trees chosen by our ancestors many centuries ago. A *nahual* is not always only one animal. With dogs, for example, nine dogs represent a *nahual*. Or in the case of horses, three. It can vary a lot. You don't know how many, in fact, or rather, only the parents know the number of animals which go to make the *nahuals* of these ten special days. For us the meekest days are Wednesday, Monday, Saturday, and Sunday. Their *nahuals* are sheep, or birds, or animals which don't harm other animals.

All this is explained to young people before they get married so that when they have children they know which animal represents each day. One very important thing they have to remember is not to tell the child what his *nahual* is until he is grown up. We are only told what our *nahual* is when our personalities are formed and our parents see what our behavior is normally. Otherwise a child might take advantage of his *nahual*. For example, if his *nahual* is a bull, he might like fighting and could say, "I behave like this because I'm such and such an animal and you must put up with me." If a child doesn't know his *nahual* he cannot use it as an excuse. He may be compared to the animal, but that is not identifying him with his *nahual*. Younger children don't know the *nahual* of their elder brothers and sisters. They are told all this only when they are mature enough and this could be at any age between ten and twelve. When this happens the animal which is his *nahual* is given to him as a present. If it is a lion, however, it is replaced by something else. Only our parents, or perhaps other members of the community who were there when we were born, know the day of our birth. People from other villages don't know and they are told only if they become close friends.

A day has a special meaning only if a child is born on it. If no baby is born on any one Tuesday, it is of no interest to anyone. That is, there is no celebration. We often come to love the animal which is our *nahual* even before we know what it is. Although we love all the natural world, we are often drawn to one particular animal more than to others. We grow to love it. Then one day we are told that it is our *nahual*. All the kingdoms which exist on this earth are related to man. Man is part of the natural world. There is not one world for man and one for animals; they are part of the same one and lead parallel lives. We can see this in our surnames. Many of us have surnames which are the names of animals. *Quej*, meaning horse, for example.

We Indians have always hidden our identity and kept our secrets to ourselves. This is why we are discriminated against. We often find it hard to talk about ourselves because we know we must hide so much in order to preserve our Indian culture and prevent it being taken away from us. So I can tell you only very general things about the *nahual*. I can't tell you what my *nahual* is because that is one of our secrets.

Ceremonies for Sowing Time and Harvest: Relationships with the Earth

....

Sown to be eaten, it is the sacred sustenance of the men who were made of maize. Sown to make money, it means famine for the men who were made of maize.

　　　　　—Miguel Angel Asturias, *Men of Maize*

The seed is something pure, something sacred. For our people the seed is very significant.

　　　　　—Rigoberta Menchú

There's another custom for our twelfth birthday. We're given a little pig, or a lamb, or one or two chickens. These little animals have to reproduce and that depends on each person, on the love we give our parents' present. I remember when I was twelve, my father gave me a little pig. I was also given two little chickens and a lamb. I love sheep very much. These animals are not to be touched or sold without my permission. The idea is for a child to start looking after his own needs. I intended my animals to reproduce but I also intended to love the animals belonging to my brothers and sisters and my parents. I felt really happy. It's one of the most wonderful things that can happen. I was very pleased with my little animals. Years and years can go past without us eating beef. With us, eating a chicken is a big event.

It wasn't long before my little pig grew and had five little piglets. I had to feed them without neglecting my work for my parents. I had to find food for them myself. So what I used to do was, after work in the fields, I'd come back home at six or seven in the evening, do all my jobs in the house for the next morning, and then at about nine o'clock I'd start weaving. Sometimes I'd weave until ten. When we'd stop for our food out in the fields, I'd hang my weaving up on a branch and carry on weaving there. After about fifteen days, I'd have three or four pieces of cloth to sell, and I'd buy maize or other little things for my pigs to eat. That's how I looked after my little pigs. I also started preparing some ground with a hoe to sow a bit of maize for them. When my pigs were seven months old, I sold them and was able to sow a bit of maize for the mother pig so she could go on having piglets. I could also buy myself a *corte* and other things to put on, and enough thread to make or weave a blouse, a *huipil.* That's how you provide for your needs and, in the end, I had three grown-up pigs, ready for me to sell. At the beginning it's difficult. I didn't know what to give them to eat. I'd collect plants in the fields to give my piglets and when I made the dogs' food, I used to take a bit for them too. By the time the first little animals are born, our parents can tell if our *nahual* gives us the qualities for getting on well with animals. I was one of those who loved animals, and they always turned out very well for me. Animals loved me too. Cows, for instance, were never awkward with me. My parents were very pleased with me.

For us women, Sunday was the day we went to the river to wash clothes. Mother or father would go to market to buy things, but some Sundays they didn't have to go because we don't eat very much that comes from the market. We mostly eat maize and plants. We go there to sell, when we harvest our beans. We grow little beans but we don't eat them. They all go to market so we can buy the few provisions we use from market, like soap, salt, and some chile. Sometimes we can't sell our beans because nobody buys them. Everyone is selling the beans they've grown, so the traders come and pay what they choose. If we ask a little more, they don't buy. But for us it's almost a day's walk to the town, and it's difficult to get horses because only two or three people have horses. When we need one we ask a neighbor to lend us one, but many people want to borrow and some are left without horses. So we have to carry our beans on our backs. I used to carry forty or fifty pounds of beans or maize from our house to the town. We'd sell maize too when there was something we needed to buy.

Most villagers hardly ever go down to the town. We only go when we're needed to carry all our goods to town, and then two or three of my brothers and sisters would go. Otherwise, just my father, or my mother, or a neighbor would go. It's the custom with us on Saturday nights to go from house to house asking if any neighbor is going to town next day and if they say, "Yes," we say, "Will you bring us this thing or that thing?" And that neighbor buys what the whole community needs. So when my mother goes to town, she shouts very loud to all the neighbors: "I'm going to market," and they say,

"Buy us soap, buy us salt, buy us chile," and tell her how much she should buy. Then another neighbor will come and offer a horse, if a horse is needed. So we all help one another. This is how we sell things as well. Most people in our village make straw plaits for hats, or they make mats, or weave cloth, so at the weekend they get it all together for one person to sell. This way we don't all have to go to market.

The times we spend up in our village are happy times because we're there to harvest the maize, and before we harvest the maize, we have a fiesta. The fiesta really starts months before when we asked the earth's permission to cultivate her. In that ceremony we burn incense, the elected leaders say prayers, and then the whole community prays. We burn candles in our own houses and other candles for the whole community. Then we bring out the seeds we will be sowing. With maize, for instance, the seeds for the coming year are picked out as soon as the cobs start to grow. We choose them and put a mark on them. The cob is peeled or left in its leaves but those grains are taken off, and the big ones are wrapped in the leaves and made into a little ball. The small ones are cooked straight away and made into a *tortilla* the next day and eaten, so we don't waste even the smallest part of these cobs. The big seeds, wrapped in the leaves in little balls, are left in the branches of a tree to wait, to be dried as carefully as possible. It has to be a place where none of the women pass over them, or jump on them or anything, nor where the hens and chickens or any other animal can walk on them—where dogs, for example, can't get them. In front of our house there is a big tree where we put everything like that. A child stands watch to see that nothing gets at them.

Before the seeds are sown in the ground, we perform a ceremony. We choose two or three of the biggest seeds and place them in a ring, candles representing earth, water, animals, and the universe (that is, man). In our culture, the universe is man. The seed is honored because it will be buried in something sacred—the earth—and because it will multiply and bear fruit the next year. We do it mainly because the seed is something pure, something sacred. For us the word seed is very significant. The candles are lit in every house. We put in some *ayote* too, because that will be sown together with the maize. And we do the same with beans. It is like an offering to the one God. This will be our food for the coming year. During the fiesta, prayers are given up to the earth, the moon, the sun, the animals, and the water, all of which join with the seed to provide our food. Each member of the family makes a vow and promises not to waste the food.

The next day everyone calls to each other to go and start sowing. The whole community rejoices when we begin to sow our maize. When we reach the fields, the men sow the maize and the beans. The seeds go in the same hole. The women follow, planting the *ayotes* in between the furrows to make the most of every bit of land. Others, children usually, follow sowing gourds, *chilacayote*, or potatoes. Children like sowing potatoes. We plant everything at the same time. Then we have to look after the maize because there are many kinds of animals in the mountains and, at sowing time, they come and dig up the seeds. So we take it in turns to keep watch in the fields, taking a turn around the fields now and again during the night. Raccoons, squirrels, *taltuzas*, and other rodents are the ones that come at night. During the day, it's the birds. We're happy to take turns keeping watch because we fall asleep by the tree trunks. We like setting traps everywhere we think an animal is likely to come. We set traps but when the poor animals cry out, we go and see. Since they are animals and our parents have forbidden us to kill them, we let them go after we've given them a telling off so that they won't come back. If the dogs kill them, we eat them but, generally, we don't kill animals. We only kill them accidentally. When the leaves start sprouting, they stop digging up the seeds.

When the maize starts growing, we all go back down to the *fincas* on the coast to work. When we come back, the maize has grown and needs attention. It needs weeding out. When that's done, we go back to the *finca*. When the maize is high, it needs attending to again. These are the two most difficult parts of growing maize; after that it can be left to itself. We have to put little pieces of earth round the roots so that the stalks don't get knocked over by the wind. While it is growing, the women often don't go to the *fincas* but stay and look after the beans, putting in little sticks for them to wind round so they don't interfere with the maize. They look after the *ayotes* too, and all the varieties of gourds.

Maize is the center of everything for us. It is our culture. The *milpa* is the maize field. *Maíz* is the grain. The *mazorca* is the body of the maize, the cob. The *tuza* is the leaf which envelops the cob, especially when it's dry. The *xilote* is the core. That's why we called it *xilotear* when the fruit begins to grow. Maize is used for food and for drink, and we also use the *xilote* for bottle stoppers and food for the dogs and pigs.

The animals start coming into the maize fields again when the cobs appear. The birds eat them and the animals come from the mountains for them.

So we have to keep guard again. It's usually the children who look after the fields; shouting and throwing earth all day to keep the birds away. All the neighbors are in their fields shouting. When the cob starts to grow, we have other customs. One custom is when we start using the leaves of the maize plant to make *tamales*. We don't cut them or use them straight away, but have a special ceremony before we cut the first leaf. All our village sows their maize in the same way but it doesn't always grow the same. Some turn out small, some big, and some even bigger. So the neighbors with the most maize must share their big leaves with the others. For us, using a maize leaf for our *tamales* makes them very tasty, and we want to give some meaning to it, so that's why we celebrate the first leaves. Then comes the fiesta. After we've used the first leaves, when we've eaten the *tamales* inside, we don't throw the leaves away but make a pile of them. We roll them up and hang them in a corner of the house in remembrance of the first harvest the earth gave up. Then comes the ripe maize cob. Sometimes we eat it when it's still very young but only if we really need to because it's bigger when the cob has matured. But it's mountainous there and the cobs fall off with the winds. We have to pick up the maize which falls and eat that too.

At harvest time, we also celebrate the first day we pick the maize cobs, and the rest of what our small plots of land yield. The women pick the beans and the men pick the maize; we all harvest the fruits of our labor together. But before we pick them, we have a ceremony in which the whole community thanks the earth and the God who feeds us. Everyone is very happy because they don't have to go down to the *finca* and work now that they have food. The ceremony to celebrate the harvest is nearly the same as the one where we ask the earth's permission to cultivate her. We thank her for the harvest she's given us. Our people show their happiness, their gratitude for this food, this maize, which took so long to grow. It's a victory for the whole community when they harvest their crops and they all get together for a feast. So we have a celebration at the beginning of the *tapizca*; and at the end of the *tapizca* we have another.

Every village has a community house which is used for meetings, for prayers, for fiestas, or anything else. It's a big house which can hold a lot of people. It has a kitchen and a *tapanco* to store the communal maize. The whole community assembles there to celebrate our faith, to pray. If we don't do it every Friday, then it's every Monday. So the whole village gets together, even when there are no special ceremonies or fiestas to celebrate. We get together to pray or just to talk to each other. We tell each other our experiences. We don't need an agenda; it's a dialogue between us. We also play with the children for a while. This happens once a week. Either on a Friday or a Monday.

At the beginning everybody works communally, clearing the bush in the mountains. How many years would that take one family? We work together: the women pulling out the small plants below and the men cutting down trees on the mountainside. When sowing time comes, the community meets to discuss how to share out the land—whether each one will have his own plot or if they will work collectively. Everyone joins in the discussion. In my village, for example, we said it was up to all of us if we wanted our own plot or not. But we also decided to keep a common piece of land, shared by the whole community, so that if anyone was ill or injured, they would have food to eat. We worked in that way: each family with their own plot and a large piece of common land for emergencies in the community or in the family. It was mostly to help widows. Each day of the week, someone would go and work that common land.

The Natural World: The Earth, Mother of Man
• • • • • • • • • • • • • • • • • •

We must respect the one God at the heart of the sky, which is the Sun.

—Rigoberta Menchú

Tojil, in his own natural darkness, struck the leather of his sandal with a stone, and from it, at that very moment, came a spark, then a flash, followed by a flame, and the new fire burned in all its splendour.

—Popul Vuh

From very small children we receive an education which is very different from white children, *ladinos*. We Indians have more contact with nature. That's why they call us polytheistic. But we're not polytheistic . . . or if we are, it's good, because it's our culture, our customs. We worship—or rather not worship but respect—a lot of things to do with the natural world, the most important things for us. For instance, to us, water is sacred. Our parents tell us when we're very small not to waste water, even when we have it.

Water is pure, clean, and gives life to man. Without water we cannot survive, nor could our ancestors have survived. The idea that water is sacred is in us children, and we never stop thinking of it as something pure. The same goes for the earth. Our parents tell us: "Children, the earth is the mother of man, because she gives him food." This is especially true for us whose life is based on the crops we grow. Our people eat maize, beans, and plants. We can't eat ham, or cheese, or things made with equipment, with machines. So we think of the earth as the mother of man, and our parents teach us to respect the earth. We must only harm the earth when we are in need. This is why, before we sow our maize, we have to ask the earth's permission.

Pom, copal, is a sacred ingredient for our people. We use it to express our feelings for the earth, so that she will allow us to cultivate her. *Copal* is the resin of a tree. It has a smell like incense. We burn it and it gives off a very strong smell: a smoke with a very rich, delicious aroma. We use the candle, water, and lime a great deal in our ceremonies. We use candles to represent the earth, water, and maize, which is the food of man. We believe (and this has been passed down to us by our ancestors) that our people are made of maize. We're made of white maize and yellow maize. We must remember this. We put a candle out for man, as the son of the natural world, the universe; and the members of the family join together in prayer. The prayers usually ask the earth for permission to plant our crops at sowing time, to give us a good harvest, and then to give thanks with all our might, with all our being, for a good harvest.

The prayers and ceremonies are for the whole community. We pray to our ancestors, reciting their prayers which have been known to us for a long time—a very, very long time. We evoke the representatives of the animal world; we say the names of dogs. We say the names of the earth, the God of the earth, and the God of water. Then we say the name of the heart of the sky—the Sun. Our grandfathers say we must ask the sun to shine on all its children: the trees, animals, water, man. We ask it to shine on our enemies. To us an enemy is someone who steals or goes into prostitution. So, you see, it's a different world. This is how we make our pleas and our promises. It doesn't refer so much to the real world, but it includes part of our reality. A prayer is made up of all this. We make a definite plea to the earth. We say: "Mother Earth, you who gives us food, whose children we are and on whom we depend, please make this produce you give us flourish and make our children and our animals grow . . . ," and other things as well. Or we say: "We make our vows for ten days so that you concede us permission, your permission, Mother Earth, who are sacred, to feed us and give our children what they need. We do not abuse you, we only beg your permission, you who are part of the natural world and part of the family of our parents and our grandparents." This means we believe, for instance, that the sun is our grandfather, that he is a member of our family. "We respect you and love you and ask that you love us as we love you"—those prayers are specially for the earth. For the sun, we say: "Heart of the sky, you are our father, we ask you to give your warmth and light to our animals, our maize, our beans, our plants, so that they may grow and our children may eat." We evoke the color of the sun; and this has a special importance for us because this is how we want our children to live—like a light which shines, which shines with generosity. It means a warm heart and it means strength, life-giving strength. It's something you never lose and you find it everywhere. So when we evoke the color of the sun, it's like evoking all the elements which go to make up our life. The sun, as the channel to the one God, receives the plea from his children that they should never violate the rights of all the other beings which surround them. This is how we renew our prayer which says that men, the children of the one God, must respect the life of the trees, the birds, the animals around us. We say the names of birds and animals—cows, horses, dogs, cats. All these. We mention them all. We must respect the life of every single one of them. We must respect the life, the purity, the sacredness, which is water. We must respect the one God, the heart of the sky, which is the sun. We must not do evil while the sun shines upon his children. This is a promise. Then we promise to respect the life of the one creature, which is man. This is very important. We say: "We cannot harm the life of one of your children; we are your children. We cannot kill any of your creatures, neither trees nor animals." Then we offer up a sheep or chickens, because we believe sheep to be sacred animals, quiet animals, saintly animals, animals which don't harm other animals. They are the most tranquil animals that exist, like birds. So the community chooses certain small animals for the feast after the ceremonies.

The Day the Mountain Said No

··

Pablo Santos
AETA, PHILIPPINES

When Mount Pinatubo in the Philippines erupted in June 1991, in what has turned out to be this century's most violent volcanic explosion, the Aeta people thought it was the end of their world.

The Aeta, an indigenous people who settled on the present-day island of Luzon some twenty thousand years ago, had long known their way of life was threatened—but they were sure it was going to be man's abuse of nature that would eventually deal the final blow.

They were not prepared for the day Mount Pinatubo literally blew its top off, spewing out more than eight cubic kilometers of searing rocks, lava, and dust high into the atmosphere before coming to rest within a fifty-kilometer radius of the mountain.

It was the elders who saw the eruption as the sign that Mount Pinatubo— Apo Mamalyari (Creator)—had finally said no to its desecration by man.

For thousands of years, the Aeta people had lived in the thick rain forests of the Zambales Range, a jagged ridge that forms the spine along Luzon's southwestern coast. Many lived in the thick jungles on the slopes of Mount Pinatubo, and its relative remoteness sheltered the Aeta from persecution by the lowland settlers—first Malay, then Spanish. Their lives on and around what modern-day geologists had declared to be a dormant or extinct volcano, which last erupted about six hundred years ago, revolved around a fundamental principle: "Land is life."

It is a phrase that to outsiders often has sounded like a cliché or slogan. But to the indigenous people of the Philippines these are three words that describe their sacred bond with Mother Earth.

All the indigenous people of the Philippines believe they are the sons and daughters of the Earth. "The Earth is the breast that feeds us," in the words of Datu Mandagese of Agusan on the island of Mindanao over five hundred kilometers to the south of Luzon. "The land is an extension of our body. Anything that causes damage to the Earth causes the same to the Lumad (non-Muslim hill tribes in Mindanao). When the land is abused, so are the Lumad." For the Aeta people, land cannot be bought or sold, it cannot be owned by just one person—the Earth is for everybody so that everyone can live. Why can't the Aeta sell land? Because land was created by the supreme deity for their parents, themselves, and their children. The Earth is sacred.

Long before the government officials came along, the Aeta had laws of the land through the leaders, chief, warriors, and priests that marked boundaries using mountains, streams, rivers, and old trees. The land was where the ancestors were born, where they died, and were buried. On Aeta land, the destruction of the forests began with the arrival of people who did not respect the trees and mountains. Tall, sturdy trees were replaced by smaller, fast-growing trees; and when these were harvested the land eroded. The rivers became dirty and the fish scarce. Then even the fish disappeared because of silting in the lakes and lagoons.

For the indigenous people of the Philippines, respect for land is respect for life itself. Land and life are one and the same.

But land has always been a source of conflict. This is especially true when it has come to relations with the authorities, where the value attached to land by indigenous people is exactly the opposite of that of the government. While the indigenous people look at land as life itself, governments, past and present, look at land as a commodity. While the indigenous people look at land as a source of life for all generations, the government looks at land as a source of huge profits for a few.

Land provides not only for the physical needs of the indigenous people, it provides a line of continuity from the past to the present. It mirrors a history of struggle in defense of a homeland. Land is home. It defines the relationship of people within and outside the community.

The difference spells conflict between the government and the indigenous people, with the latter at a disadvantage. After all, the government has all the means—from laws to arms—to enforce its programs and facilitate the operations of profit-making corporations within the confines of the communal territories of the indigenous people.

Intrusion into ancestral lands and exploitation of their natural resources

began as early as the country's colonization by Spain in the mid-sixteenth
century.

To legitimize such plunder, land laws were enacted during the Spanish
period, institutionalized during the U.S. regime toward the end of the nineteenth century, followed to the letter by succeeding pseudo-independent
Philippine governments, made more repressive and exploitative under the regime of Ferdinand Marcos, and vigorously implemented under the present
authorities.

These laws virtually rendered the indigenous people squatters on their
own lands. And it was these laws that gave the Philippine government the
"right" to prospect for geothermal energy on Mount Pinatubo, drilling deep
into the mountain to tap the heat in its bowels.

Not only that, the sides of the mountain were full of illegal loggers and
poverty-stricken lowland peasants nibbling away at Pinatubo's last remaining
forests. At the same time, war planes from the nearby U.S. Clark Air Base
used a valley below the mountain for target practice, and the Aeta had long
grown accustomed to the thunder of low-flying jets and earthshaking
explosions.

So our elders were not surprised when the earth heaved and the mountain
threw its bowels out into the surrounding atmosphere, some of the dust circling the globe and reddening sunsets on the other side of the planet.

No one yet has a precise count, but as many as one hundred Aeta perished
as the first pyroclastic flows snuffed out the forests and enveloped their flimsy
huts. Those who ran to nearby caves or fled down the mountain were saved.
Of the estimated thirty thousand Aeta living on Pinatubo, about seventeen
thousand are now in an evacuation center in Baquilan on the coast. Here the
Philippine government is trying to assimilate the Aeta into life in the
lowlands.

For a community that was already at the threshold of cultural extinction,
the eruption of Pinatubo has hastened the demise of the tribal ways in which
the natural environment meant everything.

The Aeta's strong oral tradition passed knowledge and skills about jungle
survival from generation to generation. Every valley, river, rock, outcrop, or
tree in Pinatubo had a significance in Aeta lore.

Today, deposits as thick as two hundred meters cover some valleys. Military helicopter pilots who have flown over the crater describe scenes like

those seen on other planets. Aeta elders say Apo Mamalyari (the Creator) was angry at man's abuse of nature, like the geothermal drilling, the bombing by the jets, and the denudation of forests on the sacred mountain. Their alien and squalid life in the camps is now seen as the punishment of Pinatubo.

The Aeta themselves were nomadic and later practiced shifting agriculture—burning a small area of forest, growing root crops in the ashes, and moving on. But their traditional slash-and-burn practice has always been carefully done to give time for nature to regenerate itself. All natural things, living and nonliving, are believed to be inhabited by spirits that cannot be offended.

Modern Western anthropologists have studied the Aeta, and the U.S. military even used their knowledge of jungle survival to train U.S. soldiers during the Vietnam War. The Aeta have a vast storehouse of knowledge of the species of plant and animal life on the mountain and are able to identify four hundred and fifty types of plants and even twenty species of ants.

But, after generations of freedom, the Aeta now have a hard time coming to grips with camp life. They even look uncomfortable in the trousers and T-shirts supplied by relief agencies. Almost six hundred Aeta, mostly children, died in the camps in the five months following the eruption. They lack immunity to lowland diseases like measles, pneumonia, and malaria, and many have succumbed to diarrheal dehydration. Without access to their forest herbs, the Aeta have not been able to administer their traditional medications. Aeta shamans are also hesitant to perform their healing rituals because camp officials make fun of them.

Looked at in historical perspective, the eruption of Mount Pinatubo seems like the final crushing blow against the Aeta. These people, described by anthropologists as a small, black, kinky-haired people who are ethnic cousins of the Australian aborigines, had already suffered enough.

Lowland chauvinism, discrimination, and greed for land had already forced the Aeta to retreat farther and higher up the mountains. Aeta ancestral grounds, even in the early nineteenth century, were eyed for housing, agriculture, and commercial settlements for the lowlanders—the Unat, or "people with straight hair."

Since then, the appropriate laws in place, and bombs and bullets ready, transnational and multinational corporations have ravaged the resources within the ancestral lands of the indigenous people. A long list of corporations—in the logging, mining, agribusiness, and plantation sectors—cling like leeches to Aeta ancestral lands, considered by the government the final frontier for extracting resources to make a profit.

Seeing one's land raped by foreigners is enraging. For it to be done with the full blessing of the government is unbearable. To facilitate and attract corporate profit-making, the government has built dams, geothermal plants, roads, and bridges as support and complementary mechanisms. All of this is viewed by the indigenous people as an assault on life itself, a direct cause of environmental destruction. It is a case of greed subverting life, they say.

Take the case of another of the Philippines' mountains, Mount Apo, or Apo Sandawa to the tribes living in the area. Mount Apo, the Philippines' highest mountain peak, is not just a tourist spot or a laboratory for the scientist interested in biodiversity. To the Lumad of the area it is much more— it is a sacred place, similar to the Christian's cathedral. But the government did not consider it sacrilegious when it allowed blasting on parts of the sacred mountain and felled hundreds of trees to put up a geothermal plant to supply 23 percent of Mindanao's electricity requirements. All in the name of development.

Under the administration of Ferdinand Marcos, mining and timber companies, plantation owners, settlers, and traders were given first priority. Back in Luzon, reservations established by the government in the province of Pampanga were sorry substitutes for resource-rich ancestral lands. The Aeta had been resisting "development aggression" on Mount Pinatubo long before it erupted.

In the 1980s, the Philippine national oil company dug three wells to prospect for geothermal energy sources, evicting Aeta from the region in the process. When the wells proved unproductive, the oil company abandoned them but did not bother to prevent or monitor the possible environmental consequences of the drilling. Aeta elders say the vents of the three wells have been emitting sulphuric steam. They think there is a connection between this and the cataclysmic eruption of June 1991.

The forests immediately surrounding the wells had already been killed by the vapors, the soil had become powdery white and acidic, and the rivers that provided the Aeta with water had become muddy and foul-smelling. One nine-year-old girl even died after drinking the water.

Then there is the problem of the U.S. military bases. Although it has been decided not to renew their leases, much damage has already been done. The Aeta have birthright claims over vast areas occupied by the big U.S. military bases in the Philippines—the air force base at Clark and the Subic Bay naval base. In 1910, the establishment of the Clark air base led to massive land-grabbing schemes and forced the Aeta to move higher up the slopes of Mount Pinatubo.

In 1954, during the laying of the foundations for the Subic naval station, scores of Aeta communities succumbed to promises of better livelihood chances in resettlement areas. Since 1900 they have been forced to relocate four or five times.

Aeta living on the fringes of the camps have been shot and killed indiscriminately by U.S. guards while scavenging among the garbage. Records of how Aeta children were shot after being mistaken for wild boar, or how elderly tribeswomen were bitten by fierce guard dogs, only serve to highlight the extensive suffering and humiliation inflicted on the Aeta by the Americans—long after the Philippines became officially independent of U.S. colonial rule.

The resistance of the indigenous people to these so-called developments is often viewed as an expression of nothing more than sentiment for days and times gone by. The indigenous people reply that they are neither sentimentalists nor antidevelopment. If there is a segment of the population that wants development, it is theirs. What they do not want are the projects rammed down their throats by the government. "Projects implemented by the government and those they allow to operate in ancestral areas are not for development," says Kalipunan Ng Mga Katutubong Mamamayan Ng Pilipinas (KAMP), the National Federation of the Indigenous People of the Philippines. "How could these projects lead to development if they cause the displacement of the people who are supposed to be their beneficiaries?"

In January 1990, KAMP, together with minority rights advocacy groups, launched the Campaign against Development Aggression to call the attention of the government and public to the various development projects mushrooming in ancestral areas. "The so-called development projects being implemented by the government only deplete the remaining resources of the country, in addition to causing environmental degradation that adds to the debt burden of the country," KAMP argues.

Even the government's Integrated Social Forestry Program (ISFP), supposedly one of the pillars of the government's campaign for reforestation, has been criticized by the indigenous people because it is being implemented with blatant disregard for ancestral land rights. In essence, the logic of the program is to render indigenous people squatters and to reduce their role to mere caretakers instead of owners of the land. The so-called development projects cause massive problems among indigenous people, who end up as sacrificial lambs on the governmental altar of development.

A slain indigenous leader, Macliing-Dulag, once said: "If life is threatened, what should a man do? Resist. This he must do, otherwise he is dishonored, and that is a worse death. If we do not fight . . . we die anyway. If we fight we die honorably. I exhort you all then—fight."

The indigenous people of the Philippines believe land must be defended against the continued rape by foreign and local big business engaged in logging, mining, chemical-dependent agribusiness plantations, and destructive government projects that continue to threaten the life of all Philippine residents.

"We have always been careful with the Earth," says Datu Makalipay of Agusan in Mindanao. "We will struggle to make sure no one takes what remains of our forests. I will defend our land to prevent further abuse and exploitation of its remaining wealth."

To defend land is to defend life. This is the heart of the indigenous people's struggle. Already there have been some small victories. In Mindanao, for example, there are some six thousand hectares of ancestral lands in South Cotabato that have been reoccupied by B'laan, Bagobo, and Manobo people.

"These lands were taken from us through brute force and deception," says Lumad Mindanaw, the regional alliance of indigenous people in Mindanao.

Land reoccupation signals a new level in the struggle of the indigenous people of the Philippines, who are tired of the government's empty promises and the endless cycle of petition letters to government representatives. In the words of Lumad Mindanaw, it is an "assertion of our ancestral rights."

The problem is that these efforts are not welcome. The people are harassed and silenced. In November 1990, some one hundred ninety houses were strafed and burned in Laconon, South Cotabato, and fourteen T'boli and B'laan were tortured.

"We know now that our struggle to survive exacts a high price. But we are willing to sacrifice anything to defend the source of our life—our land. It will ensure the existence and the future of the next generations," says Lumad Mindanaw.

As Macliing-Dulag said, "To claim a place is the birthright of every man. The lowly animals claim their place. How much more man?" That birthright became all the more difficult to claim the day after the mountain heaved its boiling intestines into the Philippine skies.

Tension has been building between the Aeta and the lowland refugees of Mount Pinatubo, with lowlanders maintaining that the Aeta have been given preference in relief efforts. Some lowlanders have threatened to harass and bomb Aeta evacuation centers. The hostility has led some Aeta to retreat back into what remains of the forests on the foothills of the volcano, where they are trying to pick up the pieces of their lives among the skeletons of the scarred trees on the slopes of ash-covered hills. History has documented that rather than come into conflict with the people of the lowlands, the Aeta would rather go farther back into the forests and live once again as a docile and peace-loving people.

The Aeta, like the other indigenous groups of the Philippines, and indeed of much of Southeast Asia, consider the land to be their life, particularly ancestral lands where natural objects and landmarks are part of their tradition and lore. Having lost their last bastion, the Aeta face an uncertain future in the refugee camps that ring the mountain. And many Aeta have shown that instead of leading a diminished life in the evacuation centers, they would rather risk the desolate landscape and return to their ancient lands to start again to live as their ancestors did.

The Circle Closes in
on the Nomads

•••

Kamoriongo Ole Aimerru Nkongoni
MAASAI, KENYA

*I*n the beginning, God was alone. His Maasai name was Ngai and he was omnipresent and self-reliant. Heaven and Earth were one, joined by water.

After a time, the water started sinking and Heaven and Earth parted. On top of the sinking water floated nests of all sizes, each containing a male and female of a different species. A little nest carried two safari ants, while a huge nest had two elephants. In yet another, there were two human beings, a boy and a girl. God provided food for all these creatures.

Gradually, the water disappeared. Some of it went to the south and some to the north. Mountains rose up and vegetation started growing. As the water sank, the nests came to rest on Earth and they broke, releasing the various animal species—lions, giraffes, flies, and, of course, human beings. All these creatures could speak and they all spoke the same language.

But then a problem arose—what to eat? In the beginning, they all ate fruit, but gradually some of them started to eat grass and some flesh.

It was then that God sent the cows down from Heaven on a ladder. They were sent to Maasinta, the first Maasai, who was told by God, "This is the last time I will do this for you, so you had better love these cattle the same way I love you." Ever since, the Maasai have been devoted to cattle.

The Maasai, a traditionally nomadic people of what is now East Africa, have stayed with their cattle and have loved them as instructed by God. They know that in order to remain healthy, cattle need enough grass and water, and that means continual migration to new pastures.

Today, however, land is no longer for everyone. Land has been sold off in lots, and if the Maasai no longer have grazing grounds, what will they do? A Maasai without cattle is no Maasai.

I belong to the Ilaiser clan of the Purko Maasai and my age-set is Ilterito. Like many traditional peoples of East Africa, the Maasai practice geronto-cracy, the rule of old men, in which social promotion is based on a stratified system of age, with each age-set lasting about fifteen years.

Many members of the Ilterito age-set are now dead, but a few of us still survive. We are the ones who give permission for ceremonies like circumcision to be carried out; we help in cases where people have forgotten the proper ways to do things; we chair the meetings that decide general policies for the community; and we arbitrate in disputes or hand down judgment in criminal cases.

The group that follows us is called Linyangusi, and they are gradually taking over our duties because we are now old (I was born at the beginning of the century). The next age-set is called Eseuri, and this is the group the government prefers if it wants to appoint someone to a position of responsibility, like chief.

The youngest group of elders is called Ilkitoyiip. They are the ones who work the hardest since they are young and strong. They might be required to fight lions, drive the cattle long distances, or look for lost cows.

The cows are always at the center of the Maasai way of life. When God first sent down the cows to Maasinta, the women were jealous because the cows had more milk. One day, a woman was talking to a cow. She said, "My breasts do not have enough milk for my child." The cow replied: "You can milk two of mine but leave two for my calf."

Then the woman said, "My child needs meat," and the cow said, "Take a bow and arrow. Tie my neck with a rope and shoot the arrow at my vein. Take out my blood. It will clot and be like meat."

The woman said, "My child needs fat," to which the cow answered, "Put my milk in a gourd and let it become sour. Then shake it and you will have fat."

Finally, the woman said, "My child needs bone marrow." Replied the cow: "Now I see what your aim is. You want to bewitch me. Well, you can bewitch me if you want, but before you do I am going to tell you the four things that love me and the four that hate me.

"The four things that love me are man, who always defends me from wild animals; the rainy season, which gives me grass; moonlight; and, lastly, a flat place. The four things that hate me are women, who cannot even bother to protect me; famine, which can bring about my death; darkness, where danger lurks; and the jungle, where wild animals abound.

"I have spoken," the cow concluded. "If you want to bewitch me now, you can."

So the woman went to the man and told him, "The cow is trying to curse our child. We must bewitch her." The man followed the woman's advice and bewitched the cow. From that moment on, the cow and all the other animals could no longer speak.

When God saw what had happened to the animals, he gave them the sense of smell so they could help protect themselves. Man was not given the sense of smell since God knew that if he had that sense as well as the ability to speak, he would have finished off everything on Earth.

After some time, there was a famine. The people were hungry and they started quarreling over food. God decided to create tribes. He gave each tribe wise men and a language and declared what food they should eat. The Kikuyu were given crops, and the Somali and Maasai cows.

For the community to be prosperous, the animals have to get enough to eat, and this is why it is necessary to move around. In the past, a Maasai was able to go and establish his home wherever he wanted if no one was living there. If there was someone there, permission could be sought from that person or from the elders. Where the Maasai went depended on the seasons.

In the rainy season, you move far away from the rivers because animals can drink from pools. This means building different *manyatta* (fenced enclosures with huts and an open space in the middle where the cattle sleep). In the dry season, you have to stay near the rivers because the animals have to drink every other day, or, if the grass is in very short supply, every third day. This means that one or perhaps two days are for grazing and the third for going to the river. Donkeys accompany the cattle and bring back water for the people in the *manyattas*.

Generally, one should try to graze animals as far away from the rivers as possible. If the animals remain too near the rivers, the grass is destroyed. This explains why many *manyattas* are located far from the rivers, in the grasslands. This may be inconvenient for the people but it is better for the animals. It is also important that people live together in one place and that the rest of the area be left for the animals. If people live all over the place, there will not be enough space left for grazing.

I first came to live in the lowlands because it was good for the cows—there was a lot of grass and it was warm. I could not stand seeing my cows dying of tick fever up in the highlands. In those days, this place was good and I was alone here. Now, there are too many people and there is not enough grass. We have to send the cows back up into the hills to get enough to eat.

People stay too much in one place these days. They want to be near water, but the government also wants them to stay in one place. It says this area belongs to this clan and that area to that clan. Now, you can even find land belonging to an individual, which was never the case before. Even then, the Maasai allow others to graze on their land. If they do not, what will happen when they experience drought? They may need to graze on others' land then.

It is obvious that we have to help each other. In the old days, after a drought, if a person was fortunate enough to have had some of his own livestock survive, he was compelled to give some to kinsmen that had lost theirs. This is not so common today.

Cattle will always die off during a drought. That is why it is important to have many. A Maasai who has fewer than fifty cattle is a poor man. One of my age-mates has over two thousand and as a result is highly respected.

People need to be a part of a community, and for the Maasai this begins at circumcision, the first important event in the life of a young man. After he has been circumcised, the young man goes to stay with his fellow *moran* in the bush, facing dangers together. They hunt, become physically strong, and learn how to endure hardship without complaining. Most important, they become part of a group.

But things are changing. In the old days, warriors used to carry out cattle raids (on non-Maasai, naturally). These were acts of bravery, of courage, that took place in broad daylight. Nowadays, they go sneaking about and stealing at night. This is a disgrace to the Maasai.

In my days, the *moran* used to spend a full seven years in the bush. In that way, members of the age-set really got to know one another and to feel like members of a group. Now, with many of the young going to school, they spend much less time on their "*moran*ship" training. So the old discipline and feeling of group solidarity is bound to be less.

When the period of "*moran*ship" is finished, the *eunoto* ceremony is organized to introduce the young warrior as a full member of the community. He can then be given his inheritance by his father and have authority over his own cattle, goats, and other property. He can make his own arrangements for grazing them or even selling them. He may decide to set up his own *manyatta*, or if he continues to stay in his father's *manyatta*, he makes his own gate through which his property passes.

The next important step for a young man is to get married. He may take advice from his father or from his friends about a suitable girl, who must not be of his age-group or clan or be related to him. An ideal wife should come from a good family, one that is wealthy. She should be sociable, kind, hard-working, and tidy. If she likes cows and is good at counting animals, she will be an asset to her husband.

When the new bride arrives in her husband's *manyatta*, he allocates a number of animals she has to milk and take care of. In addition, each of the husband's immediate relatives will give her an animal, and from then on she will be known to these relatives by the gift they gave her. For example, the person who gave her a goat will refer to her as "owner of the goat," while the person who gave her a sheep will call her "owner of the sheep."

The husband will not allocate all his animals to his wife. He will retain some for himself, and should he wish to marry again, he will give the new wife animals from his own stock. It would be wrong to take an animal from one wife and give it to another. But the husband can sell or slaughter an animal he has already allocated to any of his wives.

A young man who has gone through the *eunoto* ceremony is considered a junior elder. He has the right to attend the elders' meetings. There are several types of meetings, those called by individuals to discuss a dispute, for example, and those to discuss general matters concerning the community, such as grazing arrangements or plans to move to another place. If bad grass needs to be burned just before the rains, a meeting will be called to appoint a junior elder to supervise the operation and make sure it is done properly so that trees are not destroyed.

Maasai learn to always treat members of their own age-set, and all other Maasai for that matter, as equals. That is why the Maasai hate the idea of being employed. Each man should depend on his own property. Of course, there are always some people who are poor. In such cases, it is better to ask such a man to look after your animals, and after some time, you give him a gift of a cow or a goat. In this way, he will get his own property, and eventually he will no longer be poor.

Nowadays, everything is different. When I was young, there was a lot of rain. The rivers used to overflow; now the weather is changing. Sometimes I wonder if God is not punishing us for our sins, but only he knows the answer to that. We believe many of these problems have been brought to us by outsiders (people of other tribes). As Maasai, we are not allowed to cut trees or bushes on the riverbanks. Some outsiders divert streams into their properties for irrigation. The Maasai believe this is why streams and swamps are drying up now. It is bad to break the soil and destroy the vegetation that could otherwise support a number of livestock.

It is becoming more and more difficult to move from one place to another for grazing, because people have been given certain pieces of land, and some have been allocated a dry area, meaning they will be forced to depend on those who have been given a good area. For the Maasai, it is important to have one *manyatta* for the dry season and another for the wet season. How can this be possible if each person has only one piece of land? The animals might have to travel long distances to get good grass, and they will be tired. At the same time, if they end up staying in the same place, pastures will not recover and the animals will be weak. This is what is happening now. Animals are weak, and they don't give much milk. As a result, children suffer.

Some of the places where we used to take our animals have now been made national parks, and we are not supposed to go there any more. This is unfair. We should be allowed to take our animals there, at least during the dry season. The Maasai do not bother the wild animals; we leave them in peace because they are part of God's creation.

When I was young, the land used to belong to everyone, but now some people have title deeds, and then they start selling the land, sometimes for very little money. Some of those who have sold their land are grazing their animals on the land that belongs to other people or that belongs to the government, some are working for others, all of which is bad for the Maasai.

What I have seen is that, nowadays, people do not respect one another as they used to do. They have become greedy and they think only about money. Some have become very rich while their kinsmen and age-mates remain poor. Instead of helping each other as they should, they look after themselves.

I have seen all these bad things, but what I know is that the Maasai were given the rules of upright conduct and social organization by Maasinta, the first Maasai. He is the one who named all the plants and animals and who gave us our proverbs. Whatever happens we should continue to follow what he taught us.

Not only that, the Maasai should continue to respect their elders. We have a proverb that says, "The neck cannot go above the head," meaning that those who are older need to be above the younger people.

In the end, a Maasai without cattle is no Maasai. He is powerless and is not respected by society. We have to continue to live with our animals because that is the life we know. Cattle were given to us by God, so we must continue looking after them in accordance with his will.

The Man Made of Words

••

N. Scott Momaday
KIOWA, CENTRAL UNITED STATES

I want to try to put several different ideas together this morning. And in the process, I hope to indicate something about the nature of the relationship between language and experience. It seems to me that in a certain sense we are all made of words; that our most essential being consists in language. It is the element in which we think and dream and act, in which we live our daily lives. There is no way in which we can exist apart from the morality of a verbal dimension.

In one of the discussions yesterday the question "What is an American Indian?" was raised.

The answer of course is that an Indian is an idea which a given man has of himself. And it is a moral idea, for it accounts for the way in which he reacts to other men and to the world in general. And that idea, in order to be realized completely, has to be expressed.

I want to say some things then about this moral and verbal dimension in which we live. I want to say something about such things as ecology and storytelling and the imagination. Let me tell you a story.

One night a strange thing happened. I had written the greater part of *The Way to Rainy Mountain*—all of it, in fact, except the epilogue. I had set down the last of the old Kiowa tales, and I had composed both the historical and the autobiographical commentaries for it. I had the sense of being out of breath, of having said what it was in me to say on that subject. The manuscript lay before me in the bright light. Small, to be sure, but complete, or nearly so. I had written the second of the two poems in which that book is framed. I had uttered the last word, as it were. And yet a whole, penultimate piece was missing. I began once again to write.

During the first hours after midnight on the morning of November 13, 1833, it seemed that the world was coming to an end. Suddenly the stillness of the night was broken; there were brilliant flashes of light in the sky, light of such intensity that people were awakened by it. With the speed and density of a driving rain, stars were falling in the universe. Some were brighter than Venus; one was said to be as large as the moon. I went on to say that that event, the falling of the stars on North America, that explosion of meteors which occurred 137 years ago, is among the earliest entries in the Kiowa calendars. So deeply impressed upon the imagination of the Kiowa is that old phenomenon that it is remembered still; it has become a part of the racial memory.

"The living memory," I wrote, "and the verbal tradition which transcends it, were brought together for me once and for all in the person of Ko-sahn." It seemed eminently right for me to deal, after all, with that old woman. Ko-sahn is among the most venerable people I have ever known. She spoke and sang to me one summer afternoon in Oklahoma. It was like a dream. When I was born she was already old; she was a grown woman when my grandparents came into the world. She sat perfectly still, folded over on herself. It did not seem possible that so many years—a century of years—could be so compacted and distilled. Her voice shuddered, but it did not fail. Her songs were sad. An old whimsy, a delight in language and in remembrance, shone in her one good eye. She conjured up the past, imagining perfectly the long continuity of her being. She imagined the lovely young girl, wild and vital, she had been. She imagined the Sun Dance:

There was an old, old woman. She had something on her back. The boys went out to see. The old woman had a bag full of earth on her back. It was a certain kind of sandy earth. That is what they must have in the lodge. The dancers must dance upon the sandy earth. The old woman held a digging tool in her hand. She turned toward the south and pointed with her lips. It was like a kiss, and she began to sing:

"We have brought the earth.
Now it is time to play.

As old as I am, I still have the feeling of play. That was the beginning of the Sun Dance."

By this time I was back into the book, caught up completely in the act of writing. I had projected myself—imagined myself—out of the room and out of time. I was there with Ko-sahn in the Oklahoma July. We laughed easily together; I felt that I had known her all of my life—all of hers. I did not want to let her go. But I had come to the end. I set down, almost grudgingly, the last sentences:

"It was—all of this and more—a quest, a going forth upon the way of Rainy Mountain. Probably Ko-sahn too is dead now. At times, in the quiet of evening, I think she must have wondered, dreaming, who she was. Was she become in her sleep that old purveyor of the sacred earth, perhaps, that ancient one who, old as she was, still had the feeling of play? And in her mind, at times, did she see the falling stars?"

For some time I sat looking down at these words on the page, trying to deal with the emptiness that had come about inside of me. The words did not seem real. I could scarcely believe that they made sense, that they had anything whatsoever to do with meaning. In desperation almost, I went back over the final paragraphs, backwards and forwards hurriedly. My eyes fell upon the name Ko-sahn. And all at once everything seemed suddenly to refer to that name. The name seemed to humanize the whole complexity of language. All at once, absolutely, I had the sense of the magic of words and of names. Ko-sahn, I said, and I said again KO-SAHN.

Then it was that that ancient, one-eyed woman Ko-sahn stepped out of the language and stood before me on the page. I was amazed. Yet it seemed entirely appropriate that this should happen.

"I was just now writing about you," I replied, stammering. "I thought— forgive me—I thought that perhaps you were . . . that you had . . ."

"No," she said. And she cackled, I thought. And she went on. "You have imagined me well, and so I am. You have imagined that I dream, and so I do. I have seen the falling stars."

"But all of this, this imagining," I protested, "this has taken place—is taking place in my mind. You are not actually here, not here in this room." It occurred to me that I was being extremely rude, but I could not help myself. She seemed to understand.

"Be careful of your pronouncements, grandson," she answered. "You imagine that I am here in this room, do you not? That is worth something. You see, I have existence, whole being, in your imagination. It is but one kind of being, to be sure, but it is perhaps the best of all kinds. If I am not here in this room, grandson, then surely neither are you."

"I think I see what you mean," I said meekly. I felt justly rebuked. "Tell me, grandmother, how old are you?"

"I do not know," she replied. "There are times when I think that I am the oldest woman on earth. You know, the Kiowa came into the world through a hollow log. In my mind's eye I have seen them emerge, one by one, from the mouth of the log. I have seen them so clearly, how they were dressed, how delighted they were to see the world around them. I must have been there. And I must have taken part in that old migration of the Kiowa from the Yellowstone to the Southern Plains, near the Big Horn River, and I have seen the red cliffs of Palo Duro Canyon. I was with those who were camped in the Wichita Mountains when the stars fell."

"You are indeed very old," I said, "and you have seen many things."

"Yes, I imagine that I have," she replied. Then she turned slowly around, nodding once, and receded into the language I had made. And then I imagined I was alone in the room.

Once in his life a man ought to concentrate his mind upon the remembered earth, I believe. He ought to give himself up to a particular landscape in his experience, to look at it from as many angles as he can, to wonder about it, to dwell upon it. He ought to imagine that he touches it with his hands at every season and listens to the sounds that are made upon it. He ought to imagine the creatures that are there and all the faintest motions in the wind. He ought to recollect the glare of noon and all the colors of the dawn and dusk.

The Wichita Mountains rise out of the Southern Plains in a long crooked line that runs from east to west. The mountains are made of red earth, and of rock that is neither red nor blue but some very rare admixture of the two like the feathers of certain birds. They are not so high and mighty as the mountains of the Far West, and they bear a different relationship to the land around them. One does not imagine that they are distinctive in themselves, or indeed that they exist apart from the plain in any sense. If you try to think of them in the abstract they lose the look of mountains. They are preeminently in an expression of the larger landscape, more perfectly organic than one can easily imagine. To behold these mountains from the plain is one thing; to see the plain from the mountains is something else. I have stood on the top of Mount Scott and seen the earth below, bending out into the whole circle of the sky. The wind runs always close upon the slopes, and there are times when you can hear the rush of it like water in the ravines.

Here is the hub of an old commerce. A hundred years ago the Kiowa and Comanche journeyed outward from the Wichitas in every direction, seeking after mischief and medicine, horses and hostages. Sometimes they went away for years, but they always returned, for the land had got hold of them. It is a consecrated place, and even now there is something of the wilderness about it. There is a game preserve in the hills. Animals graze away in the open meadows or, closer by, keep to the shadows of the groves: antelope and deer, longhorn and buffalo. It was here, the Kiowa say, that the first buffalo came into the world.

The yellow grassy knoll that is called Rainy Mountain lies a short distance to the north and west. There, on the west side, is the ruin of an old school where my grandmother went as a wild young girl in blanket and braids to learn of numbers and of names in English. And there she is buried.

Most is your name the name of this dark stone.
Deranged in death, the mind to be inheres
Forever in the nominal unknown,
The wake of nothing audible he hears
Who listens here and now to hear your name.

The early sun, red as a hunter's moon,
Runs in the plain. The mountain burns and shines;
And silence is the long approach of noon
Upon the shadow that your name defines—
And death this cold, black density of stone.

I am interested in the way that a man looks at a given landscape and takes possession of it in his blood and brain. For this happens, I am certain, in the ordinary motion of life. None of us lives apart from the land entirely; such an isolation is unimaginable. We have sooner or later to come to terms with the world around us—and I mean especially the physical world; not only as it is revealed to us immediately through our senses, but also as it is perceived more truly in the long turn of seasons and of years. And we must come to moral terms. There is no alternative, I believe, if we are to realize and maintain our humanity; for our humanity must consist in part in the ethical as well as the practical ideal of preservation. And particularly here and now is that true. We Americans need now more than ever before—and indeed more than we know—to imagine who and what we are with respect to the earth and sky. I am talking about an act of the imagination essentially, and the concept of an American land ethic.

It is no doubt more difficult to imagine in 1970 the landscape of America as it was in, say, 1900. Our whole experience as a nation in this century has been a repudiation of the pastoral ideal which informs so much of the art and literature of the nineteenth century. One effect of the Technological Revolution has been to uproot us from the soil. We have become disoriented, I believe; we have suffered a kind of psychic dislocation of ourselves in time and space. We may be perfectly sure of where we are in relation to the supermarket and the next coffee break, but I doubt that any of us knows where he is in relation to the stars and to the solstices. Our sense of the natural order has become dull and unreliable. Like the wilderness itself, our sphere of instinct has diminished in proportion as we have failed to imagine truly what it is. And yet I believe that it is possible to formulate an ethical idea of the land—a notion of what it is and must be in our daily lives—and I believe moreover that it is absolutely necessary to do so.

It would seem on the surface of things that a land ethic is something that is alien to, or at least dormant in, most Americans. Most of us in general have developed an attitude of indifference toward the land. In terms of my own experience, it is difficult to see how such an attitude could ever have come about.

Ko-sahn could remember where my grandmother was born. "It was just there," she said, pointing to a tree, and the tree was like a hundred others that grew up in the broad depression of the Washita River. I could see nothing to indicate that anyone had ever been there, spoken so much as a word, or touched the tips of his fingers to the tree. But in her memory Ko-sahn could see the child. I think she must have remembered my grandmother's voice, for she seemed for a long moment to listen and to hear. There was a still, heavy heat upon that place; I had the sense that ghosts were gathering there.

And in the racial memory, Ko-sahn had seen the falling stars. For her there was no distinction between the individual and the racial experience, even as there was none between the mythical and the historical. Both were realized for her in the one memory, and that was of the land. This landscape, in which she had lived for a hundred years, was the common denominator of everything that she knew and would ever know—and her knowledge was profound. Her roots ran deep into the earth, and from those depths she drew strength enough to hold still against all the forces of chance and disorder. And she drew therefrom the sustenance of meaning and of mystery as well. The falling stars were not for Ko-sahn an isolated or accidental phenomenon. She had a great personal investment in that awful commotion of light in the night sky. For it remained to be imagined. She must at last deal with it in words; she must appropriate it to her understanding of the whole universe. And, again, when she spoke of the Sun Dance, it was an essential expression of her relationship to the life of the earth and to the sun and moon.

In Ko-sahn and in her people we have always had the example of a deep, ethical regard for the land. We had better learn from it. Surely that ethic is merely latent in ourselves. It must now be activated, I believe. We Americans must come again to a moral comprehension of the earth and air. We must live according to the principle of a land ethic. The alternative is that we shall not live at all.

Ecology is perhaps the most important subject of our time. I can't think of an issue in which the Indian has more authority or a greater stake. If there is one thing which truly distinguishes him, it is surely his regard of and for the natural world.

But let me get back to the matter of storytelling.

I must have taken part in that old migration of the Kiowa from the Yellowstone to the Southern Plains, for I have seen antelope bounding in the tall grass near the Big Horn River, and I have seen the ghost forests in the Black Hills. Once I saw the red cliffs of Palo Duro Canyon. I was with those who were camped in the Wichita Mountains when the stars fell. "You are very old," I said, "and you have seen many things." "Yes, I imagine that I have," she replied. Then she turned slowly around, nodding once, and receded into the language I had made. And then I imagined that I was alone in the room.

Who is the storyteller? Of whom is the story told? What is there in the darkness to imagine into being? What is there to dream and to relate? What happens when I or anyone exerts the force of language upon the unknown?

These are the questions which interest me most.

If there is any absolute assumption in back of my thoughts tonight, it is this: We are what we imagine. Our very existence consists in our imagination of ourselves. Our best destiny is to imagine, at least, completely, who and what, and *that* we are. The greatest tragedy that can befall us is to go unimagined.

Writing is recorded speech. In order to consider seriously the meaning of language and of literature, we must consider first the meaning of the oral tradition.

By way of suggesting one or two definitions which may be useful to us, let me pose a few basic questions and tentative answers:

(1) What is the oral tradition?

The oral tradition is that process by which the myths, legends, tales, and lore of a people are formulated, communicated, and preserved in language by word of mouth, as opposed to writing. Or, it is a *collection* of such things.

(2) With reference to the matter of oral tradition, what is the relationship between art and reality?

In the context of these remarks, the matter of oral tradition suggests certain particularities of art and reality. Art, for example . . . involves an oral dimension which is based markedly upon such considerations as memorization, intonation, inflection, precision of statement, brevity, rhythm, pace, and dramatic effect. Moreover, myth, legend, and lore, according to our definitions of these terms, imply a separate and distinct order of reality. We are concerned here not so much with an accurate representation of actuality, but with the realization of the imaginative experience.

(3) How are we to conceive of language? What are words?

For our purposes, words are audible sounds, invented by man to communicate his thoughts and feelings. Each word has a conceptual content, however slight; and each word communicates associations of feeling. Language is the means by which words proceed to the formulation of meaning and emotional effect.

(4) What is the nature of storytelling? What are the purposes and possibilities of that act?

Storytelling is imaginative and creative in nature. It is an act by which man strives to realize his capacity for wonder, meaning, and delight. It is also a process in which man invests and preserves himself in the context of ideas. Man tells stories in order to understand his experience, whatever it may be. The possibilities of storytelling are precisely those of understanding the human experience.

(5) What is the relationship between what a man is and what he says—or between what he is, and what he thinks he is?

This relationship is both tenuous and complicated. Generally speaking, man has consummate being in language, and there only. The state of human *being* is an idea, an idea which man has of himself. Only when he is embodied in an idea, and the idea is realized in language, can man take possession of himself. In our particular frame of reference, this is to say that man achieves the fullest realization of his humanity in such an art and product of the imagination as literature—and here I use the term "literature" in its broadest sense. This is admittedly a moral view of the question, but literature is itself a moral view, and it is a view of morality.

Now let us return to the falling stars. And let me apply a new angle of vision to that event—let me proceed this time from a slightly different point of view:

In this winter of 1833 the Kiowa were camped on Elm Fork, a branch of the Red River west of the Wichita Mountains. In the preceding summer they had suffered a massacre at the hands of the Osage, and Tai-me, the sacred Sun Dance Doll and most powerful medicine of the tribe, had been stolen. At no time in the history of their migration from the north, and in the evolution of their plains culture, had the Kiowa been more vulnerable to despair. The loss of Tai-me was a deep psychological wound. In the early cold of November 13 there occurred over North America an explosion of meteors. The Kiowa were awakened by the sterile light of falling stars, and they ran out into the false day and were terrified.

The year the stars fell is, as I have said, among the earliest entries in the Kiowa calendars, and it is permanent in the Kiowa mind. There was symbolic meaning in that November sky. With the coming of natural dawn there began a new and darker age for the Kiowa people; the last culture to evolve on this continent began to decline. Within four years of the falling stars the Kiowa signed their first treaty with the government; within twenty, four major epidemics of smallpox and Asiatic cholera destroyed more than half their number; and within scarcely more than a generation their horses were taken from them and the herds of buffalo were slaughtered and left to waste upon the plains.

Do you see what happens when the imagination is superimposed upon the historical event? It becomes a story. The whole piece becomes more deeply invested with meaning. The terrified Kiowa, when they had regained possession of themselves, did indeed imagine that the falling stars were symbolic of their being and their destiny. They accounted for themselves with reference to that awful memory. They appropriated it, recreated it, fashioned it into an image of themselves—imagined it.

Only by means of that act could they bear what happened to them thereafter. No defeat, no humiliation, no suffering was beyond their power to endure, for none of it was meaningless. They could say to themselves, "Yes, it was all meant to be in its turn. The order of the world was broken, it was clear. Even the stars were shaken loose in the night sky." The imagination of meaning was not much, perhaps, but it was all they had, and it was enough to sustain them.

One of my very favorite writers, Isak Dinesen, said this: "All sorrows can be borne if you put them into a story or tell a story about them."

Some three or four years ago, I became interested in the matter of "oral tradition" as that term is used to designate a rich body of preliterate storytelling in and among the indigenous cultures of North America. Specifically, I began to wonder about the way in which myths, legends, and lore evolve into that mature condition of expression which we call "literature." For indeed literature is, I believe, the end-product of an evolutionary process, a stage that is indispensable and perhaps original as well.

I set out to find a traditional material that should be at once oral only, unified and broadly representative of cultural values. And in this undertaking, I had a certain advantage, because I am myself an American Indian, and I have lived many years of my life on the Indian reservations of the southwest. From the time I was first able to comprehend and express myself in language, I heard the stories of the Kiowa, those "coming out" people of the Southern Plains from whom I am descended.

Three hundred years ago the Kiowa lived in the mountains of what is now western Montana, near the headwaters of the Yellowstone River. Near the end of the seventeenth century they began a long migration to the south and east. They passed along the present border between Montana and Wyoming to the Black Hills and proceeded southward along the eastern slopes of the Rockies to the Wichita Mountains in the Southern Plains (southwestern Oklahoma).

I mention this old journey of the Kiowa because it is in a sense definitive of the tribal mind; it is essential to the way in which the Kiowa think of themselves as a people. The migration was carried on over a course of many generations and many hundreds of miles. When it began, the Kiowa were a desperate and divided people, given up wholly to a day-by-day struggle for survival. When it ended, they were a race of centaurs, a lordly society of warriors and buffalo hunters. Along the way they had acquired horses, a knowledge and possession of the open land, and a sense of destiny. In alliance with the Comanche, they ruled the Southern Plains for a hundred years.

That migration—and the new golden age to which it led—is closely reflected in Kiowa legend and lore. Several years ago I retraced the route of that migration, and when I came to the end, I interviewed a number of Kiowa elders and obtained from them a remarkable body of history and learning, fact and fiction—all of it in the oral tradition and all of it valuable in its own right and for its own sake.

I compiled a small number of translations from the Kiowa, arranged insofar as it was possible to indicate the chronological and geographical progression of the migration itself. This collection (and it was nothing more than a collection at first) was published under the title *The Journey of Tai-me* in a fine edition limited to one hundred hand-printed copies.

This original collection has just been reissued, together with illustrations and a commentary, in a trade edition entitled *The Way to Rainy Mountain*. The principle of narration which informs this latter work is in a sense elaborate and experimental, and I should like to say one or two things about it. Then, if I may, I should like to illustrate the way in which the principle works, by reading briefly from the text. And finally, I should like to comment in some detail upon one of the tales in particular.

There are three distinct narrative voices in *The Way to Rainy Mountain*— the mythical, the historical, and the immediate. Each of the translations is followed by two kinds of commentary; the first is documentary and the second is privately reminiscent. Together, they serve, hopefully, to validate the oral tradition to an extent that might not otherwise be possible. The commentaries are meant to provide a context in which the elements of oral tradition might transcend the categorical limits of prehistory, anonymity, and archaeology in the narrow sense.

All of this is to say that I believe there is a way (first) in which the elements of oral tradition can be shown, dramatically, to exist within the framework of a literary continuance, a deeper and more vital context of language and meaning than that which is generally taken into account; and (second) in which those elements can be located, with some precision on an evolutionary scale.

The device of the journey is peculiarly appropriate to such a principle of narration as this. And *The Way to Rainy Mountain* is a whole journey, intricate with motion and meaning; and it is made with the whole memory, that experience of the mind which is legendary as well as historical, personal as well as cultural.

Without further qualification, let me turn to the text itself.

The Kiowa tales which are contained in *The Way to Rainy Mountain* constitute a kind of literary chronicle. In a sense they are the milestones of that old migration in which the Kiowa journeyed from the Yellowstone to the Washita. They recorded a transformation of the tribal mind, as it encounters for the first time the landscape of the Great Plains; they evoke the sense of search and discovery. Many of the tales are very old, and they have not until now been set down in writing. Among them there is one that stands out in my mind. When I was a child, my father told me the story of the arrowmaker, and he told it to me many times, for I fell in love with it. I have no memory that is older than that of hearing it. This is the way it goes:

"If an arrow is well made, it will have tooth marks upon it. That is how you know. The Kiowa made fine arrows and straightened them in their teeth. Then they drew them to the bow to see that they were straight. Once there was a man and his wife. They were alone at night in their tepee. By the light of a fire the man was making arrows. After a while he caught sight of something. There was a small opening in the tepee where two hides had been sewn together. Someone was there on the outside, looking in. The man went on with his work, but he said to his wife, 'Someone is standing outside. Do not be afraid. Let us talk easily, as of ordinary things.' He took up an arrow and straightened it in his teeth; then, as it was right for him to do, he drew it to the bow and took aim, first in this direction and then in that. And all the while he was talking, as if to his wife. But this is how he spoke: 'I know that you are there on the outside, for I can feel your eyes upon me. If you are a Kiowa, you will understand what I am saying, and you will speak your name.' But there was no answer, and the man went on in the same way, pointing the arrow all around. At last his aim fell upon the place where his enemy stood, and he let go of the string. The arrow went straight to the enemy's heart."

Heretofore the story of the arrowmaker has been the private possession of a very few, a tenuous link in that most ancient chain of language which we call the oral tradition; tenuous because the tradition itself is so; for as many times as the story has been told, it was always but one generation removed from extinction. But it was held dear, too, on that same account. That is to say, it has been neither more nor less durable than the human voice, and neither more nor less concerned to express the meaning of the human condition. And this brings us to the heart of the matter at hand: The story of the arrowmaker is also a link between language and literature. It is a remarkable act of the mind, a realization of words and the world that is altogether simple and direct, yet nonetheless rare and profound, and it illustrates more clearly than anything else in my own experience, at least, something of the essential character of the imagination—and in particular of that personification which in this instance emerges from it: the man made of words.

It is a fine story, whole, intricately beautiful, precisely realized. It is worth thinking about, for it yields something of value; indeed, it is full of provocation, rich with suggestion and consequent meaning. There is often an inherent danger that we might impose too much of ourselves upon it. It is informed by an integrity that bears examination easily and well, and in the process it seems to appropriate our own reality and experience.

It is significant that the story of the arrowmaker returns in a special way upon itself. It is about language, after all, and it is therefore part and parcel of its own subject; virtually, there is no difference between the telling and that which is told. The point of the story lies, not so much in what the arrowmaker does, but in what he says—and indeed that he says it. The principal fact is that he speaks, and in so doing he places his very life in the balance. It is this aspect of the story which interests me most, for it is here that the language becomes most conscious of itself; we are close to the origin and object of literature, I believe; our sense of the verbal dimension is very keen, and we are aware of something in the nature of language that is at once perilous and compelling. "If you are a Kiowa, you will understand what I am saying, and you will speak your name." Everything is ventured in this simple declaration, which is also a question and a plea. The conditional element with which it begins is remarkably tentative and pathetic; precisely at this moment is the arrowmaker realized completely, and his reality consists in language, and it is poor and precarious. And all of this occurs to him as surely as it does to us. Implicit in that simple occurrence is all of his definition and his destiny, and all of ours. He ventures to speak because he must; language is the repository of his whole knowledge and experience, and it represents the only chance he has for survival. Instinctively, and with great care, he deals in the most honest and basic way with words. "Let us talk easily, as of ordinary things," he says. And of the ominous unknown he asks only the utterance of a name, only the most nominal sign that he is understood, that his words are returned to him on the sheer edge of meaning. But there is no answer, and the arrow-maker knows at once what he has not known before; that his enemy is, and that he has gained an advantage over him. This he knows certainly, and the certainty itself is his advantage, and it is crucial; he makes the most of it. The venture is complete and irrevocable, and it ends in success. The story is meaningful. It is so primarily because it is composed of language, and it is in the nature of language in turn that it proceeds to the formulation of meaning. Moreover, the story of the arrowmaker, as opposed to other stories in general, centers upon this procession of words toward meaning. It seems in fact to turn upon the very idea that language involves the elements of risk and responsibility; and in this it seeks to confirm itself. In a word, it seems to say, everything is a risk. That may be true, and it may also be that the whole of literature rests upon that truth.

The arrowmaker is preeminently the man made of words. He has consummate being in language; it is the world of his origin and of his posterity, and there is no other. But it is a world of definite reality and of infinite possibility. I have come to believe that there is a sense in which the arrowmaker has more nearly perfect being than have other men, by and large, as he imagines himself, whole and vital, going on into the unknown darkness and beyond. And this last aspect of his being is primordial and profound.

And yet the story has it that he is cautious and alone, and we are given to understand that his peril is great and immediate, and that he confronts it in the only way he can. I have no doubt that this is true, and I believe that there are implications which point directly to the determination of our literary experience and which must not be lost upon us. A final word, then, on an essential irony which marks this story and gives peculiar substance to the man made of words. The storyteller is nameless and unlettered. From one point of view we know very little about him, except that he is somehow translated for us in the person of an arrowmaker. But, from another, that is all we need to know. He tells us of his life in language, and of the awful risk involved. It must occur to us that he is one with the arrowmaker and that he has survived, by word of mouth, beyond other men. We said a moment ago that, for the arrowmaker, language represented the only chance of survival. It is worth considering that he survives in our own time, and that he has survived over a period of untold generations.

The Kill Hole

•••

Linda Hogan
CHICKASAW, CENTRAL UNITED STATES

*I*n New Mexico there were an ancient people called the Mimbres. They were skilled potters. What they made was far superior to the work of later potters in the Southwest. The Mimbres formed bowls out of rich, red clay that held generations of life, and they painted that shaped clay with animals, people, plants, and even the dusty wind that still inhabits the dry New Mexico land.

Like the Anasazi and other ancient nations, these were people of the mystery, having abandoned their place and vanished into a dimension that has remained unknown to those of us who have come later. But before they disappeared into the secret, the Mimbres "killed" their pots by breaking a hole in the center of each one. It is thought that the hole served to release the spirit of the pot from the clay, allowing it to travel with them over land and to join them in their burial grounds. It is called a "kill hole."

At the third death I attended, I thought of these earlier people, and wondered about the kill hole, how life escapes the broken clay of ourselves, travels away from the center of our living. It's said that at death, the fontanelle in the top of the skull opens, the way it is open when we are born into the world. Before her spirit escaped through the crown, I wanted to ask that dying woman what she could tell me about life. But dying is hard work and it leaves little time for questions. That afternoon, there was time only for human comfort as the woman balanced those last hours between the worlds of life and raspy death.

That woman died in California, not far from the place where Ishi, the last Yana Indian, was found in 1911. Ishi came from a small group of Indians who lived undiscovered for over fifty years in the Mill Creek area, concealed by forest. They knew the secret of invisibility. Not even a cloud of smoke had revealed their whereabouts. But as the settling of the continent expanded to the west, and as the logging of the forests continued, Ishi was found, finally, by surveyors who must have believed he was not a man in the way they were men, for they carried away his few possessions as souvenirs for their families.

For the next four years Ishi lived in a museum as a living exhibit. He offered scholars his tools, his crafts, and his language. His was a tremendous gift to the people who were near him, but during that time he was transformed from a healthy man into a wasted skeleton. He died from tuberculosis, one of the diseases of civilization. But sometimes death has such a strange way of turning things inside out, so that what is gone becomes as important as what remains. Such an absence defines our world as surely as a Mimbres pot contains a bowl of air, or as a woman's dying body holds a memory and history of life. This is especially true in the case of Ishi; his story illuminates the world of civilization and its flaws. It tells us what kind of people we are, with our double natures. It speaks of loss and of emptiness that will never again be filled, of whole cultures disappeared, of species made extinct, all of these losses falling as if through a hole, like a spirit leaving earth's broken clay.

In our own time, there have been events as striking as the discovery of Ishi, events that, in their passing, not only raise the question of what kind of people we are, but give us reason to ask what is our rightful place within the circle of life, we beautiful ones who are as adept at creation as we are at destruction?

■ ■ ■

One of these events, one that haunts us like a shadow from the dark periphery of our lives, is the recent research where apes were taught American sign language. Through that language of the hands, a dialogue began between signing chimpanzees and human beings, a dialogue that bridged the species barrier for perhaps the first time. Within a relatively short time, the chimps learned to communicate with humans and with one another. They asked questions, expressed abstract thought, and combined signs and symbols to create new words they had not been taught by their human teachers. With their hands, they spoke a world of emotion, of feelings similar to our own.

One angry chimp called his handler, "dirty." Another one, Ally, developed hysterical paralysis when separated from his mother. Later, one of the subjects had to be tranquilized as he was taken away, distraught and protesting, and sold into scientific research.

From these studies, we learned that primates have a capacity for love and resistance, that they not only have a rich emotional life, but that they are able to express their pain and anguish. This is an event whose repercussions astonish us with their meaning, whose presence throws us into an identity crisis equal to that in Galileo's time when the fabric of belief was split wide open to reveal that earth was not the center of the universe. This event bespeaks our responsibility to treat with care and tenderness all the other lives who share our small world. Yet the significance of this research has gone largely unheeded. Many members of the scientific community played down the similarities between apes and humans, ignoring the comfort of such connections. They searched instead for new definitions of language and intelligence, ones that would exclude apes from our own ways of speaking and thinking. They searched for a new division, another wall between life and life. In itself, this search sheds light on us, and in that light, we seem to have had a failure of heart.

But perhaps this armor of defense comes from another failure, from the downfall of our beliefs about who and what we are as human beings. One by one, in our lifetimes, our convictions about ourselves and our place within the world have been overturned. Once the use of tools was considered to be strictly a human ability. Then it was found that primates and other species make use of tools. Then altruism was said to be what distinguished us from other species, until it was learned that elephants try to help their sick, staying the long hours beside their own dying ones, caressing and comforting them. And we can't even say that art is an activity that sets us apart, since those same compassionate elephants also make art. In fact, when the artist de Kooning was shown anonymous paintings by elephants, he thought the artist to be a most talented individual, one who knew how to "finish" and compose a drawing. On hearing that the artist was an elephant, he said, "That's a damned talented elephant." Jane Goodall, also on the subject of art, says that not only do chimpanzees make and name paintings, but that when shown their artwork as much as a year later, they remember the title they originally gave it.

▣　▣　▣

Even humor is not entirely limited to humans. Recently Jane Goodall also related an exchange between the signing gorilla Koko and trainer Penny Patterson. A researcher was visiting them, and Penny wanted Koko to exhibit her intelligence.

Penny held up a piece of white cloth.

"Koko, what color is this?"

Koko signed, "Red."

Because the gorilla made an error, the woman asked again. "Koko, what color is this?"

Koko again replied, "Red."

Exasperated, the trainer said, "Koko, if you want to eat supper, you'd better answer the question. What color is this?"

Koko leaned forward and picked a tiny piece of red lint off the white cloth, looked her caretaker in the eye, showed her the lint, and laughed. "Red, Red, red, red!"

Still wanting a place of our own, a place set aside from the rest of the creation, now it is being ventured that maybe our ability to make fire separates us, or perhaps the desire to seek revenge. But no matter what direction the quest for separation might take, there has been a narrowing down of the difference between species, and we are forced to ask ourselves once again: what is our rightful place in the world, our responsibility to the other lives on the planet? It's a question of crucial importance as we live in this strange and confusing time, when so many of our scientists prefer to meddle with the creation of new life forms rather than to maintain and care for those, even human lives, who are already in our presence. Oren Lyons, Iroquois traditionalist, has said, "We forget and we consider ourselves superior, but we are after all a mere part of this creation. And we must consider to understand where we are. And we stand somewhere between the mountain and the ant, somewhere and only there as part and parcel of the creation."

We are of the animal world. We are part of the cycles of growth and decay. Even having tried so hard to see ourselves apart, and so often without a love for even our own biology, we are in relationship with the rest of the planet, and that connectedness tells us we must reconsider the way we see ourselves and the rest of nature.

A change is required of us, a healing of the betrayed trust between humans and earth. Caretaking is the utmost spiritual and physical responsibility of our time, and perhaps that stewardship is finally our place in the web of life, our work, the solution to the mystery of what we are. There are already so many holes in the universe that will never again be filled, and each of them forces us to question why we permitted such loss, such tearing away at the fabric of life, and how we will live with our planet in the future.

◧ ◧ ◧

Ishi is just one of those losses. Ishi was what he called himself, and the word meant only "man." Ishi kept his real name to himself. It was his only possession, all that remained for him of a lost way of life. He was the last of a kind of human being. His absence left us wondering about these lives of ours that unfold in the center of a tragic technology. When we wake up in the night, full of fear, we know the hole is all around us, pulling at even our dreams. We learn from what has fallen through before us. It's why we study history. It's why I wished a dying woman would balance between the worlds a moment, teetering there, and gaze backward in time to tell me any wise secret of survival. The kill hole where everything falls out is not just found in earth's or the body's clay. It is a dusky space between us and others, the place where our compassion has fallen away, our capacity for love failed. It is the time between times, a breached realm where apes inform us of a truth we fear to face. It is a broken mirror that reveals to us our own shady and dualistic natures and lays bare our human history of cruelty as well as love. What we are lives in that abyss. But we have also to ask if this research is not a great step in creating a bridge across that broken world, if these first explorations between humans and apes are not hands held out in welcome. Some of us have reached out across the solitude of our lives with care and mercy, have touched away the space between us all.

There is a Mandan story that tells how the killed buffalo left through a hole in the sky. From that hole, it's said, the grandmother still looks down at earth, watching over her children.

Today in San Diego, a young California condor is breaking a hole in an egg, pecking its way through to life. There are only twenty-eight California condors left in the world, all of them in captivity. They've been dwelling on the brink of extinction. But how amazing it is, this time a new life coming in, turning another way through that hole. A mending is taking place, a life emerging like the thread out of the labyrinth, the thread leading out of a Navajo rug's pattern of loss. The old woman in the sky is looking down on us, keeping watch.

Credits

••

1. Origins

"The Emergence" (sections 1–6), from *Diné Bahane': The Navajo Creation Story*, arranged by Paul G. Zolbrod (Albuquerque: University of New Mexico Press, 1984). Reprinted by permission of the University of New Mexico Press.

"The Creation," from *Tales of the Iroquois*, by Tehanetorens (Ray Fadden), published by *Akwesasne Notes* (1976, 1992). Reprinted by permission of Ray Fadden.

"Tangaroa, Maker of All Things," from *Legends of the South Seas*, edited by Antony Alpers (London: J. Murray, 1970; reprinted by HarperCollins, Inc.).

"In the Beginning . . .," from *The Songlines*, by Bruce Chatwin, copyright © 1987 by Bruce Chatwin. Reprinted by permission of Viking Penguin, a division of Penguin Books, USA Inc.

"The Mother of Water," from *The Kalevela or Poems of the Kaleva District*, compiled by Elias Lonnrot and translated by Francis Peabody Magoun, Jr. (Cambridge, Mass.: Harvard University Press), copyright © 1963 by the President and Fellows of Harvard College. Reprinted by permission of the publisher.

"The Origin of Different Water Animals," from *Folktales of India*, edited by Beck, Claus, Goswami, and Handoo (Chicago: University of Chicago Press, 1987). Reprinted by permission of the University of Chicago Press.

"Juruna Kills the Sun," from *Xingu: The Indians, Their Myths*, edited by Orlando Villas Boas and Claudio Villas Boas (Souvenir Press, 1973). Reprinted by permission of Souvenir Press Ltd.

"How Moon Fathered the World," from *The Origin of Life and Death: African Creation Myths*, edited by Ulli Beier (Heinemann Educational Books Ltd., 1966). Reprinted by permission of Heinemann Publishers Ltd.

"Sun and Moon," from *Folk Literature of the Nivaklé Indians*, edited by Johannes Wilbert and Karen Simoneau (Los Angeles: UCLA Latin American Center Publications, 1987). Reprinted by permission of UCLA Latin American Center Publications.

"Morning and Evening," from *The Origin of Life and Death: African Creation Myths*, edited by Ulli Beier (Heinemann Educational Books Ltd., 1966). Reprinted by permission of Heinemann Publishers Ltd.

"The Origin of Fishes," from *The Origin of Life and Death: African Creation Myths*, edited by Ulli Beier (Heinemann Educational Books Ltd., 1966). Reprinted by permission of Heinemann Publishers Ltd.

"How Gluskabe Brought the Summer," from *The Wind Eagle and Other Abenaki Stories*, as told by Joseph Bruchac (Bowman Books, 1985). Reprinted by permission of Joseph Bruchac.

"The Rollright Stones," from *Everyman's Book of English Folktales*, edited by Sybil Marshall (J. M. Dent and Sons, 1981). Reprinted by permission of J. M. Dent and Sons Ltd.

"Hailibu the Hunter," from *Favourite Folktales of China*, translated by John Minford (New World Press, 1983). Reprinted by permission of China Books and Periodicals, San Francisco.

"The Seven Sisters," first published in *The Reporter*, January 26, 1967. Reprinted from *The Way to Rainy Mountain*, by N. Scott Momaday, copyright © 1969. Reprinted by permission of the University of New Mexico Press.

"The Toad," from *The Origin of Life and Death: African Creation Myths*, edited by Ulli Beier (Heinemann Educational Books Ltd., 1966). Reprinted by permission of Heinemann Publishers Ltd.

"The Chameleon and the Lizard," from *The Origin of Life and Death: African Creation Myths*, edited by Ulli Beier (Heinemann Educational Books Ltd., 1966). Reprinted by permission of Heinemann Publishers Ltd.

"The Origin of Death," from *African Folktales*, by Roger D. Abrahams, copyright © 1983 by Roger D. Abrahams. Reprinted by permission of Pantheon Books, a division of Random House.

2. Animal Tales and Transformations

"The Jaguar and the Girl," "The Woman Who Was Married to a Jaguar," "The Man Who Married Gemini and Who Made a Trip to the World of the Thunderbirds," and "The Woman Married to Jaguar-Man," from *Folk Literature of the Nivaklé Indians*, edited by Johannes Wilbert and Karen Simoneau (Los Angeles: UCLA Latin American Center Publications, 1987). Reprinted by permission of UCLA Latin American Center Publications.

"Gratitude: The Hunter and the Antelope," from *African Genesis*, edited by Leo Frobenius and Douglas C. Fox (New York: Benjamin Blom, 1966).

"The Celestial Bear," "Trading Teeth with the Beaver," and "The Song of the Birds," from *Tyendinaga Tales*, collected and introduced by Rona Rustige (Kingston, Canada: McGill-Queen's University Press, 1988). Reprinted by permission of McGill-Queen's University Press.

"The Blossom Tree" and "The Young Man Who Refused to Kill," from *Tibetan Folk Tales*,

3. Tricksters

the Hunter and Other Tales from Nigeria, copyright © 1968 (Harcourt Brace and World, 1968). Reprinted by permission of Harold Courlander.

"T'appin (Terrapin)," from *The Book of Negro Folklore*, edited by Langston Hughes and Arna Bontemps (New York: Dodd, Mead, and Co., 1958).

"Sheer Crops," from "Brazos Bottom Philosophy," by A. W. Eddins, *Publications of the Texas Folklore Society* 9 (1931): 153–64.

"The Crocodile Man and the Heron Man," from *Primitive Reader: An Anthology of Tales by Aboriginal People*, edited by John Greenway (Hatboro, Pa.: Folklore Association, 1965).

"The Monkey-Son," from *Folktales of India*, edited by Beck, Claus, Goswami, and Handoo (Chicago: University of Chicago Press, 1987). Reprinted by permission of the University of Chicago Press.

"The Raven and the Whale," "The Raven and the Hunter," and "The Lustful Raven," from *A Kayak Full of Ghosts*, gathered and retold by Lawrence Millman, copyright © 1987 by Lawrence Millman. Reprinted by permission of Capra Press, Santa Barbara.

"The Winnebago Trickster Cycle" (sections 12–14), from *The Trickster: A Study in American Indian Mythology*, by Paul Radin (Shocken Books, 1956; reprinted by Routledge, U. K.).

"The Stealing of the Sun" and "Sun's Arrival in the Sky," from *California Indian Nights Entertainment*, edited by Edward W. Gifford and Gwendoline Harris Block (Glendale, Calif.: Arthur H. Clark, 1930).

"Coyote Juggles His Eyes," from *Coyote Stories*, by Mourning Dove (Humishuma), edited by Heister Dean Guie (University of Nebraska Press, 1933, reprinted 1990).

4. Tales to Live By

"Landscape, History, and the Pueblo Imagination," by Leslie Marmon Silko, first published in *Antaeus* 57 (1986); reprinted 1987. Reprinted by permission of Wylie, Aitken & Stone, Inc.

Excerpts from *I, Rigoberta Menchú: An Indian Woman in Guatemala*, copyright © 1984, Verso. Reprinted by permission.

"The Circle Is the Way to See," "The Day the Mountain Said No," and "The Circle Closes in on the Nomads," from *Story Earth*, copyright © 1993, Inter Press Service Third World News Agency (San Francisco: Mercury House). Reprinted by permission.

"The Man Made of Words," by N. Scott Momaday, from *The Remembered Earth: An Anthology of Contemporary Native American Literature*, edited by Geary Hobson (Albuquerque: University of New Mexico Press, 1979). Reprinted by permission of the author.

"The Kill Hole," by Linda Hogan, first published in *Parabola* 13 (1988): 50–53.

Index

BOOKS OF RELATED INTEREST FROM BEACON PRESS

Gary Paul Nabhan and Stephen Trimble
The Geography of Childhood:
Why Children Need Wild Places

In this unique collaboration, two naturalists ask what may happen now that so many children are denied exposure to wilderness.

"*The Geography of Childhood* is neither doomsday tract nor polemic, but rather an excursion into the natural world that rekindles our attachment to animals, birds, plants, open spaces, and the earth. It will connect parents with the precious resource of their children's relationship to living things, while raising consciousness of what may be missing in our own lives."

—*Salt Lake Tribune*

[0-8070-8525-1, PAPERBACK]

Scott Russell Sanders
Staying Put: Making a Home in a Restless World

"In the tradition of Wendell Berry, Sanders champions fidelity to place, informed by ecological awareness, arguing that intimacy with one's home region is the grounding for global knowledge. . . . Reflective, rhapsodic, luminous essays . . . A wise and beautifully written book."

—*Publishers Weekly*

[0-8070-6341-X, PAPERBACK]

Available at bookstores or directly from Beacon Press,
25 Beacon Street, Boston, Massachusetts 02108-2892